Audio
on
Wheels

Audio
on
Wheels

Vivian Capel

London
Newnes-Butterworths

THE BUTTERWORTH GROUP

ENGLAND
Butterworth & Co (Publishers) Ltd
London: 88 Kingsway, WC2B 6AB

AUSTRALIA
Butterworths Pty Ltd
Sydney: 586 Pacific Highway, NSW 2067
Melbourne: 343 Little Collins Street, 3000
Brisbane: 240 Queen Street, 4000

CANADA
Butterworth & Co (Canada) Ltd
Scarborough: 2265 Midland Avenue, Ontario M1P 4S1

NEW ZEALAND
Butterworths of New Zealand Ltd
Wellington: 26-28 Waring Taylor Street, 1

SOUTH AFRICA
Butterworth & Co (South Africa) (Pty) Ltd
Durban: 152-154 Gale Street

First published in 1975 by Newnes-Butterworths,
an imprint of the Butterworth Group

ISBN 0 408 00190 9

Photoset by Amos Typesetters, Hockley, Essex
Printed in England by Hazell Watson & Viney Ltd., Aylesbury, Bucks

Preface

There is at present a tremendous interest in 'in-car entertainment' as it is sometimes called; perhaps the frustrations of traffic delays and jams may have had something to do with it, or it may be a spin-off from the boom in home hi-fi.

It is therefore rather surprising that so little really useful information has been published on the subject other than catalogues of current models and brief comparisons of the various types of equipment. This book sets out to fill the gap. It contains information on all aspects of mobile audio from the basic principles of radio and tape players up to the installation of complete systems, with details of how they work and the special problems which arise with audio on wheels. To ensure comprehensive coverage of the subject, the now obsolete disc systems are described as well as mobile public-address. Equipping and setting up a specialist workshop for car audio is dealt with, and also maintenance and repair.

The radio engineer, the motor mechanic and the amateur DIY man have been catered for in the planning of this work. Part 1 deals with the basic principles and design of audio amplifiers, radio reception, and sound recording. This is intended for readers with little or no knowledge of the subjects and lays the foundation for what is to follow. The engineer on the other hand may wish to go straight to Part 2, which deals specifically with car audio equipment and related practical matters.

Motor mechanics and fitters in particular should find the book helpful, while those engaged in selling car audio should benefit from the acquisition of a sound background knowledge of the subject.

Acknowledgements

The author would like to acknowledge the cooperation of the following firms in compiling this book, and their assistance in providing technical information on their products and related matters:

Acoustico Enterprises Ltd
Antiference Ltd
Bosch Ltd
C.E.S. Ltd (Bristol)
Oscar Radio Co
Radiomobile Ltd
Valradio Ltd

Contents

Part 1

Basic Principles

Chapter 1

Audio Amplification

Whatever the audio system, the electrical output from the tape-head, pickup-cartridge, radio-unit or microphone is very small, ranging from a few thousandths of a volt to around 1 volt at the most. These *signals*, as the audio or radio electrical currents are called, are far too small to drive a loudspeaker, hence amplification is needed. A perfect audio amplifier would increase the magnitude of the applied signal without changing it in any other way, either by losing part of it or by adding anything to it in the process. So far, such an amplifier has not been devised, although there are a number of hi-fi amplifiers that get quite close.

There are a number of modifications that all practical amplifiers make to the signal being amplified. These are: curtailment of certain frequencies, usually the higher and lower ones; over-emphasis of other frequencies; production of spurious frequencies giving rise to *harmonic distortion* as it is termed; the interaction of various frequencies when amplified simultaneously producing what is known as *intermodulation distortion;* the generation of noise, usually hum or hiss; and the introduction of time delays for some frequencies so that there is a *phase difference* in the amplifier output compared to the input signal.

It might seem from this catalogue that the output signal can bear very little relationship to that fed in at the input! However, in good amplifiers the amount of modification of the signal is not great, and to most ears the result is quite acceptable. Even trained ears have difficulty in detecting the various types of distortion in the better hi-fi amplifiers; actually it is the other links in the audio chain, the loudspeaker and the tape or disc equipment, that are likely to give most distortion. Audio equipment designed for mobile use is not usually of the standard required for home hi-fi systems. It obviously is intended as a background music-source where a high degree of concentration will not (or should not, at least while the vehicle is in motion) be given. Thus an extended flat frequency-response and low distortion are not really necessary. Noise level can also be higher as this would tend to be masked in any case by traffic noises.

It should be mentioned here that in mobile systems the audio amplifier does not have to be a separate unit; it is usually an integral part of the instrument, needed in all cases where a loudspeaker is used for the reproduction. Thus even the small transistor radio has its own audio amplifier.

Amplifying devices

Amplification can be obtained by using valves, transistors or integrated circuits. Valves were for many years the only means, but have now been superseded by transistors, which are especially suited for mobile applications. Integrated circuits are really a number of transistors and associated components formed together into one tiny chip of semiconducting material (the same as that used to make individual or discrete transistors). Although not as common as discrete transistor circuits, they are rapidly taking over in many fields and may be expected to be found increasingly in car radio and audio systems. Valves are now obsolete and are only found in older radios.

The transistor consists of a small portion of germanium or silicon crystal to which carefully controlled amounts of chemical impurity have been added. Two types of impurity are available producing N-type or P-type semiconductors. A sandwich is made by one of various methods to form a PNP or NPN configuration, so forming junctions between the N and P-type material. A small current passed from one side of the transistor to the centre, i.e. across the first junction, will control and regulate a much larger current passed across the whole transistor.

The three parts of the PNP (or NPN) sandwich are known as the *emitter*, *base* and *collector*. Generally the input signal to a transistor is applied between base and emitter, and the output is taken from the collector and emitter, although other configurations are possible. This is known as the common emitter connection, since the emitter is common to the input and the output.

A load resistor is used to develop the output signal voltage, and a coupling capacitor is also often used; this needs to be of a high value and so is usually of the electrolytic type. Biasing is generally derived from a potential divider across the supply. Figure 1.1a shows the basic circuit of a PNP type transistor; the NPN type (Figure 1.1b) is exactly the same except for reversed polarity, indicated by the arrow in the symbol being in the opposite direction. Replacements must always be of the same type as the original.

The field effect transistor (FET) operates on a different principle,

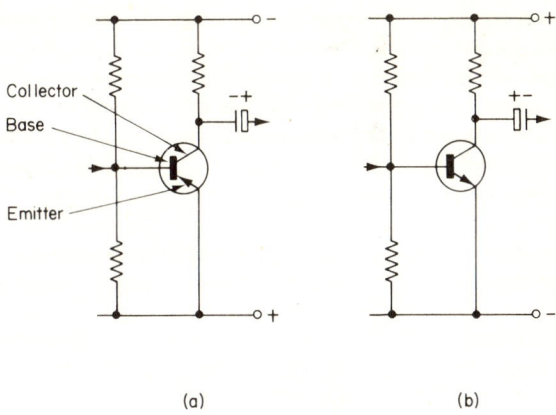

Figure 1.1. (a) PNP transistor amplifying circuit and (b) NPN transistor; note opposite polarity

the main practical difference being that the input electrode takes virtually no current from the signal source. This is an advantage when it is being driven from a high-impedance source. The electrode terminology is different from normal transistors: *source* corresponds to emitter, *gate* corresponds to base, and *drain* corresponds to collector.

Transistors can work with voltages of between 3 and 45 V, according to type and application, and a 12-V car battery is therefore perfectly suitable as a supply source; this fact together with the greatly reduced size make the transistor the ideal amplifying unit for mobile audio systems.

Amplifying stages

The circuits outlined earlier are of single stages only, several such stages making up the complete amplifier. Each stage handles the signal in turn, then passes it on to the following one, and each is designed for a specific set of conditions. The first or input stage, for example, handles a very small signal so a high degree of amplification is needed in order to pass on a reasonable signal level to the following stage. A more important requirement is that this should be done with the minimum of self-generated noise. All transistors generate noise, which appears in the output along with the amplified signal. Owing to the small signal levels, noise generated in the input stage can assume a significant proportion of the output, and the stage would be said to have a poor *signal-to-noise ratio*. Furthermore, as any noise generated here is amplified by all the succeeding stages, it has a worse effect than any noise appearing in a later stage.

Noise in a transistor depends among other things on the amount of current passing through it, so for a low noise-factor the minimum current only should be passed. However, if the current is too low the input signal may drive the device into distortion, so the current must be adequate to handle the amount of signal applied to the stage. Fortunately with input stages where noise must be kept low, the signal is also low and therefore small currents can be used. These are limited by using high values for the bias and load resistors. Because a high-value load produces a greater voltage drop across it, it will also give a high signal-voltage output, and all the requirements can thus be met.

The following and any succeeding stages will obviously be handling larger input signals, and the current through these stages must be accordingly higher. It will be noted therefore that lower-value resistors are generally used in these stages.

The conventional means of coupling one stage to the next in common emitter configuration is by connecting a capacitor between the collector terminal and the base terminal of the next stage. This passes on the audio frequencies but blocks the d.c. voltage. This is necessary because there is a d.c. voltage on the collector of approximately half the supply voltage, whereas the base voltage is much lower, about half a volt higher than the emitter (about 0.2 V with germanium transistors and 0.6 V with silicon types), and the emitter voltage is about 1 V up from the earth line. Thus for a 12-V supply we would expect the collector voltage to be around 6 V, while the following base would be about 1.5 V. Figure 1.2 shows the arrangement.

Sometimes stages are directly coupled, with the collector of the first stage connected directly to the base of the following one (Figure 1.3). The d.c. voltages are obviously different from those of capacitor-coupled stages; the first collector voltage is lower due to the

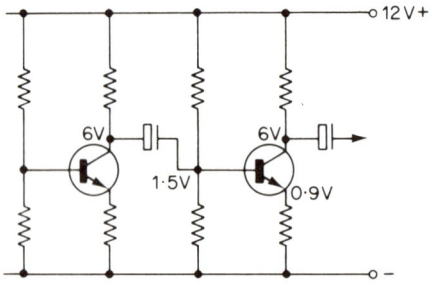

Figure 1.2.   Two-transistor circuit with capacitor coupling

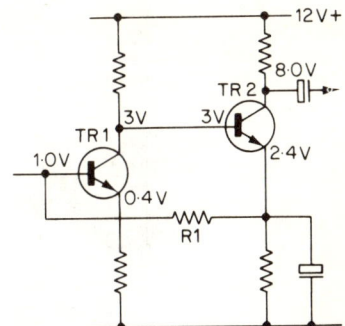

Figure 1.3. Directly coupled circuit resulting in saving of components

high value of its load resistor, while the following base (which must be at the same voltage as the previous collector) is higher than usual. As the difference between emitter and base is always about 0.6 V (for silicon transistors), the emitter voltage of the second transistor is also higher than normal. In order to make the second collector voltage higher than its emitter and base voltages, as of course it must be, the resistance of the collector load is rather lower than usual. Approximate voltages are indicated on the diagram. Since d.c. coupling avoids the necessity of a coupling capacitor and also reduces the number of resistors required, it is understandably popular with manufacturers. The phase-shift effects at certain frequencies mentioned earlier in this chapter are due mainly to coupling capacitors, so eliminating these can improve the quality.

There are numerous directly-coupled arrangements in common use, each with its own characteristics and advantages. However, there is a limit to the number of stages that can be directly coupled in the manner of Figure 1.3, because each must operate at a higher supply voltage than its predecessor, thus giving a ladder effect. This means dividing the available supply voltage (12 V in the case of car equipment) between the coupled stages.

Some designs overcome this snag by using PNP and NPN transistors in conjunction, as shown in Figure 1.4. A further method of coupling stages is by the use of transformers; the primary winding serves as the collector load of the first stage, and the secondary feeds the following one (Figure 1.5).

After the signal has been amplified to the required level, it is passed to the final (or output) stage. This stage drives the loudspeaker and it has rather different requirements from the previous ones. Rather than just amplify the signal voltage, it must supply power, and so must produce both voltage and current gain. More current is taken by the output stage than the whole of the rest of the amplifier, and so output transistors are larger, and some means of dissipating the heat thus

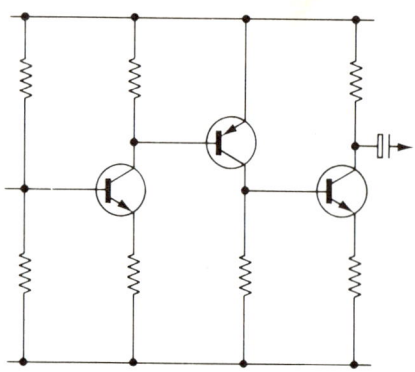

Figure 1.4. Directly coupled circuit using more than two transistors by employing both NPN and PNP types

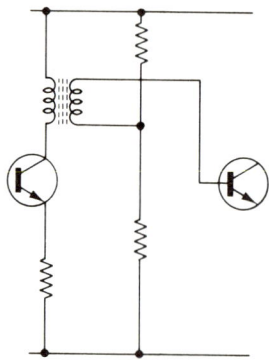

Figure 1.5. Transformer coupling between stages

generated must be provided. Small output transistors as used in battery portable radios are fitted with copper clips that conduct the heat and radiate it into the air, though some are clipped to the metalwork of the instrument to improve the heat conduction. These are known as *heat sinks* (Figure 1.6a). Larger transistors that give more power are encased in metal which is bolted to the chassis of the reproducer (Figure 1.6b). These cases are internally connected to the collector and so must be electrically insulated from the chassis. This is accomplished by fitting a mica washer between the transistor and its mounting, in order to insulate electrically but give good thermal conduction. It is important always to replace this washer when changing transistors and to ensure that it is not punctured.

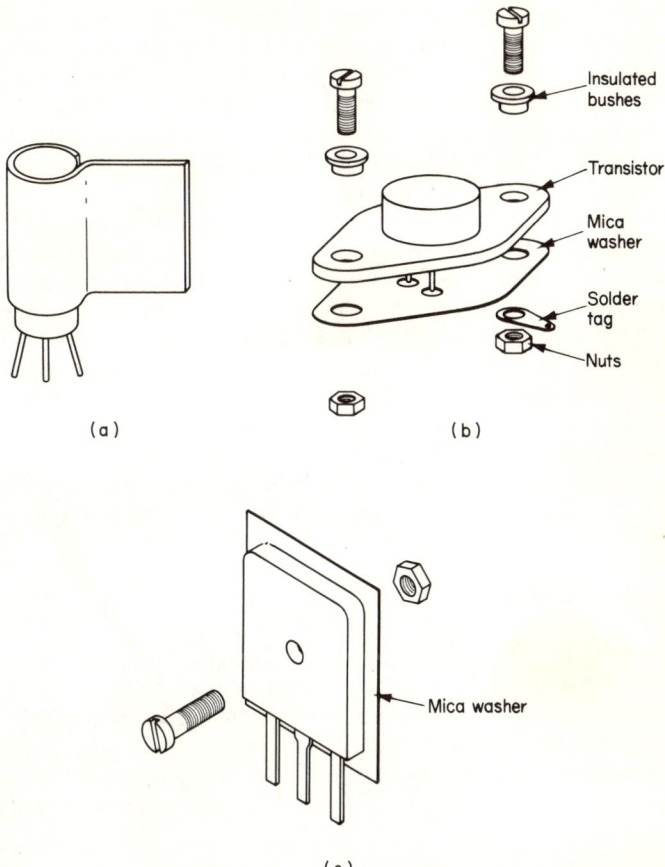

Figure 1.6. (a) Output transistor with heat sink; (b) large output transistor encased in metal, showing fixing and insulating arrangements; (c) flat type of output transistor giving heat conduction from inside surface through mica sheet to chassis member

Impedance matching

To obtain the maximum transfer of power from one circuit to another, it is necessary for the impedances of both circuits to be similar. Impedance is measured in ohms and could be described as the a.c. equivalent of resistance, that is the degree to which a circuit resists the flow of an alternating current.

A high-impedance circuit passes little current when a high voltage is applied, whereas a low-impedance circuit passes a large current at a low voltage. The same power could be present in either high or low impedance circuits. For example, a 60-W house lamp operates at 240 V and passes a current of some 0.25 A. A 60-W car bulb on the other hand operates from 12 V and passes 5 A. The power is the same yet the house lamp is a high-impedance device, whereas the car bulb impedance is low. Connecting a house lamp to a car battery would produce almost no light, while the connection of a car bulb to the mains would certainly destroy it.

Loudspeakers are rated at a certain impedance, usually from 3 Ω to 16 Ω. The output stage must deliver its power at the same impedance if there is to be no power loss. Output transistors are low-impedance devices, especially the higher-power ones, so they are generally connected to the loudspeaker via a capacitor without any form of impedance matching. However, some of the smaller output stages use an output transformer to obtain optimum matching; the transformer steps down the voltage and hence lowers the impedance. (Transformer impedance is a function of the turns ratio between primary and secondary, and almost any impedance can be converted to any other by arranging a suitable ratio between the windings.)

Push-pull output

This type of stage uses two transistors. The signal is first split in phase by the preceding stage, then fed in opposite phase to the bases of the output pair so that when one is receiving a negative signal swing, the other is receiving a positive one. The outputs are re-combined to assist each other; one method uses a split-primary output transformer (Figure 1.7). Thus one 'pushes' as the other 'pulls'. Advantages of this

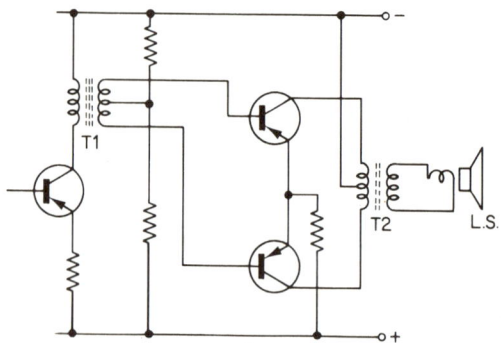

Figure 1.7. Push-pull output circuit. The signal is fed in opposite phase to the bases by means of centre-tapped transformer secondary T1. It is recombined by centre-tapped output transformer T2

type of circuit are: more than twice the output of a single valve or transistor, reduction of transformer d.c. core saturation owing to d.c. currents flowing the opposite way in the windings, and cancellation of second-harmonic distortion.

Single transistors must be operated on the straight portion of their characteristic curve. As mentioned earlier, collector-current change is proportional to base-current change only between certain limits. Above and below those limits the change is not proportional and if the device were operated in these regions distortion would be the result. Operation on the straight portion is described as *class A* working.

With a push-pull circuit we can operate much lower down the characteristic even though one half of the applied waveform encroaches on the non-linear part. This is because the negative half-waves are handled by one transistor and the positive by the other, so all parts of the applied signal will be operating on the straight portion of one or other of the push-pull pair, and in theory there will be no more distortion. This mode of operation is known as *class B*. The main advantage is that a much smaller current is passed through the transistors, which in the case of battery equipment is very useful; also the smaller current produces less heat, so there are fewer problems arising from heat dissipation.

While in theory there should be no more distortion, in practice the two halves of the waves do not fit perfectly together resulting in a slight discontinuity where they join. This *cross-over distortion* as it is called is inherent with class B systems, although in hi-fi amplifiers it is greatly reduced by special types of circuit.

Where two transistors of the same type are used there must be some means of dividing the signal so that the signal applied to one base is opposite in phase to that applied to the other. A circuit that has become popular, and that avoids the necessity of a phase splitter, uses two transistors with the same characteristics but opposite polarity (i.e. one PNP and the other NPN). Here, the signal applied to both bases is the same, but while it increases the current through one, it decreases it through the other, so we have a push-pull effect. This circuit is known as the *complementary* push-pull circuit (Figure 1.8).

The transistors are connected in series across the supply, and the loudspeaker, in series with a capacitor, is connected across one of them. The capacitor charges and discharges due to the action of the transistors, and the series-connected speaker responds to the varying charging current.

Power rating

The power output rating of an audio amplifier depends entirely on the output transistors, their current rating and the manner of operation

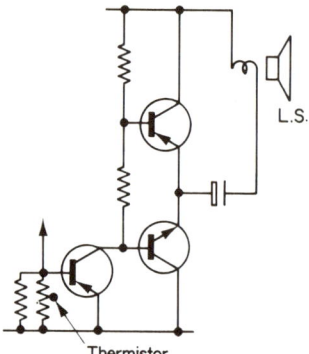

Figure 1.8. Complementary push-pull circuit. The phase is the same at both bases but it drives one transistor on and the other off. The capacitor thus alternately charges and discharges through the loudspeaker. A thermistor is included in the base circuit of the driver transistor for thermal stability, this stage being directly coupled to a preceding one

L.S.

Thermistor

(class A, B or intermediary state). It has nothing to do with volume. The volume control can be turned up until the maximum power rating is reached, whereupon the output transistors will be driven into the curved portion of their characteristic and distortion will be the result. As music constantly varies in sound level with some peaks many times higher than the average, it follows that, even when an amplifier is operated with the average level well below the maximum power, sudden peaks could drive it into distortion. With mobile equipment the average level must be fairly high to overcome traffic noise, so unless the power rating is adequate there could be frequent occurrences of distortion.

It should be noted that there are different ways of expressing power ratings. An alternating current varies in level from a peak value down to zero; therefore with a pure steady note (a sine wave) the energy in the circuit to perform work such as driving a loudspeaker is less than the peak level. This is known as the r.m.s. (root mean square) value; 1 A r.m.s. is defined as the alternating current that will produce the same heating effect as a direct current of 1 A. The r.m.s. value is the preferred way to express power output, although some makers express power in peak value; peak power rating is twice that of the r.m.s., thus a 3-W r.m.s. rating can also be described as 6 W peak. Obviously this looks better on paper. A third type of rating is that of 'music power', which is based on the fact that many amplifiers can handle very short peaks such as sometimes occur in music in excess of the normal power rating, without distortion. This rating is higher than the peak (although there can be r.m.s. and peak ratings in music power, it is usually peak music power that is quoted), but there is no arithmetical relationship to the normal peak or r.m.s. values, it depends on the individual amplifier. So a 3-W r.m.s. output could well be described as 10 W music power or more. These ratings are obviously used to make an amplifier appear better than it really is, so the ratings should always be carefully checked.

Volume and tone controls

Some provision must be included to adjust the volume level in every audio amplifier. The control consists of a potentiometer, i.e. a resistance that can be varied by means of a movable contact, connected across the signal source (either the input socket or the output of the first stage), with the movable contact connected to the base circuit of the following stage. Thus the signal voltage across the resistance is tapped off at any desired level (Figure 1.9a).

Human hearing does not respond to sounds of varying intensity in a linear manner: a sound that may seem twice as loud as another is actually many times its intensity. Thus to give a control that sounds smooth in its progression, the resistance must not be distributed over the volume-control track linearly. It must obey a logarithmic law of progression, hence all controls for this purpose are marked 'log'.

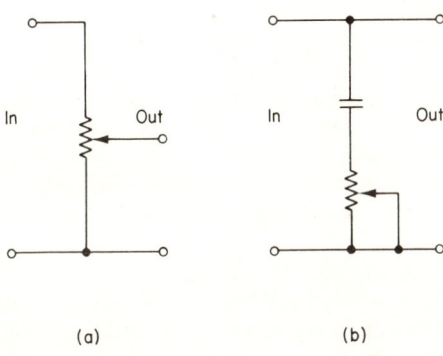

(a)   (b)

Figure 1.9. (a) Volume control circuit; (b) treble-cut tone control circuit

Tone control can be quite complicated, consisting of treble cut and boost as well as bass cut and boost. However, in mobile equipment it is nearly always restricted to a simple treble-cut control. This is based on the fact that a capacitor passes high frequencies more readily than low ones. A capacitor shunted across the signal at some point in the amplifier therefore bypasses the high frequencies, the effect getting progressively less as the frequency drops until at bass frequencies there is little difference.

The degree of treble cut can be varied by means of a variable resistor connected in series with the capacitor (Figure 1.9b). This resistor should be of the linear type unlike that of the volume control. Normally the tone control should be set at minimum cut, otherwise the brilliance and sparkle disappears from the reproduction; however, if noise or hiss become prominent it can be turned down to give a compromise between the noise reduction and loss of clarity.

Thermal stability and negative feedback

When a transistor gets warm the current through it increases; this further raises the temperature and so the current goes up even more. The cycle rapidly develops until the transistor burns out. This is known as *thermal runaway*, and steps must be taken to prevent it. It is most common in output stages, but earlier stages can be affected by upsetting their operating conditions even if the cycle does not proceed to the destruction of the transistor.

Adequate heat conduction is one important preventative, but circuit devices to ensure stability are also used. For example, R1 in Figure 1.3 supplies forward bias for the first transistor from the emitter of the second. If current through TR2 rises, so will the voltage on its emitter. This increases the forward bias on TR1, increasing its current and thereby causing a drop in its collector voltage due to the drop over its load resistor. Thus the base bias of TR2 is correspondingly reduced, decreasing its current. Any current changes therefore tend to be self-counteracting. Such d.c. feedback circuits are commonly used in one form or another to achieve stable operation.

Another method is to include a thermistor in the output circuit as in Figure 1.8. This is a resistor whose value changes with changes in temperature. Thus the bias is altered if there is a rise in ambient temperature, to reduce the current through the output stage.

Feedback is the feeding back of a signal to a previous stage. If the signal is fed back out of phase, gain is reduced as a result, but so is distortion and noise, and any non-linearities in the frequency response curve are flattened; this is known as *negative feedback*. Hi-fi amplifiers rely heavily on negative feedback to give low noise and distortion, and the gain reduction is made up by extra stages. It is less used in mobile equipment but is often found in small doses. Resistors back-coupled to a preceding stage give signal feedback as well as thermal stability if they are not bypassed by a capacitor (the one in Figure 1.3 is bypassed by the emitter capacitor). Another way of obtaining feedback is to leave the emitter resistor of a stage un-bypassed by a capacitor.

Chapter 2

Principles of Radio Reception

Although pre-recorded material is being used increasingly in mobile entertainment systems, the programme source in most widespread use is still the car radio. In this chapter, then, the main principles of radio reception and some basic circuits are outlined.

Radio waves are electromagnetic waves similar to light waves but at a much lower frequency. The normal broadcast bands range from 200 000 to 100 000 000 cycles per second or *hertz* (Hz), which is now the generally used unit of frequency. Multiples are the *kilohertz* (kHz), which is 1000 Hz, and the *megahertz* (MHz) or 1 000 000 Hz.

The distance through space between one wave crest and the next is known as the *wavelength* and is an alternative means of describing the station frequency. It is measured in metres and it increases as the frequency decreases. To find either frequency or wavelength from the other, divide the known figure into 300 million; thus the BBC long-wave transmitter at 1500 m has a frequency of 200 kHz. Metres were always used to calibrate radio scales but ironically, now everything else is going metric, metres are being dropped in favour of frequency markings!

A radio carrier-wave can be illustrated as in Figure 2.1a, but in order to convey an audio-frequency (a.f.) signal, which is of a much lower frequency, the signal must be superimposed or *modulated* on the carrier. There are two ways of doing this—*amplitude modulation* and *frequency modulation*. The former method varies the level or amplitude of the carrier in sympathy with the audio, while the latter varies its frequency. Amplitude modulation is the most common type of reception for car radios so we will deal with this in greater detail. Figure 2.1b shows the amplitude-modulated signal. The radio signal induces an electrical waveform of similar nature into the aerial, but this is of an extremely low level, a matter of a few millionths of a volt, so amplification is needed before the modulated audio signal can be extracted from it.

 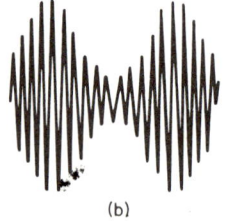

(a)   (b)

Figure 2.1.   (a) Unmodulated carrier wave; (b) amplitude modulated carrier

Tuned circuits

There is a further requirement of the radio-frequency amplifier besides amplification. Many signals will be present at the aerial, each one corresponding to the radio waves broadcast by each of the many transmitters that are receivable in the area. Some means of selecting the desired signal and rejecting all the others must be provided.

This is accomplished by means of tuned circuits. We have seen in the previous chapter how capacitors pass high frequencies more readily than low ones, so their *reactance* (resistance to alternating currents), measured in ohms, *decreases* as the frequency increases. Coils or inductors behave in the opposite manner, i.e. their reactance *increases* with frequency. Now, these two forms of reactance are opposite in nature: both cause phase displacement between applied voltage and current, but capacitive reactance causes the current to lead the voltage, while inductive reactance causes it to lag. This produces the rather strange effect that one type of reactance can cancel the other if the two are present in the same circuit. The resulting circuit reactance is the *difference* between them, rather than the sum as might be expected.

It follows from this that if reactances are equal, they cancel exactly and the result is zero. As the reactances of a capacitor and an inductor vary with frequency in opposite senses, it also follows that for any capacitor/inductor combination there is one frequency at which the reactance is in fact zero. At this point the circuit is said to be at *resonance*.

Radio tuned circuits make use of this principle, arranging matters so that the resonant frequency of the circuit coincides with that of the desired transmission. There are two basic forms of tuned circuit: one has the inductor and capacitor in series and the other has them in parallel. The series circuit is known as an *acceptor* circuit because in this form the resonant frequency is accepted by it, that is it offers the minimum impedance to it. In the case of the parallel circuit, the

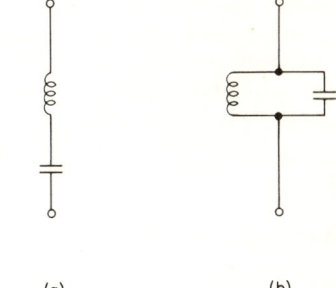

Figure 2.2. (a) Acceptor circuit; (b) rejector circuit

(a)   (b)

resonant frequency is offered the maximum impedance hence it is rejected and the circuit is termed a *rejector* circuit. (See Figure 2.2.)

The rejector circuit is commonly used across the input of a transistor (from base to emitter); connected thus it bypasses all frequencies other than the desired one, which is rejected and so is applied to the transistor for amplification. It is also used in series with the collector, to form the collector load. (See Figure 2.3.) As we saw in the previous chapter, it is the collector load over which the output signal voltage is developed, so a high-impedance load means a high output voltage; as the circuit has a high impedance only to the resonant frequency, it is only this frequency that produces an appreciable output signal voltage. It can be noted too that, as the d.c. resistance of the circuit is low, the collector voltage is unaffected, whereas with resistive loads as used for audio stages a high load value reduces the collector voltage, thus setting a limit to the maximum load resistance usable.

In order that the circuit can be tuned from one station to another, either the inductance or capacitance must be made variable. Inductance can be varied by inserting a brass or iron-dust core in the coil. A brass core decreases the inductance, which has the effect of

Figure 2.3. Basic tuned-circuit stage. Rejector circuit across the input bypasses all signals except desired one. Rejector circuit in series with collector serves as load impedance which is at maximum at desired frequency

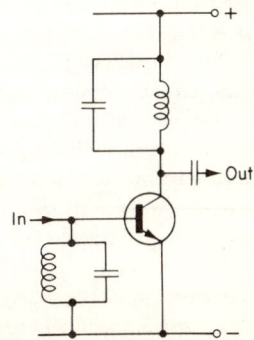

increasing the tuned frequency, while an iron-dust core increases inductance and so lowers the frequency. A variable capacitor consists of a fixed set of plates and a movable set, and as they mesh together (without touching) the capacitance increases. A fully meshed tuning capacitor gives maximum capacitance, which in turn lowers the frequency.

The superheterodyne receiver

All modern radio receivers employ the superheterodyne principle, but to see why this is so we must briefly examine its predecessor the tuned-radio-frequency circuit. With this, the signal from the aerial is passed successively through a number of stages, each with one or more tuned curcuits, until it is sufficient in level to be demodulated. Apart from supplying the needed amplification, several tuned circuits are involved. (One or two tuned circuits fail to give sufficient sharpness in tuning or *selectivity*, and adjacent stations can cause interference with the desired one. Several are needed, then, to give the required separation.) The main snag with this circuit is that all the tuned circuits have to be adjusted each time the set is tuned to a different station. While this can be done by ganging the various capacitors on a single control, it is difficult to keep them all in step over the whole tuning range; furthermore capacitance between sections leads to unwanted coupling between stages and instability.

With the superheterodyne circuit the incoming signal is mixed with a frequency generated by a local oscillator in the receiver. This results in two new frequencies, one equal to the sum of the signal and the local oscillator signal and the other equal to the difference between them. The difference signal is the one that is used; the other is ignored.

When the receiver is tuned from one station to another, the frequency of the local oscillator is altered. The local oscillator frequency is always kept spaced from the incoming signal frequency by the same amount, so that whatever the frequency of the received signal the difference signal is always of the same frequency. This is known as the *intermediate frequency* (i.f.).

It follows that successive stages of amplification need be tuned only to the one intermediate frequency and, once so tuned in the initial alignment, do not have to be altered. A number of stages can be used each with one or more tuned circuits so that ample selectivity can be obtained with the minimum of tuning problems. The only variable tuning that is really necessary to the basic principle of the circuit is that of the oscillator, but in practice the aerial input circuits are tuned at radio frequency to increase the wanted signal level input to the mixer and to reject signals at around the intermediate frequency that would otherwise break through. Tuning is accomplished either by a two-gang capacitor or by a pair of coils with sliding cores operated from the tuning control. The latter is more usual for car radios. Occasionally an r.f. stage that amplifies the signal at radio frequency may be used before the mixer, in which case three variable tuned elements are required. This affords extra sensitivity to weak stations.

Input and mixer stages

Starting with the aerial, all car radios use an external aerial to avoid interference pickup from the engine, but ordinary portable radios use a ferrite rod. This is a rod of special ferrous material similar to that used for tuning cores, on which the input coils are wound. Compactness is the main virtue of this arrangement, compared to the long external aerials used in the early days of radio.

Long and medium wavebands have separate aerial coils which are aligned initially by sliding them along the ferrite rod. Input circuits that use an external aerial, as in car radios, have separate adjustable cores to the coils. Selection of the desired waveband is made by switching.

The input tuning coils are of high impedance, whereas the transistor input impedance is low; therefore, to avoid signal loss, coupling coils are wound over or on the same former as the aerial coils to give impedance matching by transformer action.

A single transistor serves as oscillator and mixer (Figure 2.4). Oscillation is brought about by employing a coil with two or more windings, one connected in series with the emitter and the other with the collector. This results in positive feedback and oscillation. A third winding is often included to tune the oscillator by means of external capacitors. The radio input signal is applied to the base, and so

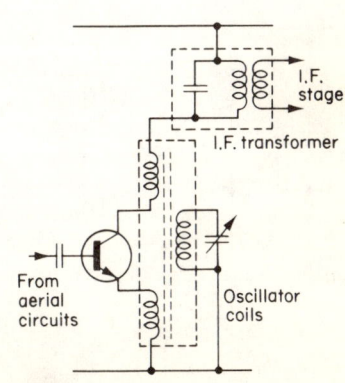

Figure 2.4. Transistor mixer stage. Oscillation is produced by emitter and collector windings, and tuned by third auxiliary winding. Aerial signal is fed into the base, and i.f. output appears across i.f. transformer

mixing occurs with the appearance of the i.f. signal at the collector. There are variants of this circuit, but the basic principle is the same.

In addition to the capacitance tuning across one of the oscillator coil windings, the coil is also provided with a tuning core. Both these tuning elements are needed in the initial alignment to enable the oscillator tuning to keep in step with the aerial tuning circuits, because the shunted capacitance affects the high-frequency end of the scale more than the low, while the core affects the low more than the high.

I.F. stages

The output of the mixer is at a fixed frequency. This is now standardised in a.m. receivers at 470 kHz, but frequencies around this, e.g. 465 kHz, may be encountered. Actually the exact frequency is not at all critical, as long as the one produced by the mixer is the same as that to which the i.f. stages are tuned.

Being single-frequency stages, i.f. stages are simple in design (Figure 2.5); with transistor receivers two or sometimes three stages of amplification are used, requiring three or four i.f. transformers. As sufficient selectivity can be obtained from this number, usually only the primaries are tuned by means of a core. The secondaries are just untuned low-impedance windings to match the impedance of the following stage. There are occasional exceptions where both primaries and secondaries are tuned.

With early types of transistors there was a large internal capacitance between the base and collector, resulting in positive feedback and instability. To balance this, an external capacitor was fitted to give negative feedback and neutralise the effect. Modern transistors have a much lower base/collector capacitance, so neutralising capacitors are not needed in modern i.f. stages.

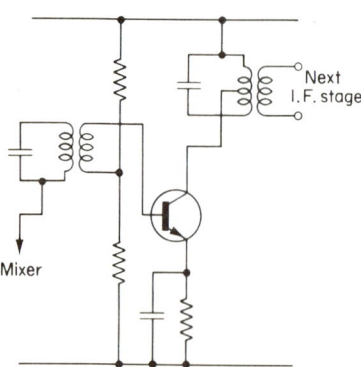

Figure 2.5. Typical a.m. i.f. stage

The demodulator and a.g.c. circuit

From the final i.f. stage, we have a 470-kHz carrier modulated with the original a.f. signal. All that now remains is to remove the modulation so that it can be applied to the audio stages. With a.m. circuits this is quite straightforward, and consists of merely suppressing the lower half of the i.f. waveform. This leaves the a.f. signal plus half-cycles of the i.f. frequency, the latter being bypassed by means of a resistor/capacitor network, leaving only the audio. The suppression or rectification is achieved by passing the signal through a diode and load resistor (Figure 2.6). Demodulation was originally described as *detection*, and this term is still sometimes used. In many circuits the load resistor is also the volume control.

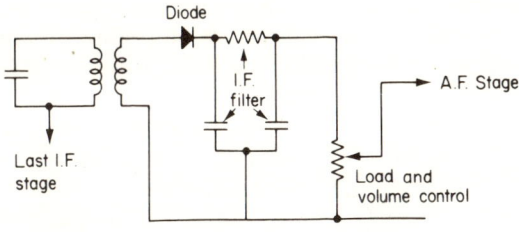

Figure 2.6. A.M. demodulator circuit showing diode, i.f. filter to remove all trace of i.f. signals, and load resistor (also volume control) across which audio signals are developed

There can be considerable variation between the signal strengths of different stations, and in the case of mobile equipment the strength of the same station can vary from one moment to the next due to changing topography. The result could be a continually fluctuating volume level, but this is kept to a minimum by the automatic-gain-control (a.g.c.) circuit—also called automatic volume control (a.v.c.). When the i.f. signal is rectified by the demodulator diode, a steady positive or negative voltage is produced in addition to the a.f. signal. The polarity depends on which way round the diode is connected, and the level depends on the level of the i.f. signal. This voltage is fed back to one of the i.f. stages to control its gain by varying its base bias. Hence a strong signal produces a large a.g.c. voltage which reduces the gain and so decreases the signal, whereas a weak signal produces a small voltage which allows the i.f. stages to operate at full gain.

Decoupling

It is important that unwanted coupling between stages in any amplifier audio, r.f., or i.f. be kept very low, otherwise positive feedback can result in instability with whistling, hooting, distortion and other undesirable audible effects. One way by which such coupling could occur is by signals from a particular stage appearing in the supply line. This can be prevented by offering a lower impedance path to earth for such signals than to the supply line.

This can be done by a simple resistor/capacitor arrangement as shown in Figure 2.7. Any signal currents originating from the stage shown will find the capacitor a lower impedance path than the resistor and will be safely bypassed. Capacitor values vary according to application; for audio frequencies the value is high, several microfarads in fact, and the capacitor is usually of the electrolytic type, while for the i.f. stages it need be no greater than 0.1 µF.

The a.g.c. voltage line must also be decoupled by this arrangement to prevent signal feedback occurring along with the steady control voltage.

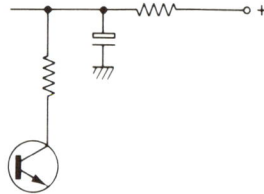

Figure 2.7. Decoupling circuit. Signals pass through capacitor to earth instead of through resistor into supply line

Frequency modulation reception

F.M. radio signals are transmitted at a much higher frequency than those of a.m., from about 80 to 100 MHz, but this is not the main difference. The amplitude of the carrier does not vary with the modulation as with a.m., but remains constant. Instead the frequency varies, both increasing and decreasing from its original mean value (Figure 2.8). The extent of this deviation corresponds to the volume level of the audio modulation, the maximum being ±75 kHz. The frequency of the audio signal is represented by the number of times per second the f.m. carrier deviates. Thus both audio frequency and amplitude are conveyed.

Prior to the demodulator, the signal is processed in the receiver in much the same way as it is for a.m. An r.f. amplifier is nearly always used before the mixer, this being the main difference. The method of connecting the r.f. and mixer transistors is slightly different: a common-base configuration is used to achieve satisfactory operation at the very high frequencies involved. The r.f. and mixer stages are usually mounted on a separate sub-assembly to form an f.m. tuner, thus enabling them to be easily identified. The positioning of components on this unit is very critical and it should not be touched by anyone other than a skilled radio engineer.

Figure 2.8. Carrier modulated with f.m. signal. Amplitude remains constant but frequency varies in sympathy with audio modulation

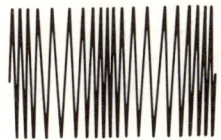

The output from the mixer is taken not to the first i.f. stage, but to the a.m. mixer. This is switched to form an additional i.f. stage when f.m. is being received so that the a.m. first i.f. becomes the f.m. second i.f. stage and so on. Thus, with an extra stage, extra amplification is obtained on f.m.

The i.f. stages must pass not just a single frequency but a band of frequencies, because the i.f. signal (like the original carrier) deviates from the standard frequency of 10.7 MHz by a maximum of ± 75 kHz. Thus they must have a pass-band of at least 150 kHz, although in practice some 200 kHz is usual to allow for sidebands and slight oscillator drift.

Separate i.f. transformers are used for the f.m. (at 10.7 MHz), but there is no need to switch these in and out of circuit when changing

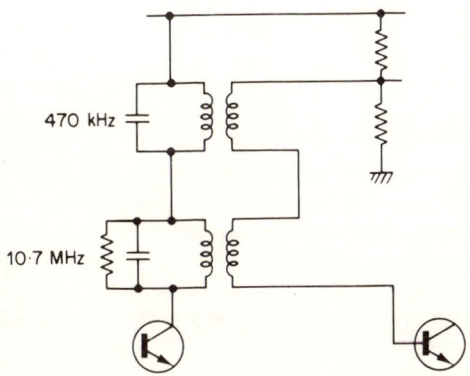

Figure 2.9. Combined a.m./f.m. i.f. stage. Transformers are series connected but switching is unnecessary because each has little effect on the circuit except at its own frequency

from a.m. to f.m. They are connected in series with the 470-kHz transformers, but offer a low impedance path at 470 kHz and have no effect on the circuit at that frequency. Similarly, the a.m. transformers have no effect at 10.7 MHz. (See Figure 2.9.)

The f.m. demodulator is quite different from that used for a.m., and switching is employed to select the appropriate one. There are several types, but the most common is known as the *ratio detector*. This employs a pair of diodes connected from each end of the last i.f. transformer secondary to a load resistor. A third winding is connected from a centre-tap on the secondary to a further load resistor, and it is across this component that the audio signal is developed. Any amplitude modulations of the carrier appear across the first resistor, and a large-value capacitor is connected across it to bypass them. The circuit is thus insensitive to amplitude modulations and any amplitude-modulated interference is suppressed. It should be noted, though, that some types of interference are rich in frequency-modulated components, one of these being car ignition. So f.m. is not suitable for car radios unless special suppression techniques are used.

Chapter 3

Sound Recordings

While radio remains at present the principal source of mobile entertainment, sound recordings are playing a large part and will undoubtedly increase further in popularity as a programme source. They offer the advantage of a choice of one's own entertainment when it is wanted, plus stereo or even quad if required.

We shall take a more detailed look at the various types of mobile play-back systems in succeeding chapters, but here we outline the basic principles involved.

Tape recordings

Without doubt the most suitable means of recording for mobile use is on magnetic tape, and the majority of car pre-recorded entertainment systems use this medium. Tape players are not unduly affected by vibration or car motion; programmes of up to an hour in length or continuously repeating programmes can be obtained, thus needing the minimum attention; players can be made physically small, often incorporated with a car radio; and stereo and even quad systems pose no problems.

Magnetic tape consists of a flexible base such as polyester or acetate on which is deposited a film of fine particles of iron oxide. These can be magnetised by an external magnetic field to form magnetic zones of varying intensity along the length of the tape, and this is precisely how a recording is made. The recording head contains a set of coils and pole-pieces to form an electromagnet, with a narrow vertical gap between the poles at the face of the head (Figure 3.1). Currents through the coils produce a field across the gap that causes a vertical strip of magnetisation across the width of the tape. The currents vary in sympathy with the audio signal, and the magnetisation of the tape follows suit (Figure 3.2).

Unfortunately, since the magnetisation characteristics of the

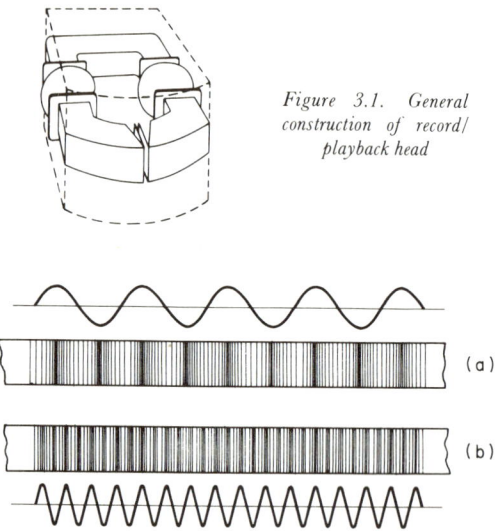

Figure 3.1. General construction of record/ playback head

(a)

(b)

Figure 3.2. The vertical magnetic zones of varying intensity produced by an applied wave.(a) Shows a low-frequency tone with a long wavelength, while (b) shows a high-frequency signal

magnetic tape particles are not linear, the magnetic pattern that is recorded would not be a faithful copy of the audio currents through the head-coils if these were applied directly. The magnetisation characteristic has both straight and curved portions (Figure 3.3), so if distortion is to be avoided only the straight parts can be utilised. This is done by use of bias in the form of a high-frequency oscillation many times higher than the highest audio frequency. The audio signal is superimposed on this and is thus lifted clear of the curved portions and applied to the straight (Figures 3.4 and 3.5). Being above the upper frequency limit of the head, the bias oscillations are not recorded and only the audio signal appears on the tape.

The high-frequency limitations of the magnetic recording system depend mainly on the tape speed and the width of the gap. Imagine for example a tape speed of 1 inch per second; it follows that for a 1-kHz note 1000 complete cycles of magnetic variations must be

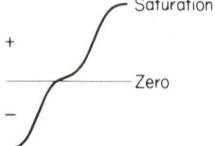

Figure 3.3. Magnetisation characteristic of recording tape. In addition to the curved portions at the saturation points of opposite polarity, there are curved parts where the characteristic goes through zero and changes polarity

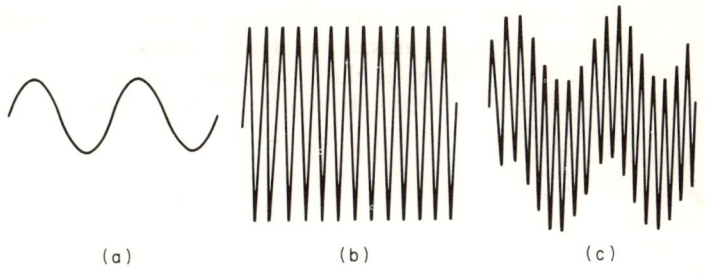

(a)   (b)   (c)

Figure 3.4. The audio waveform (a) to be recorded, is superimposed on a high-frequency bias signal (b) to give the effect shown at (c)

Figure 3.5. By being superimposed on the h.f. bias signal, the audio waveform avoids the curves and is applied only to the straight portions to produce recorded waveforms (a) and (b). As these are added in phase the result is as at (c)

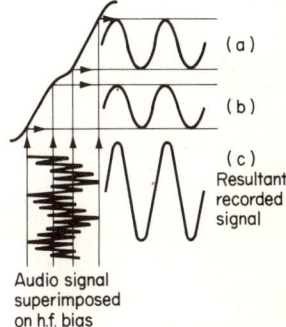

(a)

(b)

(c)
Resultant recorded signal

Audio signal superimposed on h.f. bias

accommodated within the inch, and therefore these have a wavelength of 0.001 inch. In the case of a 10-kHz note, 10 000 cycles must appear within the inch, and the recorded wavelength is 0.0001 inch. Now the gap cannot record a magnetic pattern that is shorter than its own width, any more than a thin line can be drawn with a broad pen nib (without using the nib sideways), so the effect of gap-width on high frequencies can be seen: the narrower the gap, the higher the upper frequency limit.

It follows too, that increasing the tape speed increases the recorded wavelength and thereby also extends the high-frequency response. The tape speeds used for domestic recorders are: 7½, 3¾, and 1⅞ inches per second. At one time only 7½ in/s was considered good enough for good quality recordings, while 3¾ was capable of fair results where tape economy was also required, and 1⅞ for speech only where maximum economy was the main consideration. Maximum upper frequency response was around 12 kHz for 7½ in/s, 8 kHz for 3¾, and about 4 kHz for 1⅞. In recent years there has been considerable development in recording-head design, enabling narrower and more accurate gaps to be formed. The result has been considerable improvement in high-frequency response so that the lower speeds can give acceptable results, and 10 kHz and over can be recorded at 1⅞ in/s. This in fact is the speed used in cassette recorders, while cartridges use 3¾ in/s. It should be added that not all recorders yield such figures; it depends on the head design as well as other factors.

When recording very short wavelengths (i.e. high frequencies), at slow tape speeds, the magnetic particles on the tape play an increasingly important part in the response. Recently materials other than iron oxide have been used, one of which is chromium dioxide. These particles are smaller and of more regular shape, so better results can be obtained at low speeds. A snag with this type of tape (apart from the higher cost) is increased head wear, although this is receiving attention from the tape manufacturers and efforts are being made to overcome it.

Having produced the series of magnetic patterns on the tape, playback can be achieved by simply passing the tape across the same or another similar head. As the magnetised portions traverse the gap they induce changing magnetic fields in the core that produce voltages in the coils. These voltages are very small and a high-gain amplifier is needed to reproduce them.

One very important factor is that both the recording head gap and that of the playback head should be in the same plane. For the sake of standardisation, enabling one tape to be played on another machine, this plane is vertical, but it could in theory be at any angle from the perpendicular. If the head-gap is not vertical its width is effectively

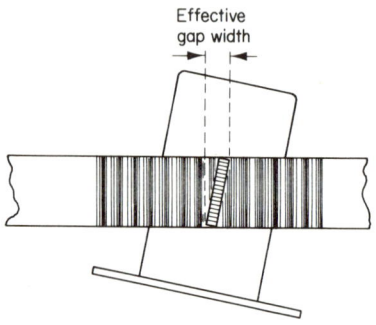

Figure 3.6. A non-vertical slit bridges adjacent magnetic zones at high frequencies, and the effective width is increased resulting in poor treble response. (The whole width of the tape is here shown recorded to show the effect; in practice only part, corresponding to one track, would be affected at a time.)

increased when viewed vertically (Figure 3.6) and bridges adjacent high-frequency magnetic zones on the tape. The result is a loss of the high frequencies giving a dull and muffled reproduction. Tape recorders have facilities for the internal adjustment of the head angle (termed the azimuth), while some, such as players using the cartridge format, have the azimuth control brought out to the control panel for user adjustment.

A recording can be erased either by wiping the tape with a permanent magnet or by running it past an erase head. This is similar to the record/playback head but is fed with a high-level high-frequency signal derived from the same oscillator that supplied the recording-bias. All tape recorders have an erase head across which the tape passes before it reaches the record head. Thus the tape is pre-erased before recording, and a recording can be made on a tape that has already got an old recording on it; there is no need to wipe it out first as this will be done automatically. Some recorders have the erase and record heads combined.

It should be noted that these remarks apply only to tape *recorders;* instruments designed only for playback have no recording-bias circuits or facilities for erasing. The majority of mobile tape systems are players only.

The types of player are considered in more detail in subsequent chapters; here it is sufficient to note the basic differences in tape width and track disposition. Reel-to-reel recorders use standard 0.246-inch width tape, and record either two or four tracks. In two-track machines the gap appears across the upper half of the tape and records on that portion; the other half of the tape is recorded by turning the tape over and starting from the other end. With four-track models, there are two gaps in the record head, one above the other, and the tracks are interposed so that tracks 1 and 3 are recorded with the tape going one way and 2 and 4 with it going the other. The more tracks there are, the narrower they must be and the smaller the induced signal on playback. Thus the signal/noise ratio is poorer on narrow tracks, and any tape irregularities producing volume fluctuations (termed *drop-out*) are more pronounced in their effect. Reel-to-reel machines, although capable of the best quality, are less convenient to use than the other types and so are not normally employed in mobile systems.

Cartridge systems use standard tape running at 3¾ in/s, but with 8 tracks recorded on it, and the tape is wound in such a way that the ends are joined to form a complete loop. Thus all the tracks run in the same direction. Tracks are selected not by electrical switching of the appropriate headgap, as with the open-reel recorders, but by physical movement of the head.

With cassettes, the tape is just over half the width of standard tape, and the running speed is 1⅞ in/s. Either four or two tracks can be recorded, the four being used to provide two stereo programmes. The tracks are started from opposite ends of the tape as with the open-reel machines, but they are not interleaved; 1 and 2 are in one direction and 3 and 4 in the other. This enables the longer gap of a mono player to 'read' the two adjacent tracks simultaneously and thus reproduce both stereo channels in mono.

Mechanical drive

All tape recorders and players need mechanical arrangements for passing the tape across the heads and spooling it up ready for rewinding or playing the other tracks. An additional facility enables the tape to be rapidly rewound or wound forward so that desired parts of the recording can be located and played.

The tape drive must be at constant speed, but this is not so easy to do as it may sound because minor speed fluctuations can and do occur even on the best machines. Any speed fluctuation causes a variation of pitch in the reproduced sound. There can be long-term variations such as a gradual change of speed from one end of the tape to the other. This is not so serious providing the change is not great, and most likely would pass unnoticed. More noticeable are variations of shorter duration known as *wow* and *flutter*. Wow is a regular variation occurring several times a second arising from uneven running in one of the rotating parts, while flutter is a much faster irregular fluctuation usually due to the tape sticking on some surface and proceeding in a rapid succession of jerks.

In order to give as steady a drive as possible, the tape drive spindle is directly coupled to a flywheel. The effectiveness of any flywheel to maintain a smooth rotation depends on its mass and speed, which is why small battery recorders cannot achieve the same speed stability as the large mains-operated units with much larger flywheels. As rotational speed is a factor, the higher tape speeds produce better wow and flutter figures than the lower ones; so, on the basis of speed stability as well as frequency response, the faster tape speeds are best. It is true that some of the more expensive hi-fi cassette decks use electronic control of the motor to sense the instantaneous speed of the tape-drive component and feed back a correcting signal to the motor, thus achieving remarkable speed stability for the tape speed. These are rarely if ever found on mobile equipment however, so the normal performance limitations hold good.

The flywheel is driven from the motor either by a rubber-tyred intermediate wheel or by a rubber or composition belt. These components are often afflicted by aging and other maladies: belts stretch or go hard, and intermediate wheels (often called idler wheels) perish or develop flats on their surface. The effect is usually slow or irregular running, or, in the case of the idler flat, knocking noises.

The motor is a small d.c. commutator unit with built-in electrical governor. This consists of a pair of contacts, to one of which is fixed a small weight. When the speed rises beyond a certain point the weight is pulled out by centrifugal force and opens the contacts. As the speed drops the weight returns and the contacts close. The tension of the outer contact is set by a screw adjustment which therefore serves as a pre-set speed control. This should not be altered unless some means of accurately checking the tape speed is to hand.

In addition to driving the tape across the heads, the player must spool it up ready for rewinding or replaying. A complication here is the fact that the take-up spool, whether an open-reel or a cassette hub, does not revolve at a uniform speed. When it is empty at the start of the tape, each revolution picks up a small quantity of tape equal to the circumference of the hub, but as it fills, the hub size increases due to previous tape layers and it picks up ever increasing quantities. It must therefore turn at a gradually diminishing speed as the tape progresses.

The solution is quite a simple one; the spool is driven through a friction clutch. This generally takes the form of a pair of plates with a felt pad in between. One plate is driven from the motor or flywheel via a belt or idler wheel, and the other driving the spool is spring loaded against the pad. Thus the spool-drive continually slips, being controlled by the tension of the tape.

.There is a refinement found on some cassette recorders whereby the motor is switched off when the cassette is finished. This can be accomplished in a number of ways. One system senses the tape-tension by a spring-loaded feeler arm. When the tape ends, the paying-spool stops because the tape is anchored to it, but as the drive continues the tension increases. This actuates the feeler arm, which releases a latch securing the 'play' button thereby returning it to the off position. Other methods cause trip mechanisms to operate when one of the spools cease to revolve, some using mechanical and others electronic means. Such devices are not needed with cartridge units since these use continuous tape.

A further mechanical function enables the tape to be wound forwards or backwards at speed. Not all players have this facility, while some include the rewind but not the fast-forward. Here, a belt or idler drive is communicated directly from the motor to the appropriate spool-carrier with a much lower gear-ratio than the flywheel drive. In some cases, the motor governor is shorted-out so that maximum motor speed and torque can be developed.

Equalising

A final point concerns the frequency response of tape systems. This is purposely tailored to emphasise and curtail various frequencies for certain reasons.

The recording head does not respond equally to currents of all frequencies, and this together with other frequency-sensitive losses means that the response is constant only between about 1 kHz and 5 kHz. Above and below there is a falling off. To compensate for this, treble frequencies are boosted during recording and bass frequencies during playback. Thus the overall record/playback response is level.

In addition to this an additional boost is given to the higher frequencies at the slower speeds in order to compensate for the falling treble response inherent at those speeds. However, this also results in a peak in the frequencies that are just below the point at which they start to fall away, and the result is an artificial brilliance which can give a harsh tone to the reproduction.

Part 2

Practical
Applications

Chapter 4

Power Supplies

The power supply circuits for a modern car radio or audio system could not be more straightforward. Transistors require a low-voltage d.c. supply and so are well-suited for running directly from the 12-V car battery. The motors used in tape players can be designed for any voltage a.c. or d.c., and so 12-V d.c. units are used for all car equipment. The design of these is quite different from those used in mains-operated players and cannot be interchanged.

The main consideration in the power circuit is to get rid of any interference that might be generated by the dynamo, voltage-regulator or any other part of the car electrical system, and that might be conducted into the radio or player along the power lead. This interference takes the form of a.c. waveforms, usually of a spiky and irregular nature, superimposed on the d.c. supply. There are two ways of preventing these from affecting the receiver circuits; one is to wire an iron-cored inductor or coil in series with the power lead, and the second is to connect a capacitor across it from the power lead to chassis.

An inductor offers an impedance to any alternating currents, the impedance rising with the frequency, yet allows d.c. to pass unhindered (except for the small d.c. resistance). Thus interference-frequencies are opposed in their path and greatly reduced. A capacitor has the opposite effect—it passes a.c. signals and blocks d.c.—so the shunted capacitor effectively bypasses interference to chassis without affecting the d.c. supply.

Practical filter circuits employ both components, usually two series inductors with a shunt capacitor taken from the junction between them. The circuit is shown in Figure 4.1; sometimes an additional inductor and capacitor are used as seen in (b) to give extra protection.

As a safeguard in case of a short-circuit developing in the receiver, a fuse is fitted. The value varies between models but 1.0, 1.5, and 2.0 A are common ratings. The fuse-holder is usually mounted in the power-lead itself, there being two halves that interlock on the bayonet

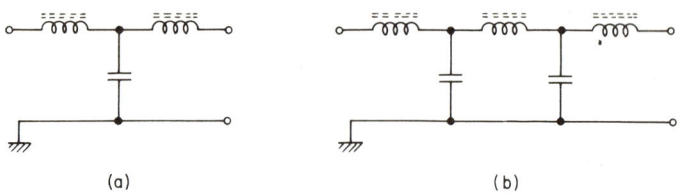

Figure 4.1. (a) Supply-line interference filter; (b) a more elaborate filter

principle, similar to the electric lamp and holder. An internal spring keeps the fuse in contact with both ends.

Occasionally another component may be encountered in the receiver power circuits although it is not often used. This is the zener diode, the symbol for which is shown in Figure 4.2. If a resistor is placed in series with a load in order to drop the voltage, the actual voltage dropped will depend on the current through the resistor, which in turn depends on the current drawn by the load. If the load current varies, the voltage appearing at the end of the resistor also varies.

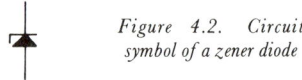

Figure   4.2.   Circuit symbol of a zener diode

A zener diode is so designed that variations of current passing through it will not produce corresponding voltage variations; the voltage remains the same within close limits. Thus in the circuit of Figure 4.3, whatever variations may be introduced by the load current or even the supply voltage, the voltage across the diode will be constant. This affords a means of stabilising voltages where required.

Although a nominal 12 V, the voltage of a car supply system can vary considerably depending on the state of the battery and the charging rate of the dynamo. If the battery is low and the vehicle stationary, the voltage can be down to 10 V or even less, yet when charging at speed the voltage can rise to 15 V or more. It follows that there must be some latitude in design to allow for such voltage variations, although where it is necessary to maintain a stable voltage to ensure steady operation of the circuit, and to ensure the safety of the transistors, a zener diode may be used.

The different types of zener diode relate to different power dissipations, but each type is available in a family of zener voltages, and the correct one must be chosen for the application required. The BZY 88 for example can be obtained in any one of 24 different voltages from 3.3 V to 30 V.

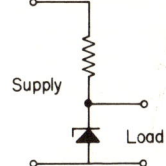

Figure 4.3. Basic stabilising circuit using zener diode; voltage is maintained across the diode irrespective of the current through it or load

Vibrator power supplies

Before the days of transistors, car radios used valves. While such equipment must be considered obsolete, the service engineer may still encounter the occasional one, and valves may be found for certain specialised applications.

Valve power supplies are not quite so simple as they are for transistors. A valve needs a high-tension voltage of 100–200 V, and also a low-voltage supply for the heater. The latter is the easiest to arrange, since 6-V valves can be connected in a series-parallel circuit (Figure 4.4) to operate from 12 V. At one time many cars used a 6-V electrical system, so car radios often had an adjustable linkage arrangement that enabled all the valves to be connected in parallel and thus run from 6 V, or changed to the series-parallel circuit for 12 V.

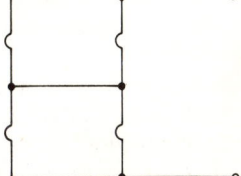

Figure 4.4. Series/parallel heater circuit as used in valve car radios

The h.t. supply is the biggest complication. While a transformer can be used to step up to any required voltage, it works only from a.c. So it is necessary to convert the d.c. battery voltage to a.c., apply this to a step-up transformer, then convert it back to d.c. again and smooth it. A rather roundabout process, but the only possible way.

The conversion from d.c. to a.c. is brought about by a *vibrator*. Current from the battery is made to flow through a coil in the vibrator via a pair of contacts. The resulting magnetic field attracts the end of a long vertical arm or reed on which is mounted one of the contacts, thus breaking the connection. The current and magnetic attraction cease, the reed returns to its former position owing to its springiness, and the cycle repeats. The operation is the same as for a d.c. buzzer or bell.

Another set of contacts is provided, one to either side of the reed and mating ones on the reed itself. The reed is connected to earth, so the reed-contacts earth each of the side-contacts alternately. The latter are connected to opposite ends of a centre-tapped transformer winding, so the polarity of the applied battery voltage is constantly being reversed between the centre-tap and one end (Figure 4.5). Thus an alternating current is applied to the transformer primary, and a stepped-up voltage appears at the secondary.

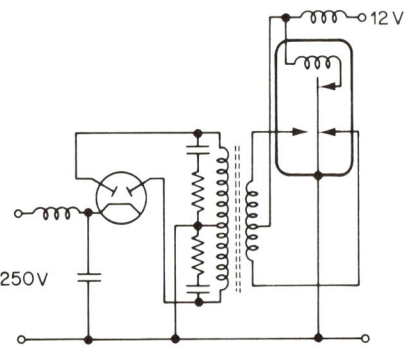

Figure 4.5. Non-synchronous vibrator circuit: vibrating reed switches supply to alternate ends of transformer primary thus generating a.c. voltage across it; voltage is stepped up by secondary winding and rectified by valve rectifier

The secondary, high-tension voltage is of course a.c., so it must be converted back to d.c., or rectified. With a simple non-synchronous vibrator, this can be done by using a valve rectifier in a circuit—very similar to the power circuits of a valve mains radio—known as a full-wave circuit. Positive pulses appear alternately at opposite ends of the secondary winding relative to the centre-tap, which is earthed. The pulses are applied to the rectifier anodes, which conduct alternately so that the cathode is always positive with respect to earth.

A disadvantage with this arrangement is that the extra valve needed, the rectifier, must be supplied with heater current. To overcome the problem, cold-cathode rectifiers were used in some radios. These were filled with mercury vapour instead of the usual vacuum. The vapour ionised with electron bombardment and became conductive without the need to heat the cathode. A characteristic of such valves was that they operated with a blue glow around the electrodes. It might be added that any such glow in an ordinary valve indicates the valve contains gas or is 'soft', and is therefore unserviceable.

. Another method of rectifying the high-tension a.c. voltage is to use a further set of contacts on the vibrator and make it self-rectifying. This is known as a synchronous vibrator, and the circuit is shown at Figure 4.6. Here, the ends of the secondary winding are alternately earthed by the reed contacts, so it is the centre-tap which is the positive in this case. As the reed that rectifies the secondary current is the same one that produces the primary alternations, there is no synchronisation problem.

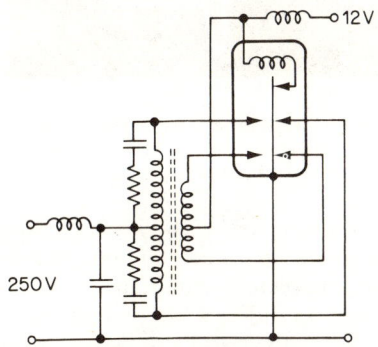

Figure 4.6. Synchronous vibrator circuit: an extra set of contacts rectifies the secondary current and so eliminates the valve rectifier

The a.c. waveform produced by the vibrator is not a smooth sine wave but a square wave, owing to the on-off switching action. The transients or sudden current changes thus involved produce what is termed 'ringing' or overshoot in the transformer windings. This results in sharp peaks appearing on the leading edges of the waves which could cause insulation breakdown in the transformer (Figure 4.7). To suppress these, a capacitor and resistor are connected across the winding. These capacitors, known as buffers, need to be of a high voltage rating (at least 1000 V d.c. or 300 V a.c.) otherwise they too would break down under the strain. They were in fact common causes of breakdown, and often needed replacement.

Vibrators themselves would also give trouble after a time, the contacts becoming pitted and burnt. While they could be filed and cleaned up, their operation was always inclined to be somewhat erratic afterwards, and as they were sealed in cans that were not easy to open the best cure was usually a replacement. The mounting consisted of a plug-in arrangement similar to a valve, so substitution was relatively easy. The first test on a dead car-radio was always to feel the vibrator to see if the vibrations could be felt. If not a tap on the side would often get a faulty one started thereby indicating the cause of the trouble.

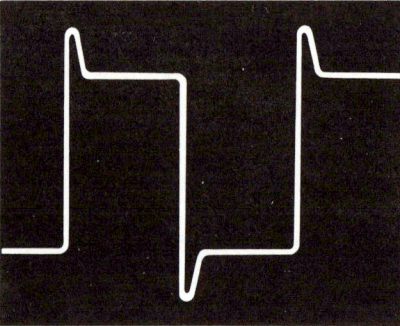

Figure 4.7. Waveform of vibrator. Peaks caused by switching surges could break down transformer; they are removed by shunted buffer capacitors

The main problem associated with vibrator power supplies is the interference caused by the sparking contacts. This is known as hash and can rarely be completely eliminated. Filter capacitors and inductors are necessary in the input and output circuits; the vibrator metal casing must be earthed and the power and receiver circuits housed in separate compartments screened from each other. Leads in and out of the power section are often screened too. An important factor is that the metal casing of the radio helps to confine radiation of vibrator interference to the power section. It is essential to replace all the fixing screws as these serve to earth the case to the receiver chassis at many different points.

Rotary converters

Another method of providing power for a valve circuit is the rotary converter. Like the vibrator, the transistor has rather rendered them obsolete, but they served a good purpose in their day, and may still be encountered for special applications. The basic principle is quite simple, that of a motor coupled on the same shaft and in the same casing as a generator. The motor is designed to operate from the battery voltage, 12 V or in some cases 24 V. The generator is rated to give 250 V d.c. or as required. The advantage over the vibrator is that rectification is not needed, nor the step-up transformer; also larger h.t. currents can be obtained.

The converter's disadvantages are its size and weight, and its lower efficiency, compared with the vibrator. Its current capacity made it specially suitable for larger applications such as public address amplifiers, but it was never used for car radio receivers.

Hybrid circuits

The noise and low gain of early transistors when operated at radio frequencies, along with stability problems arising from high internal capacitances, made them of dubious value in r.f. and i.f. stages of car radios, where the available signal is often of a low level. Valves were undoubtedly superior then, and the best application for a transistor was in the output stage.

As a result, a special range of valves was developed that would operate with a very low high-tension, down to 12 V in fact, so that they could be run directly from the car battery without a vibrator. While this is feasible for low-signal applications, a valve output stage needs a much higher voltage if sufficient power is to be available to drive the loudspeaker. So hybrid circuits appeared that used valves for all stages except the output, for which a large power transistor was employed. Valve heater ratings are 6.3 V, which enables four to be series-parallel connected to run from the car battery. Type-numbers of valves in this range are: **ECH 83** (triode heptode); **EBF 83** (double-diode pentode), and EF 98 (audio pentode).

A large number of hybrid car radios were made and put into service, and many still are, so the service engineer can expect to meet up with them quite frequently. A very popular example was the Philips N3G82. This used one ECH 83 as an r.f. amplifier and a.f. amplifier, another ECH 83 as a frequency changer, an EBF 83 i.f. amplifier, demodulator and a.g.c., and an EF 98 as an audio driver. The output transistor was either an OC 16 or, in later models, an OC 19.

Positive or negative earth

Cars differ in the polarity of their electrical system. At one time the negative earth was the most common; gradually this was superseded by the positive earth, which for many years was the standard with just a few models differing. Now, the trend is back to the negative earth once more.

Radio and audio equipment designed for car installation have but a single power lead for connection to the car electrical system, the return path being provided through the metal casing or frame which is in contact with the car chassis. This means that the equipment must be of the same earth polarity as that of the car. It often happens that a car radio is removed from one vehicle and re-fitted in another with a different earthed pole without any thought for the polarity, and the result is often damage to the transistors. In theory all the transistors could be damaged, but in practice the heavy current taken by the output transistor blows the fuse, so that the time the receiver is actually subject to the wrong polarity is short. Only the output transistor may be affected, the others having escaped, and in some cases only the emitter resistor suffers damage. Even so it is risky to connect up to the wrong polarity, and this should always be checked when fitting equipment.

Car radio polarity has, as may be expected, followed the trends in vehicle polarity. Positive earths have been the norm until recently. Some of these have been non-convertible, others convertible, and yet others dual-polarity models. The non-convertibles as their name implies cannot be converted because all the internal circuit positive connections are taken to various earthing points on the case and there is no possibility of isolating them. With the convertible models, groups of positive and negative connections are made to several terminal tags; conversion involves removing the chassis connections from one group and transferring them to the other, while negative supply line connections are removed from the second and taken to the

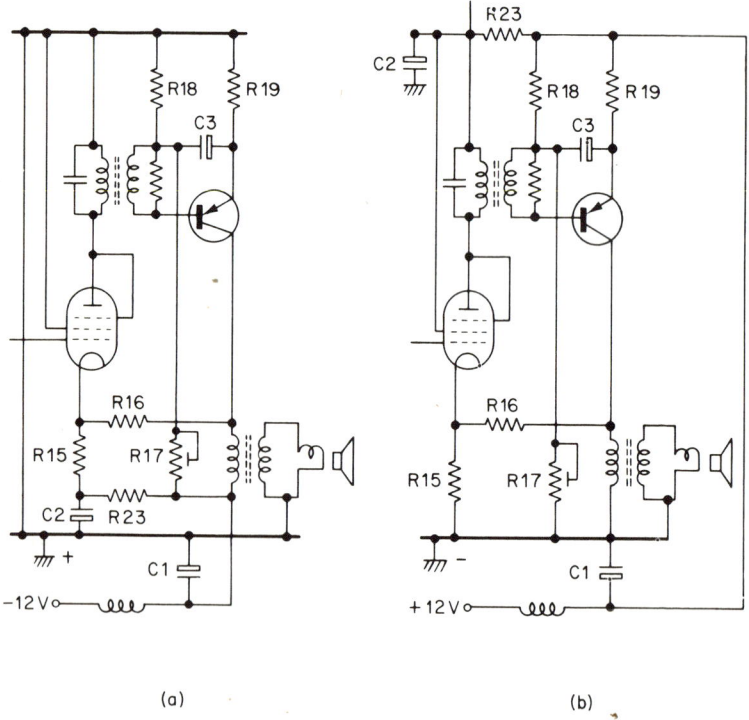

(a)   (b)

Figure 4.8.   (a) Example of what is involved in polarity conversion—part of circuit of Philips G82 wired for positive earth; (b) same circuit converted to negative earth

first. Any electrolytic capacitors that may be connected directly to the chassis must be reversed because they are polarised. On the other hand, earthed aerial-lead screening and connections to trimmer and tuning capacitors must be left intact. The process for each model is usually described in the maker's service manual, which should be followed to avoid errors or omissions. For an example of conversion, see Figure 4.8.

Dual-polarity models usually have all connections involved brought to contacts on a socket, and all that is necessary for a polarity change is to remove a plug from the socket and refit it in a different position. Some use a pair of soldered links that need to be resoldered across to different tags.

These dual-polarity receivers have been more common in recent years to enable any make of car to be equipped. However, since the swing back to negative earth by the car manufacturers radio and audio equipment is being made increasingly in non-convertible negative-earth models. Positive earth versions are in some cases available at extra charge.

Polarity converters

Non-convertible equipment can be fitted to a vehicle of opposite polarity by using a polarity converter. Cost must obviously be considered, as it would not be worth using a polarity converter with a cheap car radio; it would be more economical to change the radio. For the more expensive equipment, though, a converter is the answer.

This simple-sounding piece of equipment is rather more complicated than it may at first appear; it is not just a matter of juggling with the connections. The d.c. input is first converted to a.c. which is applied to a 1 : 1 ratio transformer. The output is rectified and smoothed back to d.c. again. Neither pole of the output is earthed within the unit: both are floating, so either can be earthed externally. Thus positive or negative earth can be obtained as required, irrespective of the polarity of the input.

Circuit details of a converter are shown in Figure 4.9. A pair of transistors are connected to a transformer so that the emitter currents pass through the primary winding. The secondary winding is connected across the bases thus providing positive feedback. This causes the transistors to oscillate in push-pull fashion, with one being driven negative while the other is driven positive due to the phase opposition of the transformer windings. Oscillation is controlled by the 500-Ω potentiometer that adjusts the base-bias.

An a.c. voltage produced by the oscillation appears across a third or tertiary winding, this being rectified by two silicon diode rectifiers

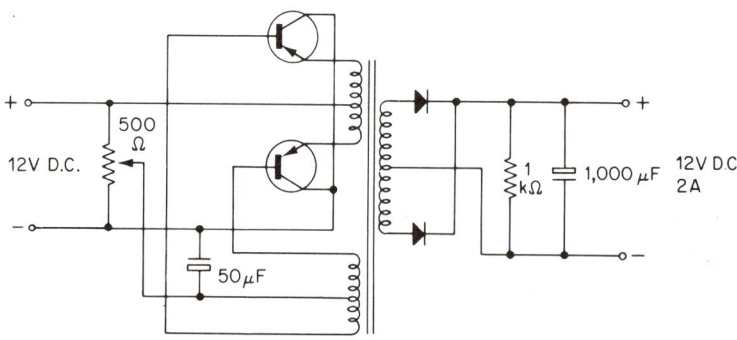

Figure 4.9.   Typical circuit of polarity converter

in a conventional full-wave circuit. A 1-kΩ resistor across the output helps to keep the voltage stable with variations of load, and the 1000-μF capacitor serves as a reservoir. The unit delivers a maximum of 2 A, which is ample for all transistor radios and most audio systems, although some of the larger quad systems may take more.

Voltage converters

The majority of car electrical systems are 12 V, but 6-V systems may occasionally be encountered not only in cars but also on motor-cycles (there is no reason why a radio should not be fitted to a sidecar). A converter can also be obtained that produces 12 V from a 6-V source. The circuit is identical to the polarity converter described above, but the transformer is wound to give double voltage output.

The larger commercial vehicles generally have a 24-V system, in which case the provision of 12 V for running a radio or audio system is much simpler. Here, the voltage converter may consist of nothing more than a resistor wired in series with the supply. A number of makers including Radiomobile list such components; however there are certain factors to be considered. The value of a resistor to drop 12 V (24 − 12) varies according to the current taken by the radio or player, and this can range from around 200 mA for a radio up to 1.8 A or more for a quad cartridge player. It follows that the value of the resistor holds good only for one current rating, and so should not be used indiscriminately for any model.

It is true that the voltage applied to car equipment varies anyway according to the state of the battery and the rate of charge, so there can be some latitude in resistor value. However, this cannot be taken too far considering the wide range of currents noted above. For example, since a resistor chosen to drop 12 V at 1.5 A would only drop 4 V at 0.5 A, a radio with this current rating would have $24 - 4 = 20$ V applied to it if used with such a resistor, and would undoubtedly be damaged.

The value of the resistor should therefore be calculated according to the current rating of the equipment to be used, which is by Ohm's Law $R = E/I$, where E is the voltage to be dropped (12 in this case) and I is the current in amps. For example, for a current of 1.5 A the resistor will be $12/1.5 = 8\Omega$. It is necessary that the resistor be capable of dissipating the power lost in the form of heat. This too can be calculated using the formula $W = EI$; in the above example, power to be dissipated will be $12 \times 1.5 = 18$ W. Thus a 20-W resistor would be required.

It may not be too easy to come by the correct value or one near to it (within 10% either way should be near enough, but no more than 15%). 10-W resistors of various values are stocked by most radio and t.v. workshops, so two of these in parallel would give a 20-W rating. The resistance of each would then have to be twice the required value; e.g. to get 8Ω two 15-Ω resistors in parallel would give 7.5Ω, which is near enough. The two resistors must be equal in resistance otherwise one would dissipate more power than the other and its individual power rating might be exceeded. If all else fails and an accurate ohmeter is available, it may be possible to make a resistor from an electric fire spiral element-wire. Choose the lowest wattage as this will have the highest resistance and so need less wire. Measure the required resistance on the meter, cut the length, and then wind it on a heat-proof former, using screw-terminals for the connections.

Whatever type of resistor is used, remember that it will get hot in use and should be protected by a shield or case and mounted clear of other wiring. The case should be ventilated by holes and if possible positioned where free air will have access to it.

There is another factor to take into account, however. Radio or audio units that have a class B output stage do not draw steady current from the supply; it fluctuates with the rise and fall of constantly varying volume level. If such a stage is fed from a low-impedance constant-voltage supply such as a car battery, the voltage across the transistors will remain the same, but if a resistance is interposed it too will fluctuate along with the current. Varying voltage with signal has two effects: it reduces the audio power delivered by the output stage on loud passages, and also introduces distortion.

The effect is less with tape players because the motor current, which is steady, is added to the amplifier current. Thus the minimum current is greater, and the difference ratio between maximum and minimum less than for a radio. Class A output stages, that is those with a single large transistor, draw a steady current with only very small fluctuations, and the series resistor has no ill effect on these.

Complete elimination of this trouble can only be achieved by using a stabilising circuit made up of a number of transistors and other components. Some useful improvement can be obtained by connecting a large-value electrolytic capacitor across the equipment supply-lead to chassis (Figure 4.10). It should be at least 10 000 µF, a value that is becoming increasingly common and should not be difficult to obtain. When the radio is switched off the full battery voltage appears across it, so it should be rated at not less than 30 V working. Mount it well away from the resistor or other heat-producing parts because the life of an electrolytic is considerably shortened by heat. Remember too to observe polarity.

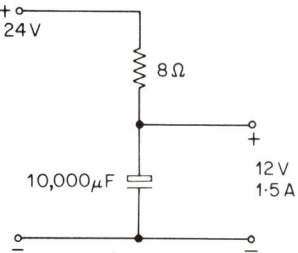

Figure 4.10. Dropping resistor for 12-V operation from 24 V at 1.5 A. Capacitor reduces distortion due to class B voltage fluctuation

This should smooth out rapid voltage fluctuations and greatly reduce the resulting distortion, but it will not do much for the longer fluctuations that reduce maximum audio power.

One snag with connecting a large-value capacitor in this manner is that it charges to full battery voltage when the radio or player is switched off, and so applies this voltage to the equipment immediately it is switched on again. This could cause damage to the transistors, but the drop in voltage as the capacitor discharges through the low-impedance equipment circuits is very rapid and it should reach its normal level within half-a-second. So the hazard, although present, is not too great. It could be eliminated entirely by wiring a switch in the top end of the resistor and using this to switch off instead of the equipment switch.

The only effective way of disposing of the problem of 24-V supplies is to use equipment that employs class A output stages, where the current is steady. Fewer of these are being made at present because of the demand for higher audio powers which can only be achieved economically by class B. Class A, then, is more likely to be found among the lower-powered radios. An alternative would be to use equipment designed for 24-V operation, but surprisingly, although the number of commercial vehicles in which radios are installed must be large, no major manufacturer at the time of writing is producing 24-V radio or audio equipment.

Tankers

While on the subject of commercial vehicles the situation affecting tankers designed for the transporting of petroleum spirit should be noted. In these, the electrical system is completely isolated from the chassis; two wires are run for all equipment, neither pole of the battery being earthed. This is to avoid the possibility of sparks should accidental contact occur between part of the system and any of the metalwork. An ordinary car radio cannot therefore be installed in the usual way. It must be completely isolated from the vehicle metalwork otherwise the electrical system would be earthed through the radio. Two wires for the power need to be run, one to the receiver's power lead as normal, and the other to the receiver case, correct polarity of course being observed.

Care is needed to see that no part of the loudspeaker or its wiring is in contact with the vehicle metalwork. The aerial lead must be watched particularly, because the screening is usually earthed to the metalwork where it is mounted and the other end is earthed to the receiver case via the outer part of the aerial plug. This screening is provided to eliminate ignition interference, but in the case of diesel engines such interference does not exist; the screening can therefore be disconnected from the aerial plug or from the metalwork at the aerial mounting point, whichever is the more practicable. Should other forms of interference prove troublesome, a 0.1 μF capacitor can be connected between the receiver case and the vehicle metalwork, thus earthing the case to r.f. currents but blocking the d.c. An easier solution is to use a radio specially designed for petrol tankers which is in fact isolated and has a two-wire power lead. Radiomobile supply such a model with the letters ISOL as a suffix after the model number. The regulations for two-wire systems do not apply to paraffin tankers, so normal installations can be made in these.

Portable tape-recorders

It may be desired to use a portable cassette recorder in a car, but to run it off the car power system to conserve its internal batteries. Most recorders have sockets for connecting an external supply. The most common battery voltage for portable recorders is 9 V, so this means dropping down from the vehicle 12-V supply.

Similar problems arise as with the 24 to 12 V drop, although they are less pronounced. All portable recorders use class B output stages, causing a voltage-fluctuations-with-volume-variation situation, but as there is only a 3-V drop the fluctuations are over a smaller range. Furthermore, portable recorders have a limited audio power, usually less than 1 W, so the current taken by the amplifier is small compared to that taken by the motor. As we saw earlier, steady current such as that taken by a motor passing through the dropping resistor along with the fluctuating current reduces the proportion of voltage fluctuations.

A further improvement in voltage stability can be made by increasing the steady current by means of a bleeder resistor connected across the recorder. This is rendered practicable by the low current taken by the instrument, usually around 300–400 mA, but would not be possible with larger currents. A bleeder can be fitted that will increase the total current to around 1 A and thus give a good degree of voltage stability.

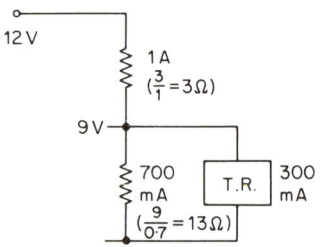

Figure 4.11.   Dropping resistor with bleeder for running 9-V 300-mA portable recorder from car

The resistors can be calculated according to Ohm's law (Figure 4.11). The top resistor must drop 3 V at a current of 1 A, so $E/I = 3/1 = 3\,\Omega$. The bottom one must drop 9 V at a current of 700 mA (assuming the recorder to take 300 mA), so $9/0.7 = 13\,\Omega$ approximately. The wattage of the top resistor will be $E \times I = 3 \times 1 = 3$ W, and that of the lower one $9 \times 0.7 = 6.3$ W. So a 5-W and a 10-W resistor respectively can be used to give a good safety margin. Values can be calculated in the same manner for recorders taking different currents, and for 6-V machines. An electrolytic capacitor across the bleeder resistor will as in the case of the 24 to 12 V conversion help, but in this case 1000 μF should be sufficient. The presence of the bleeder resistor will prevent it charging up to full battery voltage. To avoid continual drain on the battery when the recorder is not in use, some form of switch should be included to open-circuit the supply to the resistors. If this could be incorporated with the plug so that the supply is interrupted when the plug is withdrawn from the car instrument panel, it would add to the convenience and prevent the switch being accidentally left on. Alternatively, a small case containing the components could be mounted in the connecting lead between recorder and 12-V dashboard socket.

Adaptors with transistor-stabilised circuits are made for obtaining the best results from portable equipment in the car. An example is the Sony DCC 126, which has a switchable output to give 4.5, 6 or 9 V. It is compact in size and particularly useful if different pieces of equipment with difference voltage and current ratings are to be used at various times in the car.

Transvertors

It may become necessary to use, from the car, equipment that is normally mains-operated. For example, a recording may have to be made in the open air using a high-quality open-reel recorder, or it may be desired to run an amplifier or disc player where there is no mains supply. The answer for audio, as well as non-audio, applications needing mains power is the transvertor. This is a piece of equipment that provides an a.c. supply of 115 or 230 V from a 12-V car battery. An example is the range of transvertors made by Valradio, with power ratings of 50–500 W.

There are two basic types of transvertor. In the first (Figure 4.12) a pair of transistors are used in a self-oscillating push-pull circuit with transformer T1 providing feedback from one collector to the bases. The transformer reaches magnetic saturation each half-cycle, with the current rising to maximum value, remaining there until the magnetic field collapses, then rising rapidly to the opposite maximum. This produces a rough square wave, and the a.c. output is of this waveform. Repetition rate depends on the magnetic properties of the transformer, which can be varied by adjusting an air-gap in the transformer core. Hence the frequency can be adjusted, an increase in the gap producing an increase in frequency. The range is approximately 45–55 Hz.

The oscillator feeds an output transformer that produces the output voltage. There are two windings forming the secondary; in series they give 230 V, while in parallel they develop 115 V. Smaller voltage adjustments can be made by means of tappings on one of the secondaries. An inductor is connected in series with the output in order to round off the square waveform and remove the transients, which could have a detrimental effect on the equipment being operated. Both output voltage and frequency are dependent on the load as well as on the input voltage. Frequency can vary by ±3 Hz.

The second type of transvertor (Figure 4.13) uses two transistors in a low-level oscillator circuit with cross-coupled feedback capacitors.

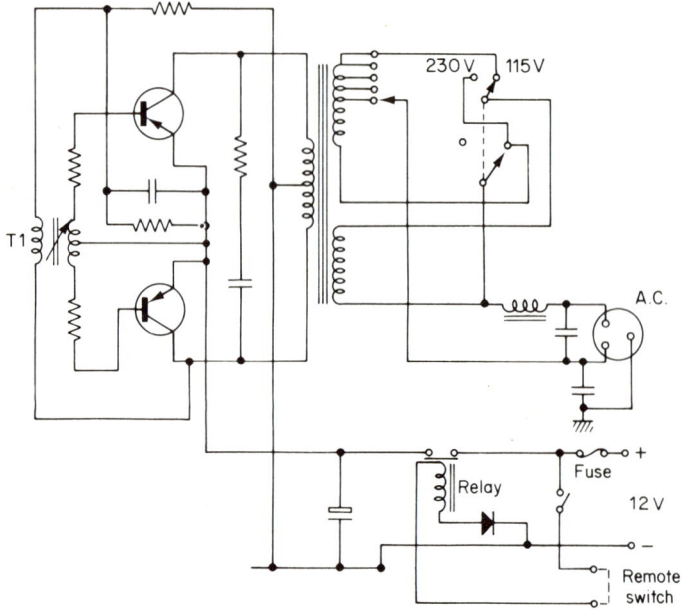

Figure 4.12. Valradio B 12/150T transvertor circuit

A coarse and fine frequency adjustment is provided by two variable resistors that alter the base bias, and a balance control is included to give a symmetrical waveform to the generated sinewave. A second pair of transistors amplify the signal, which is then applied to the two output transistors. The secondary of the output transformer is tapped to provide voltage adjustment. Frequency and output voltage are much less dependent on the load current than with the previous type, and frequency stability is generally within ±0.25 Hz. Output waveform is sinusoidal.

While the former cheaper transvertor can be used for audio equipment, it is mainly intended for power tools and similar applications. Recorder motors rely on the supply frequency in most cases to govern their speed, so they need a close-tolerance frequency supply as given by the latter type if speed and pitch variations are to be avoided in the reproduction.

Both types have a relay in the input circuit, i.e. a device that operates a switch when current is passed through an energising coil. A rectifier is connected in series with the coil so that current only flows and closes the switch when the battery polarity is correct. If the power leads are reversed, the relay does not operate and the transvertor is

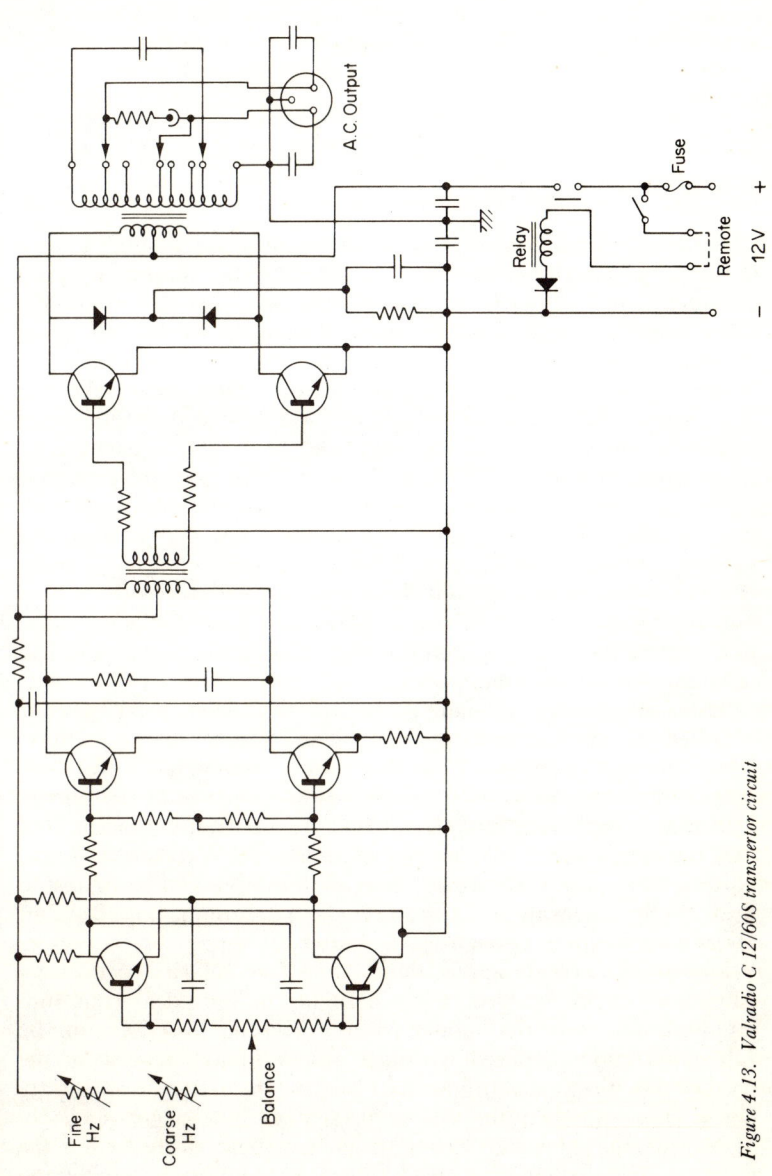

Figure 4.13. Valradio C 12/60S transvertor circuit

not switched on. Thus the transistors are protected. All transvertors generate a strong magnetic hum-field around them, a point to consider when siting them relative to tape-recorders: they should be kept not less than three feet apart. Input leads from the battery should be short as possible to avoid excessive voltage drop due to heavy input currents.

Efficiency

The basic rule of physics that power cannot be produced from nothing, although elementary, must not be forgotten when considering mobile power supplies of any kind. So whatever power is taken from the output must be supplied from the battery; changing the voltage, polarity, or d.c. to a.c. does not alter that fact, although it is often overlooked. Hence a transvertor from which a current of only 2 A is taken at 230 V is in fact supplying $2 \times 230 = 460$ W, which must come from the battery, so a current of $460/12 = 38$ A at least will be taken from the battery. Of the various power supply converters we have discussed, the rotary converter is probably the least efficient since the relatively large mass of the rotor must be kept in motion, and bearing and commutator friction overcome. The vibrator is more efficient as losses are less, but the vibrating reed must still be kept moving rapidly; while transistor oscillators are most efficient because there are no moving parts and the only losses are through electrical resistance and transformer losses.

These losses must be made good from somewhere, and they are supplied by extra current from the primary source, the car battery. Thus the wattage drawn from the battery is that taken from the output plus the conversion losses. The efficiency of an energy converter is expressed as a percentage; e.g. the transvertor is about 84% efficient, which means that of every 100 W taken from the battery, 84 appear as electrical power in the output and 16 are lost in heat. So, in our example of the previous paragraph, not 38 A but about 46 A would be taken from the battery.

For small-current applications such as polarity converters efficiency can be ignored, but where the power taken runs into hundreds of watts the total current including losses should be calculated and compared with the ampere/hour capacity of the battery. Short runs may be harmless because the battery is constantly being charged when the car is travelling, but longer spells of high-discharge when the car is stationary could easily flatten the battery. When calculating the battery's capability, remember too that the ampere/hour capacity as stated relates to a particular rate of discharge; high rates of discharge reduce the capacity considerably.

Chapter 5

Loudspeakers

It is a remarkable fact that, in spite of all the progress and invention of the last few decades in the field of sound reproduction, the basic design of the actual sound reproducer, the loudspeaker, has remained unchanged over fifty years. Whether for costly high-fidelity audio system or humble transistor radio, the loudspeaker differs only in size, materials and refinement of design.

The operating principle is known as the moving-coil movement (Figure 5.1). The actual sound waves are produced by a lightweight cone, usually made of paper composition, which is secured by a springy flexible mounting around its rim. At the apex is fixed a small cylinder around which is wound a coil of wire. The cylinder with its coil is introduced into the gap between the poles of a concentric magnet so that the centre pole is inside the cylinder and the outer pole surrounds it. The magnetic lines of force cross from one pole to the other through the coil of wire and, because the gap is small, the magnetic field is intense. A metal frame holds the magnet and the edge of the cone in their respective positions, and a ribbed flexible disc is cemented around the cone/coil junction, with the perimeter cemented to the frame or outer magnet pole. This keeps the coil in the centre of the gap and prevents it rubbing on either pole-piece. The ends of the coil are taken a short way down the cone and cemented in place where they are joined to a pair of flexible wires that are connected to a tag-strip mounted on the frame.

There then we have the complete loudspeaker; now to see how it operates. If an electric current is passed through the coil, the magnetic field set up by it interacts with that of the magnet to cause the coil to move physically either forward or backward depending on the polarity of the current. This in turn causes the cone to move forward or backward in a piston-like fashion, the motion being limited by the centering-disc at the magnet and the flexible mounting at the rim.

The output of the amplifier is an alternating current of complex

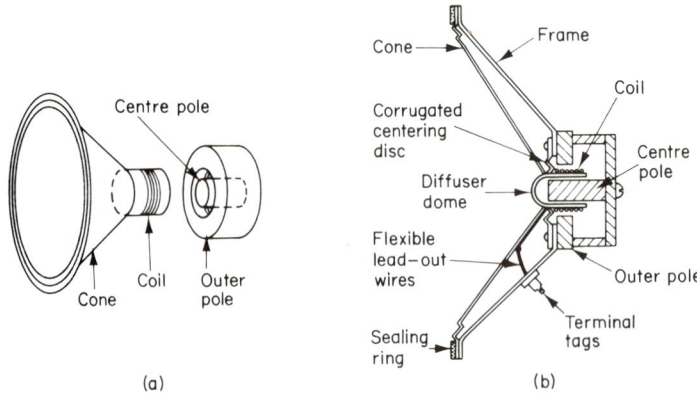

Figure 5.1. (a) Cone and magnet assembly of moving-coil speaker; (b) diagram of complete moving-coil speaker

waveforms that correspond to the sound waves of the original programme. These produce similar motions of the coil, and hence the cone, of the loudspeaker. The forward and backward motion thus produces sound waves which, if there is little distortion in the complete chain from studio to loudspeaker, resemble very closely the original sound waves in the studio.

It should be mentioned here that sound waves do not travel in an up-and-down manner like sea-waves or ripples in a pond, but with a forwards-and-backwards motion, rather like shock waves along a coil-spring that produce compression and expansion between adjacent coils. So really a sound-wave consists of alternate areas of low and high pressure. In other respects the ripple-on-the-pond analogy is a good one, because sound spreads out in all directions as ripples from a stone thrown in a pond, but in a vertical as well as horizontal plane. The number of waves per second is known as the frequency (the unit being the hertz, abbreviated Hz), high frequencies giving the treble sounds and low frequencies the bass. The wavelength, i.e. the distance between succeeding wave peaks, is also sometimes used to describe the frequency because the longer the wavelength, the lower the frequency.

Design factors

The basic design as described above is an effective one as shown by the length of time it has been used without major modification. It has a relatively high efficiency, producing a good sound level for a modest electrical input power, and responds reasonably well to a wide range of audio frequencies, although in the extreme lows and highs there are shortcomings.

There are however certain design problems. The cone should be as light as possible because it has to perform sudden changes of direction when responding to high frequencies and transient impulses. Mass results in inertia that inhibits such sudden movements. The cone must also be rigid because it should move in unison over the whole area in response to the drive applied to its centre. These requirements tend to conflict because most rigid materials tend to be heavy. Paper composition, sometimes doped with a stiffener, has been the standard compromise for years, but it is not ideal. An examination of a moving cone with a stroboscopic light at various frequencies can reveal buckling and deformation, with parts moving independently. Obviously this results in distorted sound, although it is not usually audible at lower sound levels.

To overcome this, other materials have been used, the most successful one being expanded polystyrene which combines lightness and rigidity. An example of the use of this material is the Poly-Planar range of loudspeakers made by Magitran, USA, and distributed in the UK by Highgate Acoustics. Owing to the natural rigidity of the material, there is no need even to adopt the conventional cone shape (which helps to rigidify ordinary paper composition material), and the speakers consist of flat panels of polystyrene. Concentric grooves are cut in the panels and filled with flexible material to give it the necessary compliance. There is no need of a metal frame, the panel being self-supporting, and so the whole construction is much thinner than conventional cone speakers, some being 1 inch and even less thick. This suits them particularly for car and caravan mounting, where space can be a problem especially if two or more speakers are required for stereo or quad systems.

Another method of achieving a minimum thickness is to mount the magnet inside the cone. To facilitate this, the coil cylinder must also be fixed inside the cone and the frame adapted accordingly.

Although coils are usually of copper wire, some of the more expensive loudspeakers use aluminium wire to reduce the weight. A large winding of many turns would again mean more mass and, owing to the fine wire that would have to be used, would be more fragile. The coil consists therefore of but few turns, which means it has a low electrical impedance. Impedances that have been used are 3, 4, 5, 8 and 16 Ω, but 4 and 8 Ω are the most usual ones now. Higher values up to 50 Ω have been used in some small transistor radios in order to match directly to the output stage without matching transformers, but these are not used for car equipment, where higher audio powers demand a higher signal current and hence lower impedance load to the amplifier.

Large magnets are desirable to provide a strong magnetic field and so keep the cone under control, avoiding spurious motion in the absence of an electrical signal. However with the space problems usually associated with mobile equipment, magnets have to be confined in size.

Loudspeaker enclosures

It may be thought that the only reason for putting a speaker in a box is to protect the cone and to make it look more presentable. This is not so. Sound is produced not only from the front of the loudspeaker cone but also from the back, because it too is moving adjacent layers of air, compressing and expanding them. However, because the rear air layers are being compressed while the front layers are being expanded and vice versa as the cone moves back and forth, the sound produced at the rear is in opposite phase to that at the front.

Unmounted, the loudspeaker just produces waves in the immediate vicinity of the cone which cancel each other on meeting at the rim, and so never get any farther (Figure 5.2a). When the speaker is mounted on a board with a hole in it that is just smaller than the cone so that there is no gap, the sound waves must travel farther out to the edge of the board, before they can meet and cancel (Figure 5.2b). By this time some of them have been radiated out into the listening area and the cancellation has no effect.

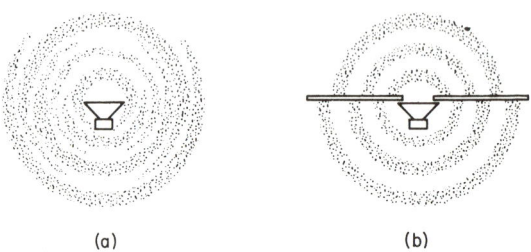

(a)   (b)

Figure 5.2. (a) Cancellation of out-of-phase sound pressure waves at the sides of unbaffled loudspeaker; (b) baffle keeps out-of-phase waves apart where wavelength is less than baffle radius

This cancelling phenomenon does not affect all frequencies alike. Sound waves with wavelengths longer than the distance between the front and back of the cone suffer, while those with shorter wavelengths do not. This means that the bass tones are affected the most. It also means that the longer we can make the path between the front and back of the cone, the better will be the bass response. So large baffles, as the mounting boards are termed, are the best. This explains why small transistor radios sound thin: the path between the front and back of the speaker cone is so limited.

The whole of the art of hi-fi loudspeaker enclosure design is to prevent cancellation without introducing other undesirable effects. One method is to completely enclose the cabinet and make it air-tight. This, known as the infinite baffle arrangement, produces a good bass from a small size, but because the cone is working against a cushion of trapped air it needs a lot more power to move it (rather like trying to work a foot-pump with a blocked air-line). With the limited amplifier powers available in mobile equipment (compared with hi-fi amplifiers) such sealed enclosures, although apparently attractive in giving good bass with small size, are not really practical. Other hi-fi types of enclosure must also be ruled out because of the size limitation, so we are left with the situation of putting mounting convenience and space availability first, and good bass response second.

Polar response

A moving-coil loudspeaker radiates sound from the front and rear and little if any to the sides. It has what is termed a figure-of-eight polar response. Low frequencies are propagated over a fairly wide angle around the front, so there is little difference if the listener is seated to one side of the speaker. As the frequency increases so the dispersion

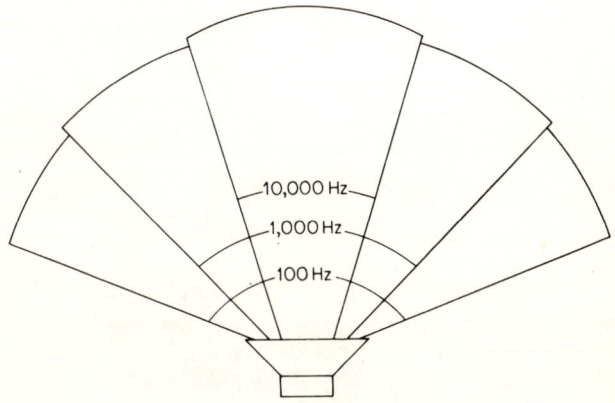

Figure 5.3. Sound dispersion angles of typical loudspeaker; angle narrows as frequency increases

angle narrows, until at high audio frequencies the output from the speaker is only a narrow beam in front (Figure 5.3). To get a balanced sound, then, the listener should sit right in front of the loudspeaker; if he is too far to one side, the treble will not be heard and the reproduction will lack clarity and brilliance.

This poses problems with car systems where the loudspeaker often must be mounted in an anything but ideal position, sometimes pointing upward from the rear parcel shelf or directed downward from underneath the front shelf. If there is a choice of position or speaker type, choose one where the speaker will to some extent be directed towards the listeners to give a good high-frequency audibility, and also one affording the maximum baffle area.

Mounting arrangements

There is a variety of mounting methods, the two main types being surface and flush mounting. The surface loudspeaker consists of a complete casing containing the loudspeaker which can be fixed to a convenient part of the car bodywork. Some are straightforward rectangular boxes of wood or plastic, others are spherical, others are angled to facilitate mounting on a sloping surface, while yet others are pod-shaped to give a semi-flush appearance (Figure 5.4). There are many variations between these and something will be available to suit almost any vehicle. The flush-mounting units are just a front cover, grille and bezel on which the loudspeaker is mounted. The whole lot is fitted over an aperture cut in the door trim, rear parcel shelf or kick-panel, the body of the loudspeaker being recessed into the shelf or trim. This takes the minimum of room and, because the trim or shelf acts as a large baffle,

Figure 5.4. Various shapes and sizes of surface-mounting loudspeaker cabinets

gives a good bass response, but the angle may not always be the best for good high-frequency coverage.

One enemy of all loudspeaker enclosures, hi-fi as well as the more modest variety, is resonance. Every physical object has a particular frequency at which it will vibrate if energy is applied to it. An example is an unbalanced road wheel which will often violently judder, but only at a certain speed when the frequency of rotation approaches the natural resonant frequency of the wheel and suspension.

Loudspeaker cones have such a frequency but it is usually well down into the bass region and gives an artificial boost to the bass response. The same is true of air trapped in an enclosure, and many hi-fi speakers make use of this to augment the bass. Objects near to or part of the loudspeaker mounting in a car may well resonate at certain musical frequencies, but because of their nature will not just augment those frequencies but will also produce an annoying rattle or buzz. Sometimes it can be quite difficult to trace the cause of such disturbances. Any loose or unsupported panels or trim should be secured in some way to damp vibrations down to a minimum.

Speaker faults

The moving-coil loudspeaker is quite a robust piece of equipment; it needs no maintenance, and rarely gives trouble. It is possible for the coil to go open-circuit but this is uncommon; what is more likely is that one of the flexible connecting leads between the cone and the terminal tag has broken. If broken at the tag end it can easily be resoldered, but make sure there is still some slack left, since it must not be pulled tight. If it has gone at the cone, it is usually possible to clean the blob where the lead joins the coil-wire, then apply some solder and solder on the broken lead. When tinning the lead preparatory to soldering, try not to tin too far along, because tinning destroys the flexibility and it is essential that the leads are flexible.

Moisture will damage the cone as well as rust the magnet pole-pieces and thereby cause them to foul the coil. Once the damage has been done there is not much that can be done to rectify it. The best course is prevention: do not mount the speakers where moisture will have access to them. Particular care must be taken in this respect when fitting to door panels.

A broken cone can be repaired without much trouble providing it is not broken too badly. The best way is to make a patch of stiff paper such as brown packing paper and glue it over the damaged area, making sure that all the broken edges are well stuck down (Figure 5.5). According to the nature of the damage, the patch can be stuck on either the front or the back of the cone.

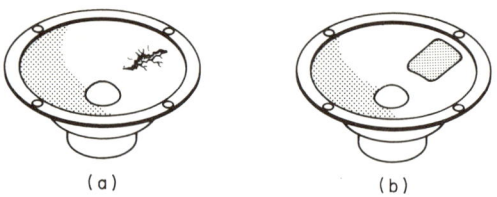

Figure 5.5. (a) Damaged cone. (b) Repair by gluing patch of stiff paper over damaged area; make sure all edges are well stuck down

Grating noises, thin reproduction and distortion can all be due to the coil rubbing against one of the magnet pole-pieces. First check with another speaker to make sure it is not an amplifier fault. Older loudspeakers have an adjustable spider across the front of the coil, which can be centred by loosening a centre screw, inserting feeler gauges inside the coil then re-tightening the screw. Nowadays, unfortunately, speakers are centred during manufacture and the coil sealed with a dome that it is claimed helps to disperse the high frequencies. An off-centre coil cannot be corrected by a simple adjustment.

What usually happens to modern speakers is not that the coil has become displaced relative to the magnet, but that the frame of the speaker has been deformed and the magnet assembly is out of true (Figure 5.6). The metalwork of modern speaker frames is less rigid than in older ones, so this is now more common than simple coil displacement.

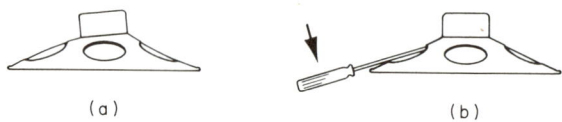

Figure 5.6. (a) Loudspeaker with deformed frame (shown exaggerated). (b) A repair can sometimes be made by levering with a strong screwdriver. Have speaker working and lever for best quality reproduction; going a little beyond optimum position will allow for slight spring-back

The angle of deviation of the magnet may be so slight as not to be discernible, yet enough because of the narrow gap to cause trouble. If the speaker is operated face upward on the bench and the fingers are gently pressed around the inside of the cone near the centre, proceeding around slowly until the starting point is again reached, it may be found that pressure at one point improves the quality of reproduction. This indicates that the magnet has been displaced in that direction. A heavy screwdriver used as a lever as shown in Figure 5.6b can often correct the deformation. Lever gently with the speaker still working; if the quality improves you know you are working in the right spot, if not or it gets worse try a different direction. Lever until the quality is normal, then go a little beyond because the frame will settle back slightly to its former position.

If this fails nothing more can be done and the speaker must be discarded.

Chapter 6

Car Aerials

The function of an aerial of whatever type is to convert the electromagnetic radio waves travelling through space into a corresponding electrical signal that can then be applied to the input circuits of the receiver. Although basically a simple piece of equipment it has an important function. It is necessary that the electrical signal produced be as large as possible, so that it will overcome the random noise signals generated in the receiver's circuits by appearing very large in proportion to them. The aerial must also be effective over the band of frequencies it is desired to receive, and if possible discriminate against noise and interference coming from outside the receiver.

The simplest aerial is a straight piece of wire, but there are a number of factors that govern its effectiveness. Length is one of them, the theoretical optimum being one-quarter of the wavelength of the desired signal. If this length is exceeded, any signal picked up by the extra wire is out of phase and so is cancelled by that in the quarter-wavelength section; so the signal presented to the receiver is less than for just the quarter-wavelength length.

A method of getting more signal is to use two quarter-wavelength sections end-to-end, the two leads being taken to opposite ends of the input coil in the receiver (Figure 6.1). Connected in this way the two signals are of opposite phase, but are added in the input coil. The arrangement is known as a dipole (two poles) and is the basis of all television and many f.m. aerials. The current and voltage distribution is also shown in the illustration, and it can be seen that the current is at a minimum and the voltage at a maximum at the ends, while at the centre it is the voltage that is at a minimum and the current at a maximum. Thus at the take-off point the impedance is low, and input circuits designed for this type of aerial take account of this.

Such an aerial being tuned to one particular frequency is only at maximum effectiveness at that frequency, but the difference in performance is not too great at nearby frequencies. The f.m. radio

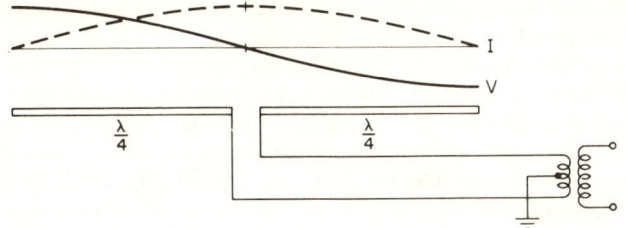

Figure 6.1. Dipole aerial with input transformer; signal voltage (solid line) and current (dotted line) distribution shown along its length

stations are grouped fairly close together between 88 MHz and 97 MHz, and dipoles designed to receive this band (band 2) are made to respond fairly evenly over this range.

If we consider some actual dimensions now, we see why dipoles are not used for the a.m. medium and long-wave bands. A quarter wavelength at 90 MHz in the f.m. band 2 is 2.73 feet, so a dipole would be double that. In practice, various factors affect the tuning of an aerial to make the optimum slightly less than the theoretical quarter-wavelength; f.m. dipoles are usually about 5 feet in length. This is quite practical for the home but rather too long for a car, although a single quarter-wavelength section of 2.5 feet is quite reasonable. At 300 metres on the medium wave, a quarter-wavelength would be 246 feet, while the 1500 metre long-wave BBC station would need 1230 feet!

Obviously even single sections are completely impractical, and a length must be used that is only a very small fraction of the actual wavelength. Such aerials are therefore untuned. Fortunately, owing to the way radio waves of various frequencies are propagated through the earth's atmosphere and environment, medium and long-wave signals suffer far fewer losses than those of the much higher frequency f.m. signals. So even with untuned, short aerial lengths, reasonable signal strengths can be obtained.

Polarisation and screening

There are other factors that affect the performance of an aerial. Theoretically, the plane of the aerial should be the same as that of the transmitter aerial. The majority of the BBC f.m. transmissions are horizontally polarised, which means that the receiving aerial should also be horizontal. In practice, propagation conditions may twist the polarisation so that a diagonal angle may prove the best. A vertical position will usually be found to be the least satisfactory for signal pickup, as it is the furthest position away from horizontal. There are, however, practical considerations in the case of car f.m. aerials. It is not easy to achieve a horizontal position without incurring other penalties, and the vertical rod may prove to be the best after all. A horizontal aerial on the roof would be ideal, but may conflict with the use of a roof rack, or be just considered aesthetically undesirable. Some vertical aerials may be given a backward rake, while others are long and flexible enough to be bent right back and clipped to the roof gutter. These should prove more satisfactory for f.m. reception, but remember that too great a length will exceed the quarter-wavelength factor; although if in a different plane, i.e. starting vertically and finishing horizontally, a greater length can be tolerated.

Polarisation has little effect on the a.m. bands due to the propagation effects, so if the radio is a.m. only there need be no problems from this source. Combined a.m./f.m. radios use the same aerial; for these, the best aerial for f.m. should be chosen and should then function quite well for a.m. also.

The performance of an aerial can be greatly degraded by screening effects. Any material if large enough can screen the aerial from incoming radio waves, but metal in particular will act as an effective screen. Thus any aerial situated inside a metal-bodied car is ineffective unless mounted across a window which happens to face toward the transmitter. In a moving car the latter condition cannot be guaranteed, although with modern cars the radio waves can pass through from the other windows with little obstruction from door pillars, etc. The window does not have to be open because glass is transparent to radio waves. Even so, the proximity of the metal body around the aerial will reduce the signal pickup. Ideally then, the aerial should be on the exterior, and mounted away from the bodywork at least for part of its length. There are also problems associated with picking up interference from the car electrical system, but this will be dealt with in more detail in Chapter 14.

Screening can also be caused by large external objects. In some towns, large buildings (many of them with steel frameworks) may at times completely surround the car and reduce the signal to a very low level, causing the programme to be lost in the general mush of background noise. The same can happen when driving through mountainous countryside.

Ferrite aerials

Ferrite aerials are not used for car radios, but since they are used in battery portables, which are sometimes operated in cars, we will take a brief look at them.

A small portable radio has an obvious problem where the aerial is concerned: there is little point in making it small enough to slip into a pocket if a long and unwieldy aerial is required. Early portables had 'throw-out aerials' consisting of a length of wire to be unrolled and draped over any nearby object, or frame aerials consisting of a frame of wire wound around the inside of the rather substantial case or its lid.

The development of ferrite material revolutionised the portable aerial situation. It consists of small particles of iron insulated from each other and is capable of being moulded into almost any shape. It is made up into rods between 3 and 7 inches in length, and coils are mounted on it, one at each end for the long and medium wavebands respectively (Figure 6.2). It has a high permeability and any stray flux is concentrated in it, so electromagnetic fields resulting from radio waves produce a relatively high-intensity field which passes through the coils.

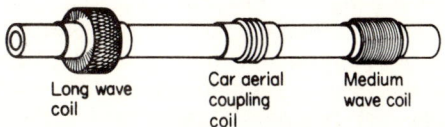

Long wave coil   Car aerial coupling coil   Medium wave coil

Figure 6.2. Ferrite aerial rod with coils as used in modern transistor radios (page 88 refers to the middle coil)

The inductance of the coils, together with the capacitance of external condensers plus some self-capacitance, forms a tuned circuit that resonates at the frequency of the desired signal. Thus we have a tuned aerial in only a few inches. A further feature is that the tuning is not fixed and has to serve over a band of frequencies; the associated capacitor is variable, being linked with the oscillator tuning-capacitor, so the aerial tuning is varied to tune exactly to the station being received. The net effect is a very efficient aerial. Unfortunately at the present state of development ferrite is not effective at high frequencies, so for reception of short wave and f.m. signals we have to rely on pull-up telescopic aerials.

The medium and long-wave coils can be slid along the rod, and this varies the inductance. So alignment of the aerial circuit, to ensure that it keeps in step with that of the oscillator tuning, is done initially by adjusting the position of the coils on the rod and then sealing with wax.

Although ideal for portable radios, ferrite aerials are not practicable for car use. If mounted inside the radio, they would suffer from the screening effect of the car body, and would also be prone to pick up interference from the ignition and other electrical circuits. If mounted outside the car, they would be very vulnerable to damage because the ferrite material is brittle and snaps easily, and the coils, being wound with fine wire, are also fragile. A number of wires would be needed to connect back to the receiver input circuit, and a further factor is that ferrite aerials are directional, having to be turned broadside-on to the transmitter, and this would be most unsuitable for use where the vehicle is constantly changing direction.

Types of car aerial

Many different shapes and sizes of car aerial have been produced. A popular one at one time was the under-car type. This was a rod or several rods mounted underneath the car, and as may be expected it was well screened by the car body. It also suffered from the effects of water thrown up from the road. It tended to be larger than the usual type of car aerial, which to some extent compensated for the screening and low position. Its proximity to the road established an earth capacitance, so the operation was partly as a capacitance aerial.

Another type was the ring aerial, consisting of a metal ring about 6 to 9 inches in diameter. It was usually mounted on the roof just above the windscreen, but is rarely seen today.

Some aerials are designed for simplicity, needing little or no installation work. One is the window aerial—a short flexible rod with a clip that slips over the top of one of the side windows, the rod projecting vertically or nearly so on the outside. The lead is brought through a small gap at the top of the window and is plugged directly into the radio. In performance these are no better or worse than properly installed aerials, but the inconvenience is rather a serious drawback. The window must be kept up otherwise there is a risk of the clip becoming dislodged and the aerial disappearing out of the window. The lead is trailed from the window across to the dashboard or wherever the radio is mounted, and this could be a safety hazard as well as getting in the way. If the lead is rather short it may have to be unplugged every time the door is opened.

Another type of aerial needing minimum installation consists of an adhesive strip in which is included metal foil or other thin electrical conductor. This is simply fixed along the top of the inside of the windscreen, the lead being taken down the windscreen pillar. It has the advantage of height, and being on the windscreen is next best to being outside. Proximity of the roof affects performance to some extent, but it can extend the whole width of the windscreen (in fact it looks better if it does), so the length can be greater than the average rod aerial, an advantage for a.m. reception. It theoretically could be divided in the centre to form a dipole for f.m. but it would tend to be directional, and in any case the receiver input circuits would need to be designed for it. The main snag is that of greater susceptibility to interference, since it is unscreened from the dashboard wiring, but this could be overcome by mounting it across the rear window. This would in most cases need an extension to the lead, but more of this later in the chapter.

The majority of car aerials are of the telescopic rod type. There are innumerable models, but the differences are mainly in mounting, retraction and angular details, as well as finish. (See Figure 6.3.)

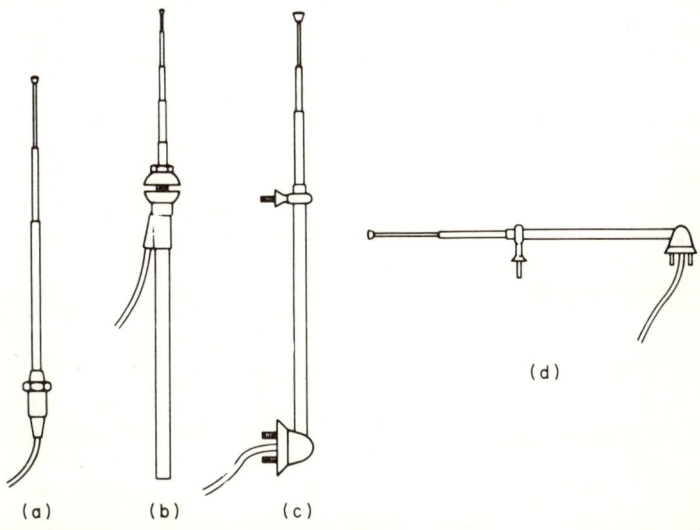

Figure 6.3. Various types of car aerial (Bosch). (a) Semi-retractable wing-mounting; (b) fully retractable wing mounting; (c) side/pillar mounting; (d) roof aerial

The *vertical mounting semi-retractable* is perhaps the most popular. It is designed for mounting on a horizontal surface such as the top of the wings, but with most models the angle can be adjusted either to accommodate a sloping mounting surface, or to incline the aerial from the vertical, or a combination of these. The maximum angle of inclination is 90° in most cases. Mounting is through a hole cut in the coach-work. An insulator passes through the hole because there must be no contact between aerial and bodywork; the cable is connected to or inside the insulator. Good aerials have the connections waterproofed to avoid trouble from water thrown up under the wings from the wheels. A plastic or metal dome covers the top part of the insulator. The aerial is often mounted in a ball-and-socket arrangement within this dome to give the variable angle. Projection below the mounting surface is just a couple of inches or so. Retraction is to the length of the lowest telescopic section, which may be around nine inches, but the length when fully extended varies from three to six feet according to the number and length of the sections. The aerial can be extended to about a couple of feet for normal operation, and left at that level. When in difficult terrain or trying to receive a weak station, it can be then extended to its full length. The extra few feet make a considerable difference under these conditions.

The unfortunate growth of vandalism in recent years has taken its toll on car aerials, as they appear to present an ideal target for those individuals who find pleasure in destroying or damaging the property of others. An answer to this problem is the *fully retractable aerial*. When retracted, the whole mast disappears below the surface and the absence of the visual stimulation of a vulnerable rod causes many potential vandals to ignore or lose interest in the aerial. More hardened types will of course not be put off by this, and will just pull it up in order to damage it. A further protection is afforded by the *lockable aerial*, which is a fully retractable model that can be locked in the retracted position.

As these aerials are retracted to below the surface level, clearance

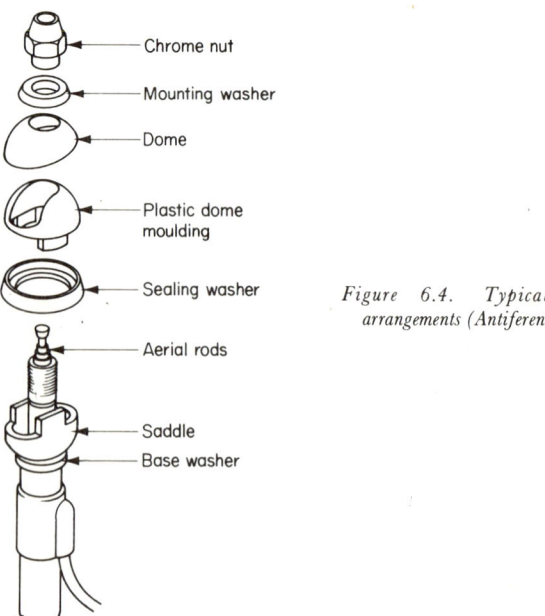

Chrome nut

Mounting washer

Dome

Plastic dome moulding

Sealing washer

Aerial rods

Saddle

Base washer

Figure 6.4. Typical mounting arrangements (Antiference antenna)

must be allowed underneath to accommodate them. This must obviously be checked before any holes are drilled in the coachwork. Clearances vary between about 9 inches and 15 inches. Another factor is the angle of inclination, which cannot be as great as with the surface mounted type. With some it can be varied up to around 40°, while others have a fixed angle. One maker has a range with the angle fixed at 57°, but this may vary with other makes. Cable entry for fully retractable aerials is at the side below the insulator, not at the bottom. A typical mounting assembly is shown in Figure 6.4.

Although a 90° angle-variation semi-retractable could be mounted to a vertical surface, there are models specially made for this position since an aerial of the normal type side-mounted near the door could become displaced and foul the door when it was opened. The special side and window-pillar models have a further insulated support at the top of the lowest telescopic section to hold it securely in place. There is also a roof model that can be mounted at the front and taken back horizontally or at an angle. This too has an extra support for horizontal mounting similar to the side-mounting type, to prevent the aerial being flattened and scratching the roof. It is in fact very much like the side model except that it is shorter.

Electrically operated aerials

The fully retractable aerials suffer from an obvious disadvantage. If the motorist wants to have the radio on whilst a journey is in progress, he must stop, get out and erect the aerial which may also involve unlocking it. If traffic is heavy and the weather inclement he may well decide not to bother!

To overcome this particular problem there is the motorised aerial, which can be erected and retracted by just switching on from inside the car. Several models are now available, but they have basic similarities. A stiff yet flexible rod about 3 mm thick made of nylon or Duracon (polyacetal resin) is fixed at one end to the uppermost section of the telescopic aerial (Figure 6.5). It passes down the hollow tubes and is wound for four or five turns around a drum at the base. The drum is driven through a gear train (Radiomobile), or a worm-drive (Nippondenso) from an electric motor. Between the drive and the drum there is a clutch to prevent the motor stalling and burning out or the drive cable breaking when the aerial is fully extended or retracted, or should the mechanism become jammed. The clutch is a ball-bearing type (Figure 6.6) consisting of two plates thrust together under the force of a compression spring, one having a pair of steel balls mounted in retaining cups and the other having a couple of indentations to match. The balls engage with the

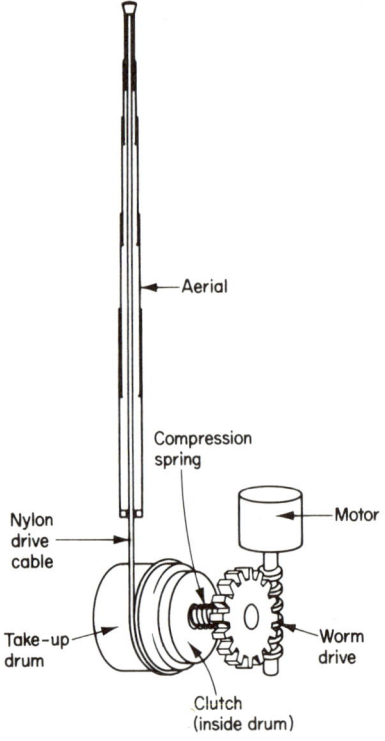

Aerial

Compression
spring

Motor

Nylon
drive
cable

Take-up
drum

Worm
drive

Clutch
(inside drum)

Figure 6.5. Basic principle of motor aerials
(Nippondenso); this uses worm-drive, others use
gear-trains and direct drive to toothed cable
(Philips)

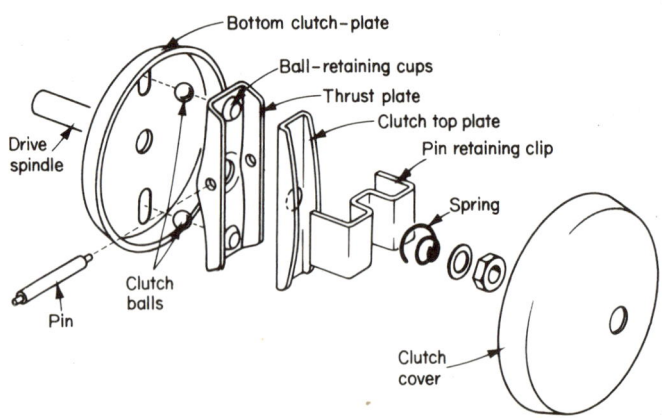

Bottom clutch-plate

Ball-retaining cups

Thrust plate

Clutch top plate

Pin retaining clip

Drive
spindle

Spring

Clutch
balls

Pin

Clutch
cover

Figure 6.6. Ball-bearing clutch exploded view, used on Radiomobile motor aerials

indentations and drive is transmitted during normal running, but they slip out if the load applied is too great. The pushing force before the clutch disengages varies between 5 and 8 lb according to the model.

Instead of driving the drum, the Philips model has teeth cut along the length of the drive-rod which engage with a toothed drive-wheel. The drum stores the excess rod as with the others and is free to revolve as the rod is paid out, but the drive is directly to the rod.

The motor and drive mechanism of electrically-operated aerials increase the space required for mounting, although this is kept to a minimum by positioning the motor parallel to the lower section of the aerial (Figure 6.7). Some models indeed are quite short; the Bosch Autojet SU for example is only 11¾ inches in depth, actually less than some ordinary retractables.

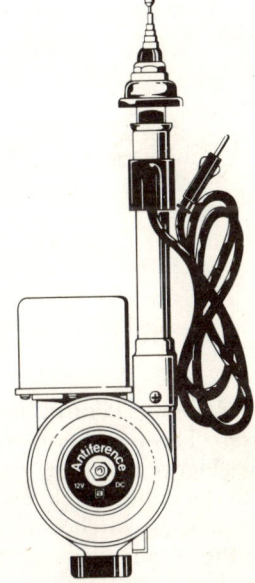

Figure 6.7. Appearance of typical complete electric aerial (Antiference antenna)

Another factor is that dirt and moisture will be thrown up over the mechanism by the road wheels if the unit is wing mounted. Close-fitting covers are used to protect the mechanisms, and drain holes are drilled at the bottom to allow the escape of any moisture that may gain entrance. It is recommended in some cases that, if the aerial is in the 'direct line of fire' of one of the wheels, a baffle plate is fixed to give further protection, otherwise it is almost certain that dirt will get inside and foul the clutch and drum even if it fails to enter the motor.

Another solution to this problem, and also to that of extra clearance, is afforded by the Radiomobile model which allows the use of an extension drive-cable so that the motor can be situated remote from the aerial. Nylon rod is used for the cable, and is encased in an outer sheath like bowden brake-cable.

The motor has three terminals, one of which (the common) is earthed. When the supply voltage is applied from common to one of the free terminals the motor runs in one direction, and when connected from common to the other the motor reverses. This enables the aerial to both extend and retract using the motor.

Control can be by one of three methods. The simplest is manual switching, where a dashboard switch is held in one position to erect and in another to retract, there being also a neutral rest position (Figure 6.8). The next is automatic switching, where the switch is pressed to start the operation which continues until the aerial is either extended or retracted fully, whereupon the motor automatically switches off.

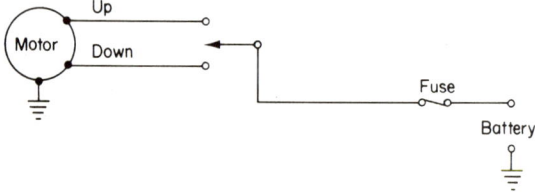

Figure 6.8. Circuit of manually-controlled motor aerial

The third method controls the aerial by means of the on/off switch on the radio. This is rather more complicated and requires a relay to operate it (Figure 6.9). The current for supplying the motor is not taken from the radio switch, only an energising current for the relay. When the radio is switched on, the relay is energised and switches a supply to the aerial 'up' circuit. When the aerial is fully extended a switch in the aerial operates, connecting the motor to the 'down' circuit and reversing the motor connection. The relay is still energised but, on switching the radio off, the energising current is removed and the relay switches back to the 'down' aerial circuit (which is its normal 'at rest' position) and the aerial retracts. When fully retracted the aerial switch is knocked back to the 'up' circuit ready for the next operation.

The supply to the aerial should be separately fused. The radio fuse need not be increased in value because the extra relay energising current is quite small. Aerial motor-current varies considerably with

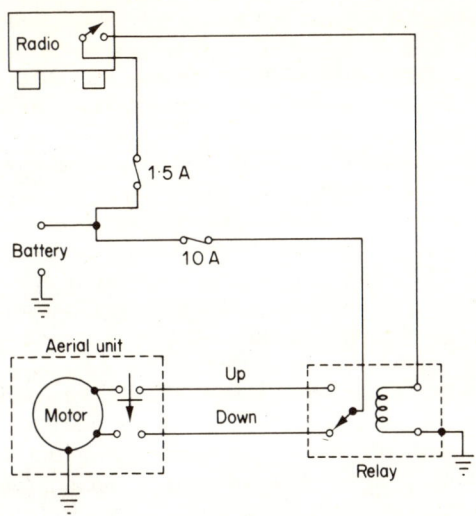

Figure 6.9. Circuit of relay operated motor aerial controlled by radio on/off switch. Current for operating motor is taken direct to relay unit, current from radio-switch just controls the relay. Shown in rest position

the make and model. It can be from as low as 1.6 A (Philips) up to 14 A for the 6-V Nippondenso (the 12-V model is 7 A).

Something that should be considered with all types of aerial is the material. Chrome-on-brass or stainless steel is the preferred material; inferior finishes often found on cheaper aerials deteriorate and this can cause a resistance to develop between the telescopic sections. Thus the upper sections can be virtually insulated from the lower ones and might just as well not be there. Even with the better finishes the rods should be kept clean to ensure good mutual contact, and a smear of oil will help. (Although oil is an insulator it improves conductivity of contact surfaces by excluding oxidisation and other contaminants that might introduce a high contact resistance.)

Aerial leads

In theory all that is needed to connect the aerial to the radio is a length of insulated wire. However, such a lead would pick up an appreciable amount of interference from the car electrical system and the result would be a very noisy background to any received programme, the weaker stations probably being completely obliterated. So in practice the connecting lead must be protected from stray interference caused by electromagnetic and electrostatic fields. This is done by enclosing the insulated wire in a sheath of copper braiding, the result being known as a *screened cable*. The screening is connected to the car bodywork at the aerial and also to the outer contact of the aerial plug by which it is connected to the casing of the radio.

Any length of screened cable is virtually a capacitor owing to the proximity of the screening to the centre conductor, separated by the insulation around the conductor. Now the input circuits of a radio are tuned, consisting of resonant circuits containing inductance and capacitance. The capacitance is made up partly of a section of the tuning ganged capacitor. If any additional capacitance is added to the aerial circuit, it will detune the radio input circuits and result in reduction of signal strength and greater proneness to interference. The capacitance of the aerial lead is allowed for in the design and alignment of the radio circuits, but as it will vary according to the make and length of the cable a small compensating trimmer is provided. This is a variable capacitor which is adjusted by a screwdriver through a hole in the radio casing. If the capacitance of the aerial cable is less than average, the trimmer is screwed in to increase its capacitance, while if it is greater, the trimmer is unscrewed. It is adjusted simply by tuning in a station, preferably a weak station on the medium wave, then adjusting for maximum volume.

A problem can arise if the aerial is mounted at some distance from the radio, such as at the rear of the car. The supplied cable will most likely be too short and must be extended. Although the best way of doing this is to fit a completely new length from the aerial to the radio, with some models access to the connections at the base of the aerial is not very good and it may prove easier to join a length on. Philips, Radiomobile, and other makers supply extension leads with socket at one end and plug at the other. Two of the available lengths are 14 and 7.5 feet. The join should be positioned somewhere where it is not likely to be kicked or pulled apart.

Cable can be joined if care is taken. The sleeving should be pushed back rather than stripped, and the two inner conductors soldered together. The joint should then be insulated, and the two sections of braiding brought down to mesh with one another and soldered at a couple of points. Do not leave the iron on the braid too long or the internal insulation will melt. Avoid having any bends near the joint when soldering because the centre wire may penetrate the softened insulation and short-circuit to the braiding. Finally tape over the completed joint. If the joint is not soldered, oxidation may occur at the points of contact and give rise to crackling and other noises later. Also, if the internal conductor is not covered by the copper braid, interference may be picked up.

Screened cable used for car radio aerials should not be of the television co-ax feeder type. This is especially designed for the input circuits of t.v. receivers and has too high a capacitance for this purpose. Audio screened cable as used for microphones and the like is even worse. The correct type is a low-capacitance cable specially made for car radios (Figure 6.10). To achieve a low capacitance the centre conductor is very thin, like 5 A fuse wire, and the insulation is not close fitting but consists of a hollow tube in which the wire has plenty of surrounding space. This construction keeps the braiding spaced away from the centre conductor. As capacitance is proportional both to the area of the conductors and to their proximity, the arrangement results in a low capacitance.

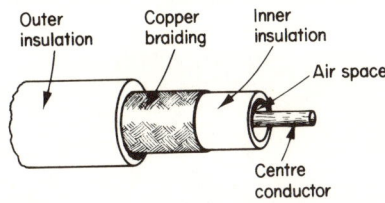

Figure 6.10. Construction of low-capacitance aerial cable

Capacitance also obviously depends on the length of cable used. Now it may be that an excessive length is necessary for some special mounting position, or the cable may have a higher capacitance than normal (perhaps because the incorrect type is being used). Detuning of the receiver r.f. circuits will cause loss of signal and the compensating aerial trimmer will be unable to make it up. The condition can be recognised by adjustment of the trimmer; unscrewing it, that is decreasing the capacitance, causes the volume to increase but it is not possible to find a peak. Normally, a peak can be found where the volume is greatest and on either side of this there is a drop.

An improvement can be obtained by adding some capacitance in series with the aerial. Capacitors connected in series give a total capacitance *less* than that of one of them; the formula is $1/C = 1/c_1 + 1/c_2 + 1/c_3 + \ldots$ For two capacitors in series that are equal in value, the total is half that of one of them.

The normal capacitance should be less than 100 pF, and values much in excess are beyond the range of the trimmer to correct. If then we have a cable that is approaching 200 pF, connecting a 200-pF capacitor in series would drop it to 100 pF. A 100-pF series capacitor would reduce it to 67 pF, bringing cable capacitances of well over 200 pF within the 100-pF limit.

It is true that the capacitor adds a series reactance that in itself reduces the signal to some extent. However the reactance is small; at 1 MHz, which is about halfway along the medium waveband, the reactance of a 100-pF capacitor is $1600\,\Omega$. The slight resulting drop in signal is more than made up by the accurate tuning of the input circuits that it makes possible. The main problem is where to fit the capacitor. It must be fully screened to avoid interference pickup. A small metal box could be made up, with a socket for the aerial plug and a short screened lead with a plug to fit the radio, but might prove somewhat clumsy and a nuisance. The best way is to fit it inside the radio itself. Simply disconnect the lead going to the aerial socket, solder on one wire of the capacitor (cut as short as possible) then join the disconnected lead to the other wire, positioning it so that there is no possibility of the joint shorting to an adjacent component or to the case. A note of the modification should be fixed to the outside of the radio, so that if it is fitted in another vehicle in the future the capacitor can be removed.

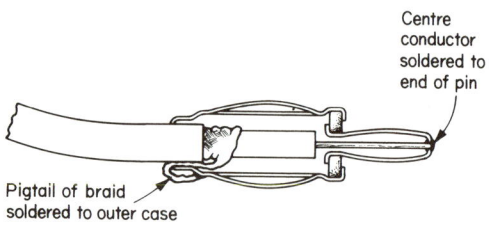

Centre conductor soldered to end of pin

Pigtail of braid soldered to outer case

Figure 6.11. Cable fitted to aerial plug

This brings us finally to the aerial plug. Fortunately, in contrast to the large variety of audio plugs, there seems to be one standard plug and socket, so there are no problems as to whether a given aerial plug will fit a certain radio. The plug and its connection is shown in Figure 6.11.

Chapter 7

Car Radios

The principles of radio reception are dealt with for beginners in Chapter 2, and of course for experienced engineers this is familiar ground. In this chapter we examine some of the special features to be found in radios designed for car operation, and how they differ from the home or portable radio.

There are of course numerous superficial differences. In most cases the radio is mounted in a slot in the dashboard or slung underneath it. Hence all the controls must be mounted on the short side facing outward, not scattered around the front, top and sides as they are with many portable radios. The loudspeaker cannot be mounted as an integral part of the radio itself because it would then be shut away behind the dashboard, so loudspeakers are separate to be mounted as taste and convenience dictate. It should be mentioned here that, in some commercial vehicles, space for mounting a separate loudspeaker can be restricted and there is no conventional dashboard to receive the radio. For such installations a special mounting kit has been produced by Radiomobile, the CVO2. This enables the loudspeaker and radio to be mounted as one unit, horizontally, vertically, on the side or front-scuttle, overhead to the cab roof or in any other convenient position.

As pointed out in the previous chapter, an internal aerial cannot be used because of the screening effects of the bodywork and the interference pickup, so all car radios have an aerial socket to which an external aerial must be connected. To prevent the internal radio circuits from being affected by interference fields, car radios are metal-cased, with the casing connected to the vehicle bodywork by mounting screws. As the capacitance of car aerials, particularly their screened feeders, varies from one type to another, a compensating trimmer is provided for adjustment with the particular aerial to avoid misalignment of the input circuits. As the trimmer must be adjusted with the radio casing in place, it is usually mounted beneath a small hole in the case through which it can be set by a small screwdriver.

 Most modern radios are quite compact and can be mounted with little difficulty. Some of the older ones, especially the hybrid models using valves and transistors, were larger and heavier, and it was necessary to support the rear end of the radio with additional mounting struts. As these were fitted well to the back of the radio compartment behind the instrument panel, access could be rather a problem and fitting and removing required considerable contortions from the unfortunate installer. Some models were split into two sections: the radio and control panel, and the power-unit consisting of the output transistors and driver stages. Older all-valve radios often had the vibrator, transformer and rectifier mounted in a separate unit.

Connection between the radio and its power-unit was made by a multi-core lead on the radio with a four or five-pin plug at the end, and a corresponding socket on the power-unit. The battery supply-lead and also loudspeaker leads were taken from the unit. Where there was room behind the dashboard, the power unit could be bolted on to the back of the radio to make one piece, but otherwise a mounting position had to be found elsewhere for it.

Power circuits

The supply voltage for car radios is a nominal 12 V, although many are now rated at 14 V because of the high charging voltage needed to keep the battery well-charged in view of the many demands on it in the modern car. This is higher than the usual 9 V of the portable transistor radio, and of course the lower 6-V receivers.

It is in the power output and the supply current that the greatest differences occur. Portable radios, supplied by dry non-rechargeable batteries, can give but a limited power if the battery is to last a reasonable time. Car radios, being run from the car battery, have no such limitation and powers many times that of the portable can be obtained. Few portables exceed 1 W, but car radios usually start at around 3 W for the cheapest models and go up to 10 W or more.

To get such high powers large output transistors are used and, as these dissipate a fair amount of heat especially at the higher powers, a heat-sink must be provided. The rear member of the radio chassis consists of a slab of metal, thicker than the other parts, on which the transistors are mounted. With some models this member is of cast-metal incorporating cooling fins (Figure 7.1).

It is only the output transistors that produce enough heat to require special dissipation arrangements; the others are small wire-mounted types as used in ordinary portables. The transistors, if of the oval TO-3 or similar encapsulation, are mounted on the outside of the chassis

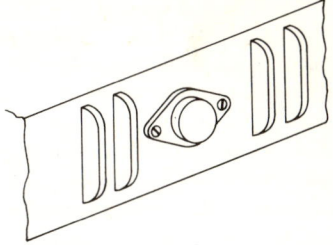

Figure 7.1.   Output transistor mounted on the outside of the rear member of a car radio; cooling fins as shown are sometimes used

member, with the connecting pins passing through holes in the chassis for connection inside the radio. The metal transistor case is however itself one of the connections, being internally joined to the collector. It must therefore be insulated from the chassis on which it is mounted, and this is done by interposing a mica washer between them which conducts heat but insulates electrically. When mounting or operating out of the dashboard for test purposes, care must be taken not to let any metalwork short against the transistor case. Some makers fit a plastic cover to prevent such an occurrence. A smaller square-shaped transistor encapsulation that is screwed to the chassis with a bolt, and has three strip-connections, is now gaining popularity as an output transistor (Figure 7.2). It is mounted inside the chassis, the connectors being fitted into holes in a printed-circuit board and soldered.

Figure 7.2.   The TO-126 type of transistor encapsulation; it is fitted to the chassis by a single bolt through the centre hole

Output-stage circuitry is very similar to that of the portable radio, with the exception of transistor type. The class B complementary push-pull is widely used, but some models use a single class A transistor. This avoids the cross-over distortion inherent with class B operation, but uses more battery current and has a limited audio power output.

The current for a class B stage is about 50 mA with no signal, whereas for a single class A transistor it ranges from about 500 to 750 mA according to transistor type. A signal drives the class B circuit into much heavier current depending on the level of the signal, the peaks reaching ten times or more the standing or quiescent current. With the class A circuit, the signal has little effect on the standing current if the transistor is correctly biased to the centre point of its characteristic. If the bias is not quite correct (which more likely than not will be the case in practice), there may be a marginal increase or decrease of current on sound peaks depending on which way the bias point deviates from the centre of the curve.

Some output stages have a preset adjustment that enables the current to be set according to the maker's specification (Figure 7.3). The adjustment alters the bias point of the output transistor(s) and must be made in conjunction with an ammeter connected in series with the collector of one of the output transistors.

The rest of the receiver circuit takes about 50–100 mA, and the dial lamp is usually a low-consumption 50-mA type.

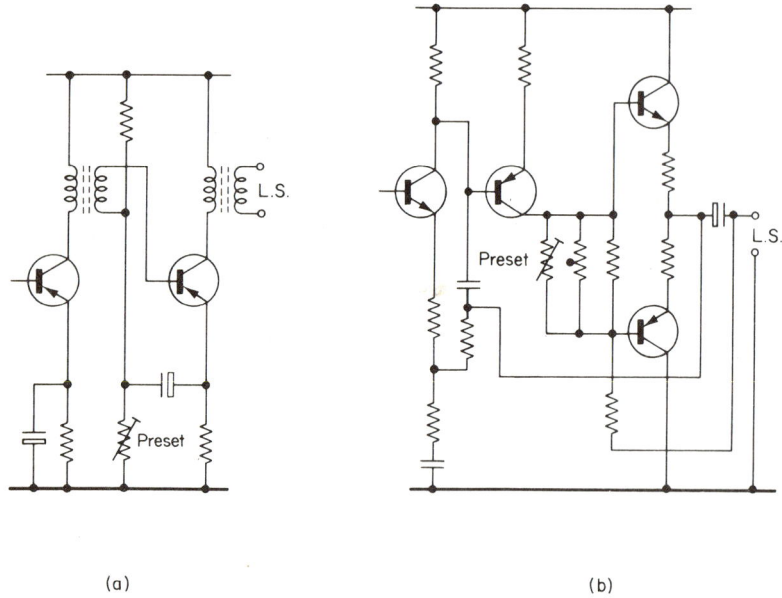

(a)

(b)

Figure 7.3. Preset bias control for adjusting the current (a) in a single-ended class A output stage, and (b) in a class B complementary push-pull output stage

F.M. reception

Although f.m. is being found on an increasing number of portable and home radios, its use on car radios is at present more limited; in fact a number of car-radio manufacturers do not have a single f.m. model in their range.

One of the advantages of f.m. reception, the better high-frequency response, is rather nullified by the modest loudspeakers used in car radio installations and by their positioning. Another advantage, the ability to receive local broadcasting stations on f.m., is now cancelled by the duplication of these services on the medium-wave.

A major disadvantage is that of interference. While f.m. is free from many types of electrical interference that affect a.m. sets, ignition interference does have frequency-modulated components and so affects f.m. reception. The effect is worse than that produced on a.m. radios, and interference suppression is more difficult. Now while it is possible to suppress interference generated by the car in which the radio is installed, the aerial will still pick up interference from every passing vehicle that is not f.m. suppressed, that is 99.9% of them. So on normal roads in the UK there is a continuous crackle of interference from other vehicles.

There is a peculiar form of distortion that affects f.m. receivers known as multipath distortion. This is caused by reflected signals arriving at the aerial slightly later than the direct one owing to the longer paths travelled. On t.v. receivers the effect is known as 'ghosting' and can be seen as a series of subsidiary images displaced to the right of the main one. Owing to the much longer wavelengths of a.m. radio signals, the effect is not detectable with these. Ordinarily, multipath distortion can be reduced or eliminated by altering the aerial location or direction to minimise the pickup of reflected signals. Obviously this cannot be done with a moving-vehicle aerial and, although the multipath reception would soon pass as the vehicle changed its position relative to the source of reflection, there would be numerous other possibilities of reflection from stationary objects and moving vehicles as the journey proceeded.

The ranges of the v.h.f. f.m. stations are much less than those of medium-wave a.m. broadcasts, so on any given journey the car is likely to pass from good to fringe reception areas in quite a short while, and frequent re-tuning to the nearest f.m. transmitter would certainly be required on a high-speed long journey.

Some makers claim to have developed circuits to overcome the interference problems on f.m., but their reluctance to supply details and performance data must lead to such claims being regarded with suspicion. It is evident that, at present, f.m. reception is not very satisfactory and offers little advantage to the mobile listener. There is one factor though which may alter the situation. Stereo broadcasting has now been extended to nearly all the BBC f.m. services in most areas. Stereo is being pushed in nearly every mobile audio system; few if any are mono only. Manufacturers, ever on the watch for new ideas to capture public interest, may well concentrate on developing technical innovations to improve f.m. reception—some in fact have already appeared—for the purpose of pushing stereo car radio. It must be noted that stereo reception is more critical and needs a stronger signal than mono, so real improvements would have to be made before stereo car radio could be a practical proposition.

Tuning and station selection

An important requirement with a car radio is that station selection and other necessary operations should be possible with the minimum of distraction, so that the driver need take his eyes off the road for the briefest moment, if at all, and his hand off the wheel for only a little longer. Switching on and adjusting the volume is straightforward enough, requiring very little attention, but tuning the desired station can be a different matter. For this reason many of the more expensive car radios incorporate some means of automatic station selection, a feature not so often found on ordinary radios.

The most usual form is the pushbutton selector. In theory selection can be done electrically by a bank of pushbutton switches, each one selecting a pair of tuned circuits, one for the r.f. and the other for the oscillator stages. Adjustment of the required station would be accomplished by tuning a coil-core or trimmer capacitor for each circuit. This was the method used in many of the old valve pushbutton radios. A multiplicity of tuned circuits is required, and the tuning range of each is limited by the amount the inductance (if coil tuned) or capacitance (if trimmer tuned) can be varied. Coils and trimmers are restricted by size considerations, so each pushbutton can serve only a part of the tuning scale. As the buttons have to be designed to cover the whole scale between them, it is not possible to set buttons to stations that happen to be near each other on the scale.

A mechanical method avoids the above difficulties and is the arrangement usually adopted. Details vary from one model to another, but the basic principle is similar (Figure 7.4). Each button has associated with it a long threaded rod on which is screwed a striking plate. The position of the plate can be set by screwing or unscrewing the rod. When the button is depressed the plate pushes against a spring-loaded bar (the thrust plate), which is linked to the tuning device and holds it in the set position. The button is prevented from returning by a latching mechanism. When another button is depressed, it releases the latch (allowing the previous button to spring out) and engages its striking plate with the thrust plate to move the tuner to a new position.

A button can be tuned by first depressing it to engage it with the tuner, then turning it until the desired station is received. Subsequent selection will bring the tuner to the same point. In order to avoid turning the button in normal use and thus detuning the selected station, it is common for the button to be disengaged from the rod, as

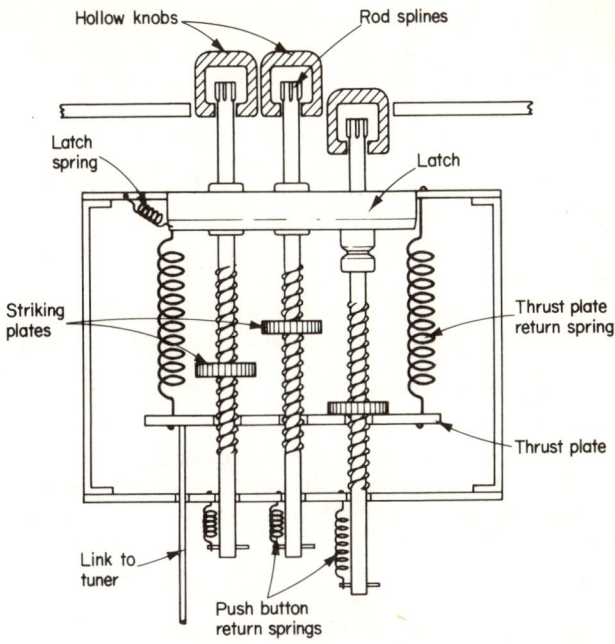

Figure 7.4. Basic pushbutton mechanism

respects rotary motion, during normal operation. Pulling the knob outwards, after depressing, engages it and enables it to be retuned. Most pushbutton radios have a tuning scale to enable initial setting up of the buttons and to identify which station is being received subsequently. Some feature manual tuning as well so that stations other than those on the pushbuttons can be tuned in.

Another method of setting the pushbuttons is to tune in the station by the manual tuning knob and then press the button. This sets a selector on the button rod so that further depressions will return the tuner to the same position. The snag here is that any alteration of the tuning knob while the button is depressed will alter the setting. Some models overcome this by taking the tuning drive from the manual knob through a clutch; pressing any button operates the clutch, thus disengaging the knob. With these sets the station must be accurately tuned manually before pressing the button to set it. There are other methods of button setting, but the basic idea is the same. Five buttons are usually provided; four for medium wave and one for long wave. In a.m./f.m. sets two or more may be devoted to f.m.

Rotary tuning scales are often to be found on portable and home radios, but the limited height of the control panel on a car radio rules them out, as the scale would have to be very small. Linear scales are therefore always used, the pointer travelling from one end to the other. It should be noted that scale markings are changing from wavelength in metres, as used for many years, to frequency in kHz or MHz (rather ironical this in view of the metrication drive). The result is that all the markings are unfamiliar to listeners who have been used to the previous wavelength calibration, and it may take a while to locate the positions of favourite stations. The pointer is carried on a cord that runs over pulleys driven from the tuning-knob spindle. The cord also controls the tuning device. (The variations of cord drives are legion, however, almost every model being different; often there is a separate cord for the tuner, and in many models the knob spindle is itself the drive spindle of the tuner.)

The tuning of any radio can be by means of a gang condenser consisting of two variable condensers on the same spindle (as commonly used in the majority of portable radios) or by permeability tuning using a coil and a core. The iron-dust core is not threaded to enable it to be screwed in and out of the coil former, but is smooth-sided and is a sliding fit inside the coil. It is mounted on a stiff wire or nylon support which is threaded into a carriage bar (Figure 7.5). There are at least two coils, one for the oscillator and the other for the input circuit; some radios with an r.f. stage have three.

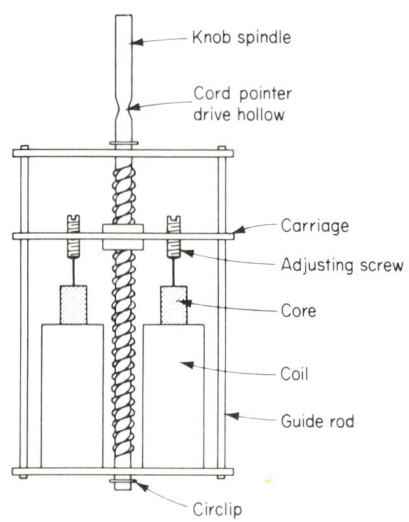

Figure 7.5. Permeability tuner with sliding cores and worm drive

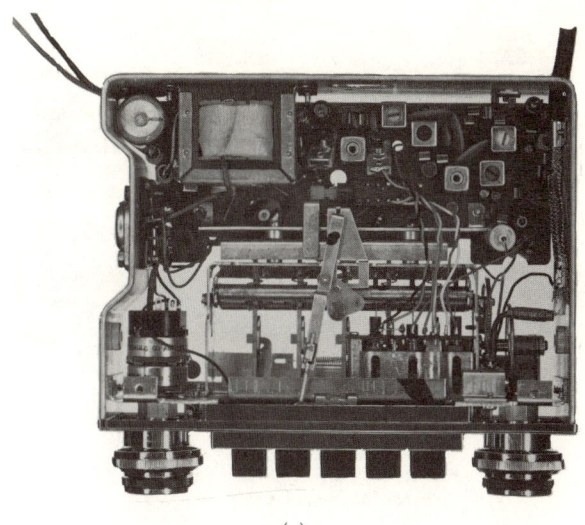

(a)

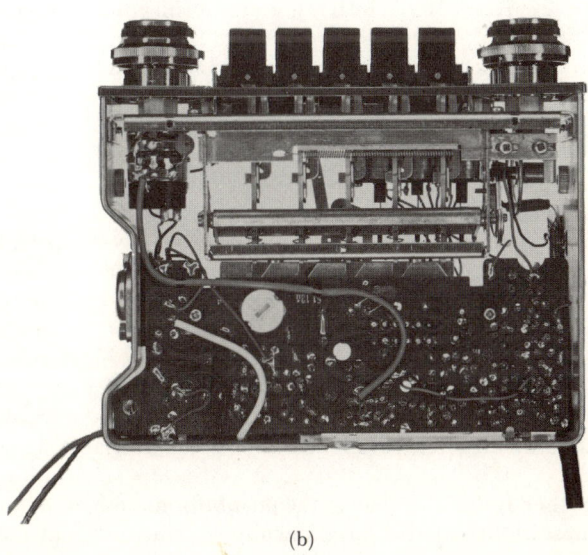

(b)

Figure 7.6. Radiomobile 1070 XB, (a) top and (b) bottom views of pushbutton radio. Tuner can be seen with mechanical pushbutton details and station scale pointer. Power output transistor can be seen on left side member (top view)

Figure 7.7.   Radiomobile 191B manually tuned radio. Pushbutton waveband and tone switching can be seen

The coils are mounted side-by-side and all the core-wires are fitted to the same carriage bar. The bar is mounted on guide rods enabling it to slide up and down plunging the cores in or out of the coils. It is driven by a worm-drive arrangement from the main tuning spindle so that a large number of turns produce a small movement of the cores to give a smooth and precise tuning control. With pushbutton radios, the worm drive is dispensed with and the bar is actuated by the pushbuttons' screwed rods.

Other methods of station selection have been used, most with a permeability tuner as a basis. One receiver used a small motor that drove the pointer over the scale and stopped whenever a station was received. The received signal or part of it was used to actuate a relay that switched off the motor. If the station was not the one desired, pressing a button restarted the motor until the next station was received, and so on. On reaching the end of the scale, the motor reversed and started the pointer back again. The circuit could be set to stop at only the strong stations so that weak unusable signals were bypassed.

In another system, similar to the pushbutton method, a number of different stations can be mechanically set but only one button is required. This arrangement, used on some Philips car radios, enables six stations to be preset. Pressing the button selects the next one in sequence, so if number 1 is tuned in and number 6 is required the button must be pressed five times to pass through the intervening ones. After number 6, number 1 is the next one up and the sequence repeats. The system enables a station to be selected without taking the eyes off the road, but hand and attention could be distracted for longer than with conventional pushbuttons. Also there is no means of station identification other than from programme material or pointer setting. Conventional pushbuttons can be selected in an instant with just a glance—no longer than needed for checking fuel, temperature, or other instrumentation—and the button allocated to each station can be remembered. They are therefore probably the best and most practical means of automatic station selection.

Input protection

When the vehicle passes near or under high-voltage power lines, which are very common in many parts of the country, a high electrostatic charge is picked up by the aerial. If the input tuning coils are connected directly from the aerial socket to chassis, the charge will be conducted to chassis through the coils with little damage. If there is no d.c. path to chassis through the coils, due to a padding capacitor at the bottom end or series instead of shunt connection of the tuned circuit, the voltage will charge up the series coupling capacitor to the base of the first transistor through the base/emitter junction (Figure 7.8a). This will very likely destroy the transistor. A resistor (R1) shunted across the circuit affords a measure of protection by discharging the aerial. The value cannot be too low otherwise it will shunt the signal, yet if too high its protection as a shunt is reduced; 2.2 kΩ is a common value.

Some further protection is necessary. One method is to wire a neon lamp across the aerial circuit. A neon lamp will strike over and start conducting at a certain specified voltage. Below that voltage it is a virtual open-circuit, while above it it offers a low resistance because it is a low-impedance device. (The high-impedance of screwdriver neon-testers is due to the high-value series resistance that is included.) When operating normally the neon has no effect on the circuit because the minute signal voltages from the aerial are way below the neon striking voltage. If a high voltage does appear on the aerial due to nearby power lines, and it exceeds the striking voltage, the charge will be conducted harmlessly through the lamp.

Another protection method is the use of a diode. This is reverse-biased, that is it is made non-conductive by the application of a small voltage of opposite polarity. In this condition it has no effect on the circuit and radio signals passing therein. A large voltage such as a static charge will overcome the bias and cause the diode to conduct the charge away. A snag with this arrangement is that diodes themselves are sensitive to large current surges, so a charge could destroy the diode and leave the set unprotected against the next one.

A simple yet effective protective device is the voltage-dependent resistor (VDR). This is a resistor without a fixed resistance value; the value decreases as the applied voltage increases. Each VDR has a quoted reference voltage that will pass a specified current. Below that voltage, the current will be very low because the resistance has increased, but above it, the current will be high. For this application a VDR is chosen that has a negligible shunting effect on the aerial circuit when connected across it, but that offers a low-resistance path to a high-voltage charge (Figure 7.8b).

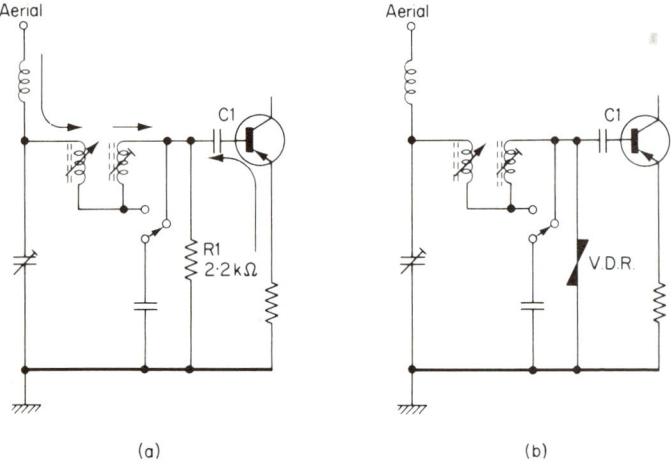

(a)   (b)

Figure 7.8.   (a) Input circuit with no d.c. path to earth through the coils. A high potential on the aerial (due to power-line induction) would charge capacitor C1 through the transistor base/emitter junction, destroying it. R1 affords some protection by providing a leakage path. (b) The same circuit protected by a VDR. At low voltages the resistance is high, giving negligible shunting effect, but at high voltage the resistance drops giving a low leakage path

Car-portable radios

The radios we have considered so far are designed for permanent installation in the car. Many portable radios feature a car-aerial socket to enable them to be used in the car by plugging in a car aerial. In most cases these are unsatisfactory. The aerial socket feeds a small winding on the ferrite-rod aerial, so signals from the car aerial are coupled directly into the radio's tuned circuits (see Figure 6.2). This reduces the directional characteristic of the portable radio to some extent so that changes in the vehicle direction do not result in so much fading. It also overcomes the screening effect of the metal body because the car aerial is outside it.

However, since the signal is not usually as great as that picked up by the ferrite rod, the sensitivity of the radio (designed for a ferrite aerial) is inadequate for use with only a car aerial. The ferrite aerial is still connected inside the set and, although it is not picking up many broadcast signals because of being screened by the car-body, it does pick up all manner of interference from ignition and other electrical circuits. The results are therefore usually weak and noisy.

Some portable radios are rather more successful when used in cars. They have a switch, usually a push-button, that switches out the ferrite aerial altogether and selects input coils designed for use with a car aerial. Such radios are usually more expensive than the normal run and may include an extra stage to give more gain. They are thus able to give good results with less interference. Some interference may be received because the radio is not totally screened in metal, unlike a proper car radio. Lining part of it with metal foil on the inside will help matters, but it cannot be completely screened otherwise the ferrite aerial would not work when it was used as a portable. Another factor is that the car in which the radio may be used will probably not be fitted with suppressors because, with the exception of the plug suppressors, suppression is usually only carried out when installing a permanent car radio. Of course anyone wishing to make regular use of such a portable in his car could have the necessary suppressors fitted (see Chapter 14).

The true car-portable radio is specifically designed for its dual role. It consists of a portable radio but with car-radio styling, controls, and station scale. When out of the car it works just like an ordinary portable with a ferrite aerial and internal dry batteries. For use in the car it slides into a special metal tray permanently fitted to the vehicle. At the back of this tray there is a row of pins that engage with a row of sockets in the bottom of the radio. These pins carry the power supply from the car battery, the connections to the car loudspeaker, and the connection to the aerial circuits (the car aerial is plugged into the tray via a normal plug and socket). There is also a plunger that enters a hole in the base of the radio and operates an internal switch. This multi-pole switch switches out the ferrite aerial, disconnects the dry battery, and switches out the internal loudspeaker. Thus all the connections are made and the functions switched by just pushing the radio home in the tray. A lock with a key is provided to secure the radio in place and prevent theft.

These car-portables enjoyed a period of popularity when it was necessary to have a separate radio licence for permanent car radios; it was believed that a car-portable radio, not being permanently installed, did not require a licence. Actually this was a fallacy because the criterion to determine whether a radio was permanent was not whether it could be removed, but whether it was run from the car battery. Car-portables were therefore liable for licence duty. As radio licences have been abolished altogether now, the issue no longer arises, but it may be of interest to note that the same rule applies in the case of portable television receivers. Those run from the car battery need a separate licence, while those operated from internal batteries do not.

There were problems with some car-portables. Failure of the plug and socket strips to marry exactly led to many broken sockets, and there were also difficulties in operating transistor output stages, designed for 9-V operation, at car-battery voltages of up to 15 V or more when the battery was charging. The frequent result was thermal runaway and burnt-out output transistors. Although the car-portable has lost its appeal to a great extent, one maker still had a current model up to quite recently.

General construction

Construction of car radio circuitry follows a similar pattern to that of portable radios. Printed circuits are used consisting of a thin insulating board on which copper foil is deposited to form the circuit connections. The various components are fitted to the board by their terminals or lead-out wires, which pass through holes in the board and are soldered to the copper print on the other side. Output transistors and some heavier components such as output transformers are mounted on the metal-frame and connected to the print by flying leads.

Where separate transistors, resistors and capacitors are used, as they generally are, the construction is said to be *discrete*. Two other constructional methods are used, although at present to a lesser extent. Some makers employ *modules*. These are complete circuit sections, mass-produced by a component manufacturer, consisting of a small printed-circuit sub-assembly totally enclosed in a metal case. A row of terminal tags is provided to fit into corresponding holes in the main printed-circuit board.

A widely used module in car radios a few years ago, although now obsolete, is the Mullard LP1166. It consists of three i.f. stages and detector, or the first stage can be used as a mixer/oscillator. A complete car-radio circuit using it is shown in Figure 7.9. The radio manufacturer need only add the tuner and input circuitry, and an audio section. Although they made matters easier for the maker, they were difficult to repair because of the lack of access.

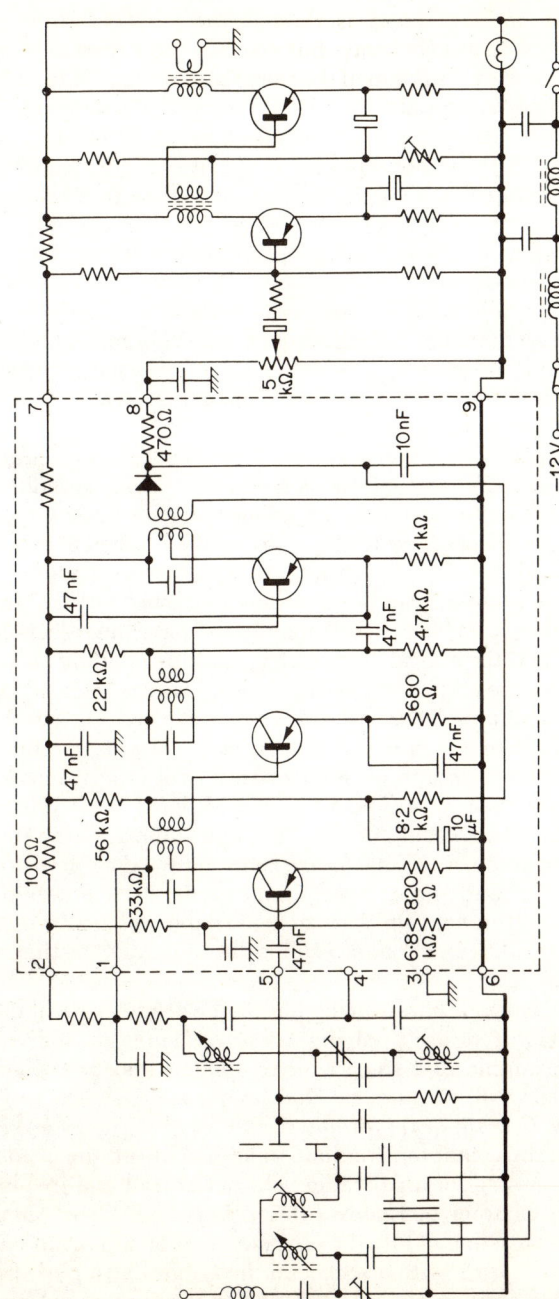

Figure 7.9. Example of complete car radio using Mullard LP1166 module (shown within dotted lines)

The other constructional method is the *integrated circuit* (i.c.). Transistors are relatively small anyway, but the actual device itself occupies a very small amount of the total space, most of it being made up with encapsulation and terminals. It follows that a large number of interconnected transistors could be accommodated in one capsule, especially if these were not separate units but were all formed on the same piece or chip of semiconductor material. (Integrated circuits are often known as 'chips'.) Diodes can also be formed on the chip and, as reverse-biased diodes possess the property of capacitance, they can be used in the place of low-value capacitors. Resistors too can be formed by layers of semiconductor material. Complete circuits of great complexity can therefore be built up in a space not much larger than that of a single transistor. The only extra components needed are coils, transformers and large-value capacitors, which cannot at present be duplicated within the i.c.

I.C.s are made by photographing large-scale circuits and then reducing them to micro-dimensions. Successive layers and diffusions of the semi-conductor materials are applied; at each stage the surface is masked with silicon-dioxide film, which is then etched to expose the correct areas for the next deposition. Although expensive to produce initially, large numbers can be subsequently turned out at relatively low cost, so they need long production runs to make them economical. An alternative is the hybrid i.c., which is made by bonding individual elements to a base and wiring with gold wire using a microscope and special manipulators. These are more expensive per unit but there is much less development involved in devising the original circuit. Thus the method is most suitable for small quantities of a special circuit. An example of the mass produced i.c. is the Mullard TAD 100, which consists of the mixer, oscillator, i.f., a.g.c. and audio pre-amp stages of an a.m. radio receiver. New i.c.s are continually being produced for radio, amplifier and many other applications; even power output stages with built-in heat sinks are now available. No doubt they will be seen increasingly in car audio and radio equipment as they are in other fields.

With increasing emphasis being put on the safety angle in the car, some manufacturers are applying safety measures to their radios. Philips for example pad some of their models and fit replaceable knobs that snap off on impact. Dial lamps are designed to give a diffused glow over the scale without dazzle.

Finally in this chapter we shall take a look at the leads and connections needed for a car radio. The aerial lead and its plug are described in Chapter 6. Loudspeaker connections vary. Some use small plugs consisting of just the pins mounted on a paxolin base on the loudspeaker lead, with a socket on the radio. Extra pins that are linked together are sometimes to be found on the plug; these complete the power supply circuit inside the radio so that if the plug is withdrawn the circuit is broken and the output stage is protected from running without the loudspeaker connected. Other radios have a short lead with a pair of socket connectors on the end into which plug connectors on the speaker-wire fit. It doesn't matter which way round the speaker is connected unless stereo is being received, but more of this in Chapter 8.

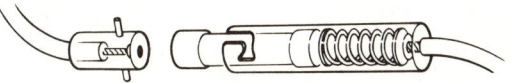

Figure 7.10. Power connector and fuse-holder

The standard power lead consists of a bayonet connector which also serves as a fuse carrier (Figure 7.10). A small bayonet plug is fitted to the lead coming from the radio, while the lead to the car electrical supply goes to a terminal at the bottom of a plastic cylinder. A compression spring fitted to this terminal has a flat contact disc at the other end, and the cartridge fuse is inserted in the cylinder to contact against the disc. The plug is pushed in against the free end of the fuse and turned clockwise to lock. Contact is maintained by the spring.

Chapter 8

Stereo and Multi-speaker Systems

The majority of home audio systems, with the exception of portable players, are now stereo, so readers will be familiar with this form of reproduction. Although the basic principle is the same there are some special problems with car installations; but first of all we shall review the way in which stereo works.

Two separate and distinct channels are used in the studios to record sounds coming from the left and from the right. While more than two microphones may be used, the result is mixed down to just two channels. On gramophone records these are carried by the two groove walls, which are modulated independently of each other, but on tape they are recorded on two tracks that run one above the other and that are picked up simultaneously by two separate magnetic coil-systems in the playback head.

When played back through a pair of amplifiers and suitably positioned loudspeakers, the direction of the original sounds can be reproduced. When a stereo system is properly set up, it is possible to identify sounds coming not only from the extreme left or right but also from points in between. A centrally placed sound in the studio appears to come from a central point between the loudspeakers, and likewise intermediate locations can be pinpointed with a fair degree of accuracy.

This ability to locate apparent sound sources between the stereo speakers is of course an illusion, and the effect is dependent on a number of factors. At whatever point in the studio the sound originates, it will be picked up by the microphones of both channels, but at different volume levels, the proportion depending on the position relative to the microphones. A central sound for example will be picked up equally by both. In addition to this there are slight time delays, with sounds reaching the nearer microphone fractionally before the farther one. This produces phase differences between the signals.

Reverberations occur in the studio as a result of sounds being reflected from the walls and ceiling. Owing to the various lengths and multiple paths of these reflected sounds, they arrive at the microphone at different times like a series of very rapid echoes, too rapid in fact to be individually distinguished. While too much reverberation makes music sound muddled and indistinct, none at all makes it dull and lifeless. A certain amount is essential and is provided for in the studio. It too is picked up by the microphones, but there are differences in level and phase which depend on the relative positions of sound-source and microphone.

All these subtle details are preserved in good stereo recording and reproduction, and they give not only directional dimension to the sound but also a sense of presence. To get the full effect, though, certain conditions must be met. There must be the minimum of 'crosstalk', the leakage of signals from one channel to another. The loudspeakers must be correctly positioned and in phase with each other, and must be balanced in response and sound level.

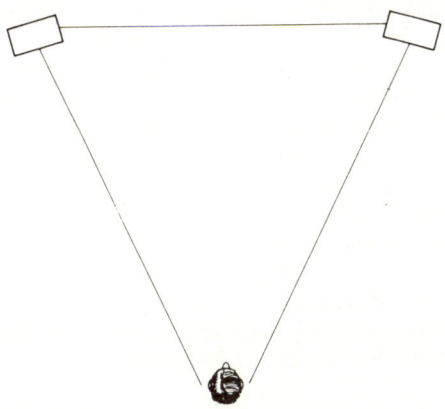

Figure 8.1. Ideal stereo configuration, speakers and listener forming an equal-sided triangle

The ideal listening set-up is an equal-sided triangle with the speakers and the listener at each corner, thus giving an equal distance between speakers and listener (Figure 8.1). Sounds will thereby be heard at the correct levels and phasing. Any major deviation from this positioning brings unbalance and degradation of the stereo effect. However, freedom of movement is restricted by this arrangement, and no more than one person can occupy the ideal listening position. Upward facing speakers that radiate in all directions

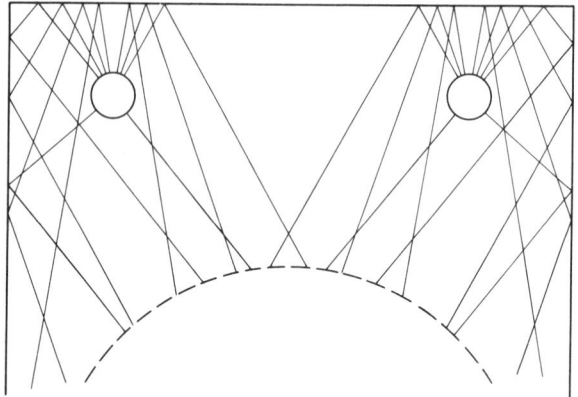

Figure 8.2. Multiple reflections from omni-directional speakers give a less-critical listening area but also less well-defined stereo image

(omni-directionals) are sometimes used to improve matters (Figure 8.2). Sound is not only received directly from these, but also from reflections from nearby walls and furniture, which makes their location and that of the listeners less critical. The penalty is, though, that the stereo image is blurred and sound locations less easy to pinpoint. Another snag is that wall-coverings and furnishings tend to absorb some frequencies and reflect others, so the frequency-response of the system is adversely affected.

A method of sound propagation adopted in some stereograms also relies on wall reflection (Figure 8.3). The main speakers are sideways-mounted in the cabinet and the gram placed across a corner of the room. Sound is bounced off the adjacent walls, thereby giving a wider stereo image than the distance between the actual speakers. To

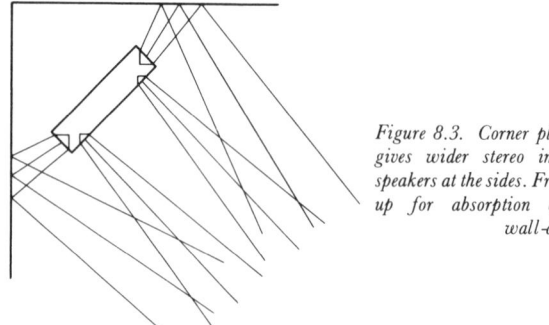

Figure 8.3. Corner placing of home stereogram gives wider stereo image from close-mounted speakers at the sides. Front-mounted tweeters make up for absorption of high frequencies by wall-coverings

compensate for loss of high-frequencies due to absorption, front-facing tweeters (high-frequency speakers) provide direct treble radiation.

Inequalities in output between the channels, due to differences in amplifier gains or speaker sensitivity, can be compensated for by the balance control. This increases the gain of one channel while decreasing that of the other, and so enables the user to adjust the centre point of the stereo image.

Car stereo

While conditions in a car are very different from those in the home, some problems are similar in nature and may thus suggest possible solutions. The speaker positioning must in most cases be dictated by space availability and convenience, and these rarely coincide with optimum stereo performance. The main problem is that, as both driver and front-seat passenger are seated very close to their respective sides of the vehicle, there can be no centre listening position. Thus if we mount a speaker on each side of the car, one will be very close to the listener and the other will be distant.

Where there is only the driver in the car, he can operate the balance control, if one is fitted, to increase the volume of the distant speaker so that it sounds about the same as that of the near one. This restores balance, but does not compensate for phase differences since the sounds from the further speaker arrive slightly later. It may be thought that this time lag is so small as to make no difference, but the ears and brain are sensitive to such phase variations and they interpret them as spatial differences, so the stereo effect is thereby confused. For a passenger, use of the balance control to favour the driver will make things worse for him, as the near speaker will be louder than the far one.

A further snag is that, while the far speaker is positioned to the left of the driver (or right of the passenger) in the UK, the near one in both cases will be almost in front or only a little to one side (Figure 8.4). Thus what stereo image there is spreads not from left to right but only from centre to one side.

This assumes the conventional speaker mounting position in or under the dashboard. Another position is on the windscreen shelf. Care must be taken here to avoid obscuring the vision of the driver, and low pod-type speaker housings are most suitable. They can be positioned as near to the side as possible in order to extend the stereo image and reduce interference with forward visibility (Figure 8.5). The basic problems remain though.

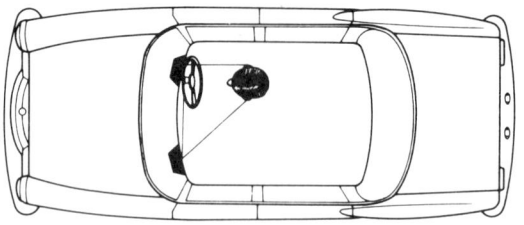

Figure 8.4. Dash-mounted car-stereo speakers. Distances are unequal and stereo image is from left to centre

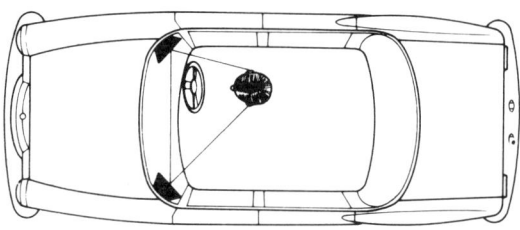

Figure 8.5. Front-shelf mounting can slightly extend the stereo image to the right

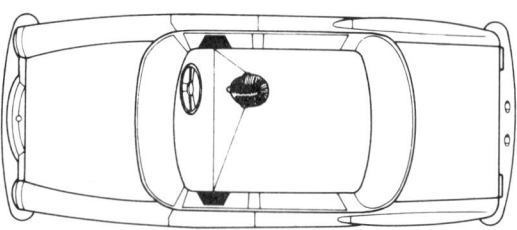

Figure 8.6. Further right-hand extension can be made by mounting the speakers in the front door panels. Can give 'hole in the middle effect' with no centrally located sounds. Speakers can also be masked by the body unless mounted well forward

Another mounting position that has gained in popularity is in the door panels (Figure 8.6). Here the stereo image is extended to either side as it should be, but the listeners are seated *between* the speakers. The result can be described as the 'hole in the middle' effect: sounds come from left or right, but there is no illusion of sound-sources at intermediate points. A further snag is that the body of the driver or his passenger will mask the sound of the speaker on his side from reaching the other listener. Both these difficulties can be alleviated to some extent by mounting the speakers well forward, near the hinge edge of the door.

A mounting arrangement devised by the author overcomes the worst effects of all those previously described. The speakers are mounted under the roof just over the heads of the driver and passenger, and are directed forward towards the windscreen (Figure 8.7). Sound is reflected back from the windscreen to the listeners; because sound radiated from the sides of a speaker is minimal, and because there is a bottom lip to the speaker-housing, very little sound appears to come from overhead.

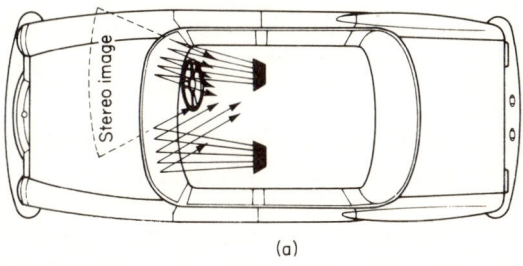

(a)

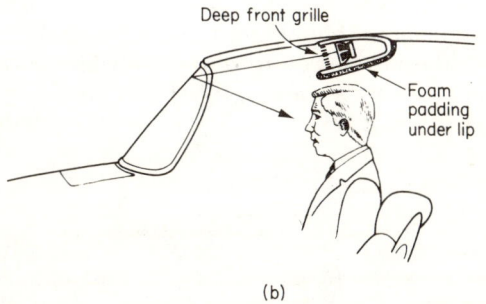

(b)

Figure 8.7. (a) Overhead mounting arrangement devised by author. Sound is reflected from windscreen giving almost equal paths from both speakers. Extending the apparent image beyond the windscreen from the points of reflection gives the driver an almost central position. Effect will be just as good for the passenger. (b) Side view of overhead speaker. Bottom lip and deep grille directs sound forward. Windscreen rake reflects it downward to listener

Glass is one of the few materials that reflect sound really well without absorbing certain bands of frequencies, so the snags encountered by using wall reflections in the home do not exist; all frequencies, treble, middle and bass, are bounced back. The backward rake of all windscreens means that the sound is reflected on a downward path, which is ideal because it is thus directed toward the heads of the listeners. The major advantage is in the relative apparent positions of the speakers, and the curvature of the windscreen plays an important part in this. Examination of the sound paths shown in Figure 8.7a reveals that those reflected from the far speaker are only a little longer than those reflected from the near one, so levels and phasing will be very close and a good stereo effect can be obtained. Furthermore, the position of the stereo image is from about the centre of the windscreen to the extreme right-hand corner, which puts the driver approximately central. The passenger likewise has a central position as the sound distribution is the same for both sides. No other mounting arrangement can achieve this result. The reflected lines can be subtended out in front of the windscreen to give the image as shown dotted in the illustration, which is little short of the ideal classic positioning of Figure 8.1.

Practical considerations are whether there is enough head room to mount speakers in this way, and the actual fitting and wiring. The latter points are dealt with in Chapter 13, but headroom could be a problem especially in smaller or lower cars. Special speakers would be required. Some very slender ones are available, one being 8 inches by 2 inches (speaker, not including cabinet); this type has been used in television receivers. A long shallow pod could be made to contain such a speaker with a total depth of less than 3 inches. Padding would be a wise provision for the bottom surface. Alternatively the speakers could be mounted nearer the centre and slightly forward of the head position. A slight outward angle may then be required (Figure 8.8). If headroom is restricted, speakers could be mounted on the windscreen shelf facing the windscreen. They would need a very wide angle of dispersion.

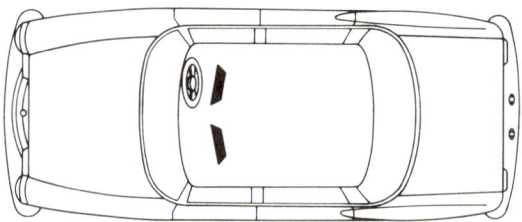

Figure 8.8. In the case of low roofs, speakers may be mounted forward,
and more central, with an outward angle

Stereo radio

Notwithstanding the vagaries of mobile f.m. reception and the even more critical nature of stereo reception on f.m., several stereo car radios have appeared, and it is very likely that more will follow. This being so we shall briefly outline the basic principle. An important factor is compatibility: the stereo signal must be receivable as a complete mono signal by mono radios. The Left and Right channels must therefore be transmitted added together (L+ R) to be received normally in mono. To enable them to be separated in the stereo receiver, a further signal (the difference between them, L− R) is transmitted, amplitude-modulated on a subcarrier of 38 kHz. This, as is the case with all amplitude-modulated signals, produces sidebands, i.e. frequencies that are equal to the carrier plus the modulating frequency and the carrier minus the modulating frequency. As the highest audio frequency to be modulated is 15 kHz, the result is a band of frequencies from 38 − 15 = 23 kHz to 38 + 15 = 53 kHz. This band from 23 to 53 kHz is then frequency-modulated on the main carrier, above the normal mono (L+ R) signal which extends only up to 15 kHz.

It can be seen then that the use of a subcarrier transforms the (L− R) signal into a band of frequencies much higher than the (L+ R) signal, although the audio frequencies in both will be similar, and thus enables separation to be achieved later in the receiver decoder. The procedure incidentally is known as *multiplexing*.

The subcarrier frequency of 38 kHz is no longer of any use because it represents zero modulation frequency. As it would require transmitter power to radiate it which would therefore be wasted, it is suppressed before transmission. Figure 8.9 shows the spectrum of transmitted frequencies and it will be noticed that there is a notch at 38 kHz.

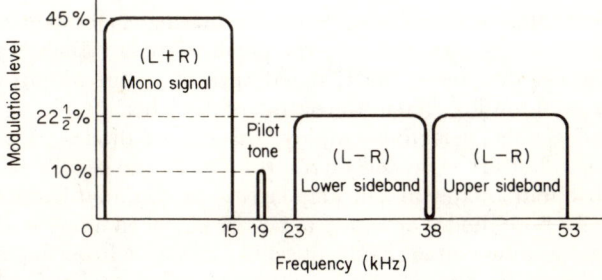

Figure 8.9. Frequency spectrum and modulation percentages of broadcast stereo signal

Now in order to demodulate the (L— R) signal we need a 38-kHz steady wave in the receiver decoder. It is comparatively easy to include a 38-kHz oscillator in the radio circuits, but the frequency and phase must be exactly the same as the original at the transmitter. To synchronise the oscillator, a steady tone at half the frequency (19 kHz) is transmitted along with the other signals, and when applied to it makes the oscillator run in step.

Why then could not the original 38-kHz carrier have been left in for the purpose? Being surrounded by its own sidebands it would be difficult to separate, whereas the 19-kHz *pilot tone*, as it is called, stands squarely in the middle of the gap between the two bands of signals (see Figure 8.9) and so can be filtered out easily. Furthermore it occupies only 10% of the modulation level, which is sufficient for synchronising purposes, and thus does not unduly take up transmitter power.

The receiver and detector circuits of a stereo radio are identical to that of an ordinary f.m. receiver; it is in the post-detector circuits that the stereo decoding takes place. The de-emphasis network that gives a decreasing treble response and that is usually connected in the detector stage must be dispensed with, otherwise the high-frequency pilot tone and (L— R) modulations would be filtered away. De-emphasis is later applied to the audio circuits, after decoding has taken place.

The pilot tone is separated by applying·the complete signal to a tuned stage similar to an i.f. circuit, but tuned to 19 kHz. The output is then fed to the 38-kHz oscillator, or it is amplified and applied to a frequency-doubler circuit thus producing 38 kHz without an oscillator.

Next, the regenerated 38-kHz subcarrier is inserted into the (L— R) signal so that the L signal modulates one half of the carrier envelope and the R signal the other. The two are then separated by a pair of synchronous detectors, supplied with some pure unmodulated 38 kHz from the oscillator; this switches one detector on and then the other alternately with each half wave, by biasing each diode in turn. Thus one detector samples only the positive-going signals, and the other the negative ones; the L signal appears at the output of one detector, and the R signal at the output of the other.

Some decoder detectors employ, instead of diodes, a pair of transistors that are switched on alternately by the oscillator, while others use four diodes in a bridge circuit. A common feature is to arrange for both diodes or transistors to be switched on permanently by a d.c. standing voltage in the absence of the synchronising signal. Thus if a mono broadcast is being received the (L+ R) signal, which is present although not used for stereo, appears at the output of both detectors and so is fed as a mono signal into both audio amplifiers.

Another method of decoding is by *matrixing*. Here the $(L-R)$ signal is detected as it stands without separation by synchronous detectors. It is then fed into a matrix circuit along with the $(L+R)$ signal and, by a process of addition and subtraction, the L and R signals are resolved.

As the pilot tone is received only during a stereo broadcast it can be used as a stereo indicator. A feed taken from the 19-kHz amplifier stage is applied to a switching transistor, which activates a lamp or a meter that then serves as a stereo beacon.

Multi-speaker mono and stereo

From that rather technical excursion, we will return to more practical matters. It is sometimes desired to fit more than one loudspeaker to a car-radio or player. Usually this means a speaker at the front and one at the rear for back-seat passengers, the rear one being flush-mounted in the rear window shelf. There are a variety of ways by which extra speakers can be controlled.

The simplest is to use a single-pole 2-way switch as shown in Figure 8.10a. By this means either speaker can be selected, but not both at the same time. If the front one is required all the time, but the rear one needed in addition occasionally, a simple on/off switch in series with the rear speaker will suffice. These switches can be either the normal toggle type, or rotary switches. If it is desired to select either speaker or both, a 2-pole 3-way rotary switch will be needed. The wiring is shown in Figure 8.10b. It can be wired for both speakers to come on in the middle position or for them to come on at the extreme clockwise setting. It depends on which is to be the normal mode of operation, the front one on by itself, or both on. This normal position can then.be the middle one with the others either side.

The sensitivity of loudspeakers varies according to the model, the impedance and the mounting method, as shown in Chapter 5. When there are rear passengers the rear loudspeaker will be situated just

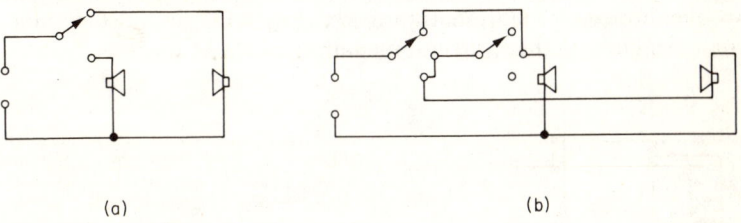

(a)   (b)

Figure 8.10. (a) Simple two-way switch to select front or back speakers; (b) two-pole three-way switch wired to select front, both, or rear speaker(s)

behind their heads, so the volume required will be less than that for the front speaker; yet on other occasions when there is no one in the back of the car it may be desired to have the rear-speaker volume higher. For all these reasons some method of adjusting the relative volume levels between the two speakers is desirable. This can be done by volume controls wired into the loudspeaker leads.

The easiest way is to connect a variable resistor in series with the rear speaker (Figure 8.11). This will reduce the volume relative to the front one, but will not make it greater. The control should be of the wire-wound variety, and be of 2 W rating minimum. The resistance is not critical, about 50 Ω should do in most cases. Lower values will not give quite so much volume reduction when fully turned back, but will be smoother in operation.

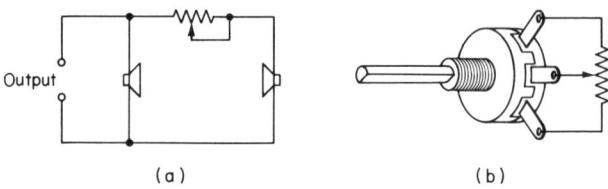

(a)   (b)

Figure 8.11. (a) Volume control for reducing level of rear speaker; (b) appearance
of control showing tag connections to internal resistance and wiper

Another method is to connect both speakers to the control as shown in Figure 8.12. In the centre position both speakers give about the same volume; turning it one way reduces one speaker and increases the other, while turning it the other way does the opposite. A drawback with this circuit is that power is dissipated in the resistor at all settings of the control. To avoid too great a loss, the resistance must be kept fairly low, although this also restricts the amount of control possible between the two speakers. When in the normal setting, about the centre of the range, half the resistance will be in circuit with each speaker. The proportion between this value and the speaker impedance represents the power loss in the circuit. The value, then, depends on the speaker impedance; for a 3-Ω speaker, the total

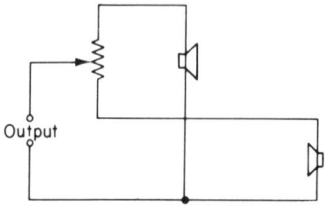

Output

Figure 8.12. Fader control wired to increase
or decrease levels of either front or rear speaker.
Centre position gives balance. There will be
power loss with this circuit

resistance of the control should not exceed 15Ω and the power rating should be not less than 3 W.

It may be desired in the case of a stereo system to install two additional speakers at the rear for the sake of rear passengers. The same control circuits we have described can be used to switch off the rear speakers; select front, back or both; control the level of the rear speakers; or fade the front or rear pair. To do this, the circuits must be duplicated so that there is one for each channel. There must be no interconnection between channels (with an exception discussed on page 108) otherwise the stereo effect will disappear and all speakers will be producing the same mono signal. So for switching off the rear speakers we need a 2-pole 2-way switch; to select either or both, a 4-pole 3-way rotary switch; and for level control and fading a pair of variable resistors ganged on the same control-spindle.

If a stereo player does not have a balance control to adjust the level of either speaker, this can be done by using a ganged control (Figure 8.13). Each section is connected in series with one speaker, but they must be so connected that the resistance of one section increases as the other decreases. To do this the centre wiper contact must be joined to the opposite end-contact to that of the other section, as shown in the illustration. If taken to the same side, the control will fade both speakers at the same time.

A variety of controls are made by car audio manufacturers such as Blaupunkt, Philips and Radiomobile and should be readily available. Some are made complete with control boxes and knobs ready to connect and screw to the dash or other convenient location, while others are available as just the component to be fitted to a control

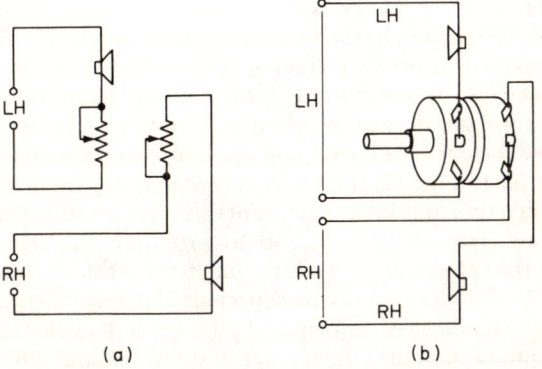

(a)   (b)

Figure 8.13. (a) Circuit of stereo balance control that can be wired into the speaker circuit if the player does not have one; (b) Control consists of two variable resistors ganged on the same spindle. These are the actual connections. There will be power loss with this circuit

panel. Most of these controls, whether toggle, rotary switch or level control, are fitted by means of a standard-sized screwed bush which is secured by a single hexagonal nut and locking washer. Spindles are of ¼-inch diameter with a flat to receive the standard knob-spring clip or grub-screw. If difficulty is experienced in obtaining a particular switch or control for a special purpose, it will probably be available from one of the radio component firms.

Quad and surround stereo

Two-channel stereo gives the illusion of a number of sound locations along a straight line drawn in front of the listener. In real life, sounds are not thus confined: they can be distant or near, to the front, sides or behind. It is to give this added illusion of reality and depth to the sound that quadrasonics (Latin, 'four sounds') has been developed. As its name implies it uses four channels instead of two. The term is to be preferred to the hybrid Latin/Greek 'quadraphonics' although the latter seems at present to be the more popular of the two.

The four channels feed four loudspeakers, two in front of the listener as with ordinary stereo, and two to the rear. Just as stereo gives the effect of sound sources between the two speakers and not just from extreme left and right, so quad creates the illusion of sound locations between adjacent pairs of speakers, hence all around the listener. The only dimension now omitted is that of height; there is no way of distinguishing whether a sound is overhead or from floor level with a conventional quad system. However, research is now going on into a new system known as 'ambisonics' which adds vertical dimension information to the four channels in such a way that it can be separated out in the reproducing system. This though is looking ahead somewhat, and is of more interest for the home system where more vertical space is available than in the car.

As noted before, studio or concert-hall reverberation plays an important part in music; it adds richness and life, and if absent the music sounds thin and lifeless. Most of this reverberation comes from the sides and rear of the hall, and so with orchestral recording in quad, the rear channels carry little but reverberation components. Although the listener may not be conscious of the rear channels when they are on, should they be switched off there is a marked difference and the reproduction in ordinary stereo seems flat and uninteresting by comparison. As all the phase differences, time delays and other acoustic characteristics are more or less faithfully preserved along with directional information, it is possible to duplicate the acoustics of the Albert Hall in a Mini!

With pop and group recordings, quad is used rather differently. Here different instruments are reproduced in each of the four channels, so the effect is of sitting in the middle of the group of performers. Whether this is good or musically satisfying is very much a matter of opinion, but at least it is a change that could add some interest to what very often is rather monotonous fare.

To get the best effect from quad, all channels should be preserved separately throughout the recording and reproducing process. This is known as 'discrete' quad, and with tape can be easily accomplished by recording on four tracks. The playback head has four magnetic circuits that read one track each and apply the output to four separate amplifiers.

The major problem with quad comes from trying to get the four channels on disc. There are many systems but they seem to have been resolved into three main ones. The CD-4 is a discrete system that records the front channels on the two groove walls in the normal way, and the rear ones on a modulated carrier-wave above the highest normal audio frequency. The method is similar in many respects to the stereo radio signal. The other two, known as the SQ and QS systems, encode the four channels into two in such a way that they can be separated later in the player. The two channels are then recorded on the two groove walls. A matrix is used for separation, but the separation is imperfect: crosstalk of a high order is present between some channels and spurious signals are generated in others. The player circuitry is simpler hence cheaper than CD-4, but complications such as logic decoders, variable blend and other devices to try to improve matters bring the complexity and cost up to the level of the discrete system.

The problems and controversies surrounding these systems need be of little concern here because for the mobile system the recording medium is tape, which is inherently discrete. There is, though, a method of enhancing ordinary stereo to give 'surround stereo' that is basically very simple. It relies on the fact that reverberation components are usually present to some extent in an ordinary stereo recording, although not separated from the main, direct sounds. Now because these reverberations travel a long path around the walls of the recording studio before being eventually picked up by the microphones, delays occur that appreciably alter the phase with the result that most of the reverberations picked up by the right microphone will be completely out of phase with those received by the left. On the other hand, sounds coming from the performers direct to the microphones of both channels will be mostly in phase, although slight phase shifts will exist. This is especially true of sounds coming from near the centre of the stage; those nearer the extremes will be more out of phase.

If then we can separate signals that are similar but out of phase from those that are mostly in phase, we shall have succeeded in isolating the reverberations from the main sound and can feed them to rear-positioned speakers. The simple way of doing this is to connect a couple of loudspeakers in series across the positive terminals of both channels—see Figure 8.14. (Note that 'positive' is used here not in the same sense as battery polarity, there being no positive or negative with a loudspeaker output because the signal is a.c.; it is used to denote the terminal where the signals from both channels are in phase.) Now when the signals are in phase, and approximately equal in level, there will be no voltage across the speakers and so no sound produced. When they are out of phase, opposite voltages will be present across the speakers and they will respond. A variable resistor can be included to reduce the level from the rear speakers if required.

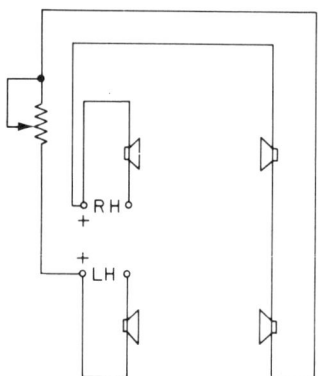

Figure 8.14. A 'surround stereo' effect can be obtained by connecting a pair of rear-mounted speakers in series, across the two live terminals of the L.S. sockets of the two stereo channels. These will then only reproduce out-of-phase signals or those with wide level-differences, such as reverberation components. Some crosstalk between channels will result

The success of the arrangement depends on the way the microphones were used at the original recording; those using the 'close mike' technique (where a large number of microphones are used close to the performers) will have fewer reverberation components than those using just a few or a single stereo mike. Unfortunately most modern recordings do use the close-mike system, so it may be expected that some recordings will give a better effect than others. Another factor is that both the rear loudspeakers are producing the same sound, being connected in series. An improved effect can sometimes be obtained by running them out of phase with each other. Try reversing the connections to one rear speaker and see which way gives the best effect. It should be mentioned that connecting speakers across the two channels in this way results in cross-talk, i.e. sounds from one front channel will also be reproduced in the other, although at about a ninth the power of their correct channel. This results in some degrading of the front stereo image, but it is not too serious.

Some quad playing systems have a facility whereby ordinary stereo tapes can be played and given a surround-stereo effect. When switched to this mode, the rear speakers are fed with the out-of-phase signals as described above, but they are supplied through separate amplifiers to prevent crosstalk taking place, so there is no deterioration of the normal front stereo image. Furthermore, other phase shifts are introduced between the two rear speakers to enhance the random reverberation effect. Results can be quite impressive, but as with the simple speaker bridging circuit they depend on the way the original recording was made.

As to mounting the rear speakers, they can be flush-fitted into the rear window shelf, one at each end. Although they face upwards, the angled rear window reflects the sound forwards. Pod-type speaker housings are quite popular for fitting to the rear shelf as they require no large hole cut in the shelf. It is important with all stereo and quad installations that the speakers be connected in phase, so that the cones all move in the same direction at the same time. Output sockets on the player units are marked usually with a + sign to denote the phase connection, and the polarity is also indicated on speakers intended for stereo use. Connecting wire must be coded in some way, such as being two-coloured or having one wire tinned and the other plain copper, so that correct phasing can be ensured.

Chapter 9

Cassette Players

There are two rival tape systems currently in use in mobile audio installations, one using cassettes and the other cartridges. The cassette was first introduced in its present form by Philips, but both cassettes and player mechanisms are now manufactured by many other makers. Until recently the cassette was used for portable tape recorders and home audio systems, leaving the cartridge as the main tape format for car players, but now the cassette system is finding increasing acceptance for mobile use.

An open-reel tape recorder has two separate reels, the tape passing from one to the other, from left to right as the recording proceeds. This is unecomonical of space because both reels must be large enough to accommodate the full amount of tape, yet only one can be full at a time. In the cassette (Figure 9.1) the reels are replaced by hubs, which because they have no side-cheeks can be placed much closer together.

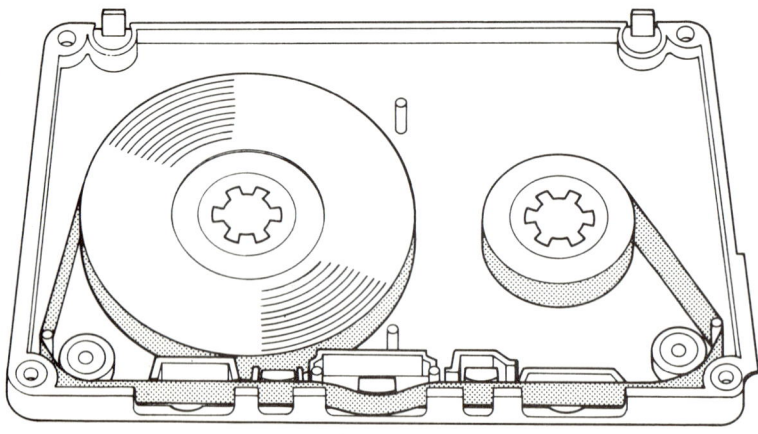

Figure 9.1. Inside view of a cassette

The tape on one hub when it is full extends more than halfway towards the other hub, but this causes no problems because as the second hub fills up the first one empties. Tape is prevented from spilling off by the walls of the cassette. Low-friction liners are placed inside the cassette walls to reduce drag on the tape as it revolves on the hubs.

Tape from one hub passes over a guide post, around a nylon pulley wheel, across an exposed area at the side of the cassette, around another nylon wheel and post and so to the other hub (Figure 9.2). At the centre of the exposed area, a felt pad is mounted on a phosphor-bronze spring; when in the playing position in the machine, the record/playback head presses against the tape at this point, the sprung pad ensuring intimate tape/head contact. The rest of the area is divided into sections: to the left is the part where the erase head would make contact in a recorder, this being absent in a playback-only machine; to the right is a similar portion where the tape-drive mechanism is engaged. Here a hole passes right through the cassette casing to accommodate the tape-drive spindle. This appears behind the tape, and a rubber pinch-wheel is applied to the front to press the tape against the spindle. The exposed erase and drive areas are identical, including the hole, because they are transposed when the cassette is turned over to play the other tracks.

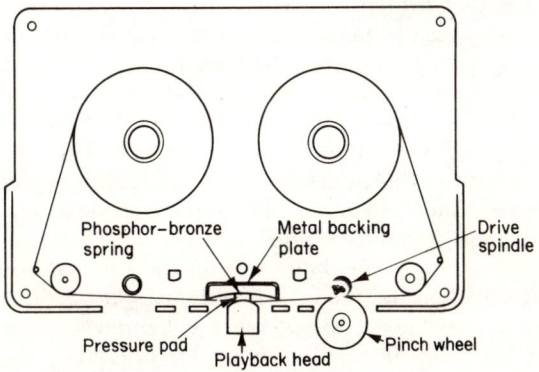

Figure 9.2. Plan view of cassette with playback head, drive spindle and pinch wheel engaged

Tape tangling

The basic cassette arrangement and dimensions are the same for all makes in spite of some slight moulding and other differences. This is essential if all cassettes are to be compatible with every player. Some makes dispense with the guide posts as these can introduce extra drag, and one uses a pair of guide arms or tusks to lightly contact the spooled tape and prevent it coming loose and tangling. Unfortunately tangling is not an uncommon experience with cassettes; tape can get in a fearful mess inside the cassette, and also outside by winding itself around the drive spindle so that it is difficult to disengage the cassette without breaking the tape.

One of the main causes of this trouble is inserting the cassette into the player with loose tape inside. Before using, tape should always be pulled taut by rotating the left-hand hub clockwise or the right-hand one anti-clockwise with a pen or match until any slack is taken up.

If a tangle should occur, the first concern is to get the cassette out of the player causing the minimum damage to the tape. If there is access to the player flywheel, it can be turned slowly by hand in the opposite direction to its normal rotation, which means turning it clockwise when viewed from the top. This may release the tape wrapped around it. If the tape is creased and wrinkled, this can be ignored, and the surplus carefully wound into the cassette by turning one of the hubs. If it is torn or stretched so that it is narrower than normal, the damaged section must be cut out and the ends joined. Where there is no access to the flywheel, the tape must be eased off as best one can.

Joining the tape is best carried out by securing the ends on a splicing block, trimming them with a blade so that they abut perfectly, and then bridging them with a length of jointing tape. The tape must be applied to the side of the tape facing into the cassette, and must not overlap the edges; if it does it must be trimmed back to the tape edge. Special tape is required for this job, because ordinary cellulose tape exudes its adhesive in time to affect adjacent layers. Tape jointing blocks or complete cassette repair kits are made by **BIB** and are readily available at modest cost from dealers or factors.

For tangles inside the cassette, the case must be taken apart. Some makes have the two halves welded together, and these can only be opened by running a sharp knife around the joint and then gluing together again when the repair is completed, an operation fraught with snags and dangers. A few more enlightened manufacturers secure the halves by five self-tapping screws which can easily be removed to provide access to the interior.

Facts and figures

The frequency response of any tape system depends in part on the tape speed. Magnetic zones are produced on the tape by the gap in the recording head and correspond to the instantaneous level of the applied electrical signal. The higher the frequency, the more rapid the succession of zones. As the frequency increases there comes a point where a new zone is created before the preceding one has moved away, so the zones merge and frequencies at and above this point will not be recorded. (For a fuller description see Chapter 3.) The faster the tape speed, the higher the upper frequency limit. Single-speed open-reel recorders operate at $3\frac{3}{4}$ inches per second, and three-speed models at $1\frac{7}{8}$, $3\frac{3}{4}$ and $7\frac{1}{2}$ in/s (4.76, 9.53 and 19.05 cm/s) so that the user can make a choice (appropriate to the material being recorded) between high frequency response and tape economy.

The cassette operates at a speed of $1\frac{7}{8}$ in/s in order to give maximum playing time with small physical size. This limits the upper frequency response and caused much criticism when cassettes first appeared. However response is also dependent on the width of the head-gap; a narrow gap can record more zones to the inch than a wider one, and thus offsets a slow tape speed. The design of heads has been developed to the point where the response of many cassette machines at $1\frac{7}{8}$ in/s is equivalent to many older tape recorders running at $3\frac{3}{4}$ or in some cases even at $7\frac{1}{2}$ in/s. While improvements have been most marked in the expensive home hi-fi units, there has been a spin-off in the form of better performance for car systems.

Another advantage of faster open-reel tape speeds is that short-term speed variations (producing the corresponding pitch changes known as wow and flutter) are reduced by the faster flywheel rotation. In the cassette player, though, the drive spindle is made much thinner than in an open-reel machine, and so must revolve faster in order to move the same length of tape. As the flywheel is directly coupled to the drive-spindle its speed too is faster—in fact little different from that in an open-reel machine operating at a faster tape-speed. However since the size, hence mass, of the flywheel is restricted, which affects its efficiency, wow and flutter remain one of the inherent problems with the cassette system. Many hi-fi systems use electronic motor control, which reduces these irregularities to extremely low levels, and this is now being used with some of the better mobile players. Examples of this type of circuit are given in Chapter 11. However for most in-car entertainment, where awareness of the smaller details is less than when listening quietly without distraction at home, the speed stability even of the cheaper players is in most cases satisfactory.

A further factor is the tape width. Standard recording tape is 0.246 inch (6.25 mm) wide, whereas that used in cassettes is 0.15 inch (3.81 mm), just over half the width. The dimensions and disposition of the tracks are shown in Figure 9.3. In the case of standard tape the four recorded tracks are 1 mm wide and the margins between them 0.75 mm. With cassette tape, the margins are drastically reduced to 0.26 mm in order to accommodate four tracks on the narrower tape

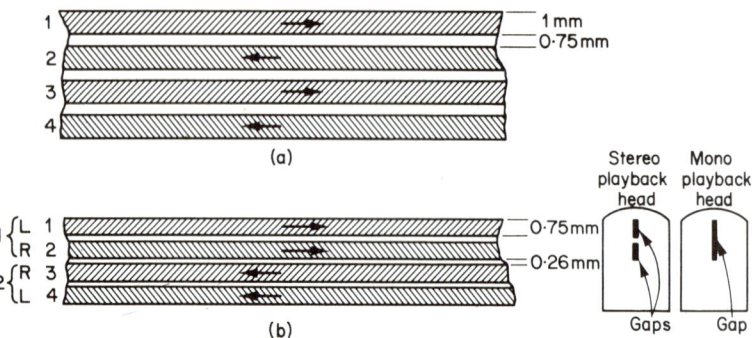

Figure 9.3. (a) Standard 0.246-inch (6.25 mm) tape as used on open-reel recorder, showing size and disposition of four tracks; (b) 0.15-inch (3.81 mm) cassette tape with stereo tracks

without too great a reduction of track width. The actual track dimension is 0.75 mm, threequarters of that of the standard tape.

Any reduction of track width increases the background noise, and this has proved a further problem in the use of cassettes for high-quality sound reproduction. Some improvement is obtained by the use of the Dolby B system. During recording, all the high frequencies at low sound levels are boosted, then during playback these same frequencies are reduced by the same amount. The result is that all frequencies are reproduced in the same proportion as they were originally. However, since the most troublesome noise frequencies are high, these too are reduced in the playback process. The result is a useful reduction in background hiss. In the case of mobile cassette systems, with high road and traffic noise, any background noise on the tape would be masked, so Dolby circuits are not at present built in to car cassette players. The reason for this becomes more apparent when it is realised that they can add up to £50 to the cost of a home hi-fi cassette deck! However, an increasing number of pre-recorded cassettes are Dolbyised, these being recognisable by the back-to-back double D design on the label. While they are intended for Dolby playback units, they can be played on non-Dolby players such as car cassette units. The main effect is a rather brighter tone; if the player has a tone control, this can be turned down a little to roughly compensate.

A feature of cassette-tape track disposition is that tracks are not interleaved as is the case with a four-track open-reel recorder. There, tracks 1 and 3 travel in one direction, tracks 2 and 4 in the other. With the cassette, tracks 1 and 2 carry the left and right channels respectively of the forward programme, and tracks 3 and 4 the right and left of the reverse one. This means that tapes can be played either on stereo or mono players. (A mono player has a wider head gap that spans the two tracks and so reproduces both channels together. A stereo head has two separate small gaps set one above the other.)

Cassette mechanics

As already mentioned, the tape is driven by means of a spindle inserted into a hole in the cassette casing behind the tape and an applied pinch wheel in front. It is also necessary to drive the take-up hub during normal running, and either hub during rewind and fast-forward functions.

To facilitate this, each hub has a hole of ⅜-inch diameter with six projecting keys. The playing compartment has a pair of matching capstans, which have a slight taper to ensure easy engagement when the cassette is inserted.

The complete mechanical transport system varies in detail between the different makers; the Philips was the original, and all the others are but variants of it. It is not easy to follow the workings because

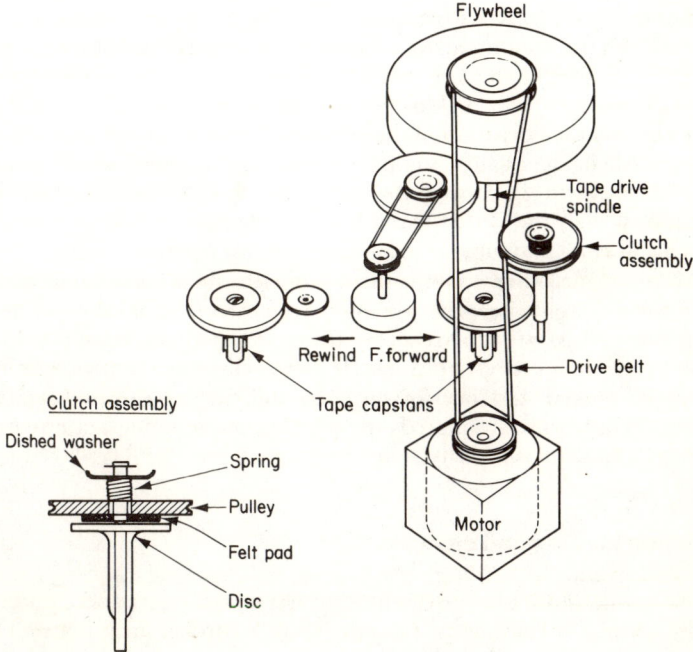

Figure 9.4. Philips cassette drive system. Positions slightly distorted to clarify operation. Clutch assembly is shown in detail in inset

numerous drive wheels are used, some mounted on one side of the sub-assembly and coupled by spindles to wheels on the other.

The basic Philips system is shown in Figure 9.4, viewed from beneath; the exact disposition of the components is slightly distorted in order to show the operation more clearly. Drive is transmitted from the motor to the flywheel by a belt, this being a factor common to most systems. In some cases the belt passes around the rim of the flywheel, but here it is taken around a pulley section which is part of the main flywheel but of smaller diameter. The flywheel spindle is also the tape-drive spindle.

The belt also drives a clutch assembly, the bottom part of which drives a rubber-tyred wheel that is coupled to the take-up capstan. Direct drive is not possible here during normal running because the take-up hub revolves more slowly as it fills up with tape, hence the need of a slipping clutch arrangement to provide the gradually decreasing speed. The clutch is shown in greater detail in the inset. A felt pad separates the bottom clutch disc from the pulley wheel, which is held against it by a compression spring. Drive is thus transmitted through the pad by friction, and the speed of the lower section can be controlled by the tape tension without slowing the drive pulley.

Another rubber-tyred wheel is driven by the flywheel rim, and is directly linked to a small pulley wheel that drives another pulley wheel via a small belt. The second pulley is coupled through a short spindle to a drive wheel. This pulley/drive-wheel assembly is moved sideways by the operation of the controls. For rewinding, it moves to the left to engage against the paying-out capstan idler-wheel, while for fast-forward it moves to the right and drives the take-up capstan-wheel, the clutch assembly disengaging for this operation. During normal playing it is in a centre neutral position.

Many of the other systems dispense with the second small drive belt, the movable idler wheel being driven directly from the flywheel rim. With a cassette tape-recorder the tape functions are selected by piano-type press keys or a single multi-position control, giving forward, rewind and fast-forward. In the case of car players the forward control is eliminated, the playing mode being actuated as soon as a cassette is inserted.

Cassette loading and ejection

A major difference between ordinary cassette recorders and car units is the method of loading the cassette. With recorders there is a well or a pop-up magazine into which the cassette is deposited and thus dropped over the projecting tape capstans and drive-spindle. The pressure roller and heads are mounted on an arm that moves in to

engage with the exposed tape at the side of the cassette when the play
or record mode is selected. This system requires a control panel at
least the width of the cassette and a total instrument height of this plus
space for heads, pinch-wheel and casing. The result would be much
too large for a car player, which must be accommodated in the limited
space afforded by the conventional radio aperture in the instrument
panel.

The solution is to use a completely different cassette housing
arrangement, where the cassette is posted sideways into a slot. This
would be impossible with the drive spindle and tape capstans in
position, so the whole drive system including flywheel and motor is
mounted on a shallow sub-chassis that is pivoted to drop below the
main chassis, on which the head and pinch-wheel are fitted. When the
cassette is pushed into the slot, a sprung retaining lever holds it in
place and a switch is operated; this activates a solenoid that lifts the
sub-chassis into position, the capstans and drive spindle ascending
through holes or cut-away portions in the main chassis to engage with
the cassette. The switch also applies power to the amplifier and
motor, so the cassette starts to play.

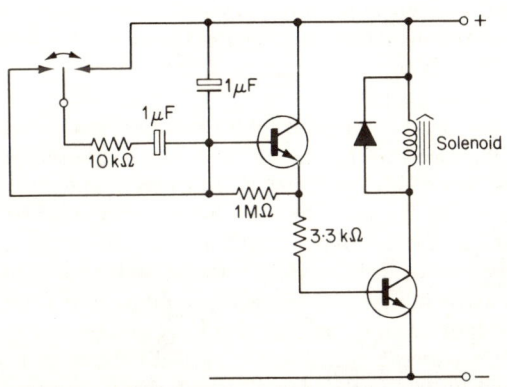

Figure 9.5. Auto-eject circuit

On reaching the end of the tape, an automatic ejection and
switch-off circuit operates. The nature of these circuits varies, but a
commonly-used one works as follows (see Figure 9.5). A switch,
actuated by a rotating cam driven by the take-up capstan, applies a
series of voltage pulses to a capacitor. This becomes partially
charged, and the voltage appearing across it is fed as forward bias to a
two-stage transistor amplifier, which then conducts. A solenoid
connected in the collector circuit of the second transistor is thus
activated. When the tape ends the capstan stops, the pulses cease and

the capacitor discharges. Forward bias being removed from the transistor, it ceases to conduct and the solenoid is de-activated. The sub-chassis is released and drops, as does the cassette-retaining lever, which allows the spring partially to eject the cassette from the slot. A cassette can be manually ejected at any time by pressing a button that shorts out the transistor bias.

Speed stability and cornering

When the vehicle is travelling on a more or less straight path there is little effect on the operation of the tape-player, but when it turns there can be a change of tape-speed. The reason for this lies with the flywheel. A rotating flywheel resists speed changes, which is the whole point of its use. This is fine as long as the equipment in which it runs does not change direction; if the equipment is turned in the same direction as the flywheel rotation, however, it will 'catch up' with the flywheel and the speed of the flywheel relative to its housing will decrease. Similarly, if the equipment is rotated the opposite way, the relative speed will increase.

Now it is not the *absolute* speed of the flywheel that governs the tape speed, but its speed *relative* to the housing, because the tape-drive components move with the housing. So when a tape player is rotated while it is running, a speed variation occurs and is heard as a rise or fall of musical pitch, depending on the direction of rotation. Obviously cornering will produce such an effect; as most flywheels run anticlockwise in tape players, a left-hand turn will cause a drop in pitch, and a right-hand turn a rise. The percentage of change depends on the ratio between flywheel velocity and vehicle-turn velocity, so the effect will be less with a fast-running flywheel and a slow turn. Normally it becomes noticeable only in high-speed tight turns, when it may well be argued that the driver has other things on his mind than the music being off-key!

However the effect can be counteracted, and has been in some cassette car players. The idea is to use two flywheels running in opposite directions, but mechanically linked together; thus rotation of the housing will have an opposite effect on each, producing cancellation. A model using this technique is the TEAC AC-9, which uses a belt drive (Figure 9.6) to operate both flywheels. Only one flywheel actually drives the tape, but the modifying influence of its partner is imparted along the belt.

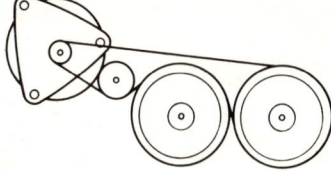

Figure 9.6. Belt-drive of contra-rotating flywheel system used in the TEAC AC-9; this gives speed stability on corners and facilitates reversal of tape

Auto-reverse

One of the drawbacks of the cassette system for car use, albeit a minor one, is the need to turn over the cassette at the end of one side in order to play the other. As starting and ejection is automatic in most models this means simply removing the partially ejected cassette from the slot, turning it over and pushing it back in. However, even this has been taken care of in some models by the provision of the auto-reverse facility. A number of makers incorporate this, including the TEAC AC-9 mentioned above; in fact the two contra-rotating flywheels lend themselves to such an arrangement. The two flywheels each have a tape-drive spindle, and both of these engage in the holes in the cassette housing. There are two pinch-wheels, each mounted on an L-shaped lever which in turn is linked to a spring-loaded solenoid plunger. When one solenoid is energised, the lever presses the pinch wheel against one drive spindle, so driving the tape; but when the other is energised, its lever and pinch-wheel engage with the other spindle and drive the tape the other way. The system is shown in Figure 9.7. Of course, when the tape direction is thus reversed, the opposite tape hub must start taking up tape. The tape capstans are each driven through an idler wheel from a flywheel. Each idler is mounted on an arm which is pulled into the engage position by a spring, but which is held off by a post on a sliding lever linked with the solenoid L-lever. Hence when one L-lever is activated by the solenoid, it not only pushes the pinch-wheel into action, but also releases the idler wheel, allowing it to drive the tape capstan. At the same time, the other solenoid is de-energised and the spring-loaded plunger moves the L-lever on that side back to release the pinch-wheel and pull away the idler. The playback head is switched by the same means to the other pair of tracks.

The changeover is initiated in a manner not unlike that described for the automatic reject circuit, but rather more complicated. A small magnetic drum is kept revolving as long as the tape is moving. This actuates a reed switch (an enclosed pair of contacts operated by a magnetic field) that keeps a capacitor charged up. When the tape ends, the drum stops and the capacitor discharges.

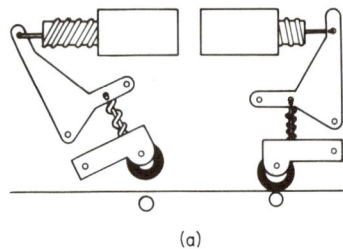

(a)

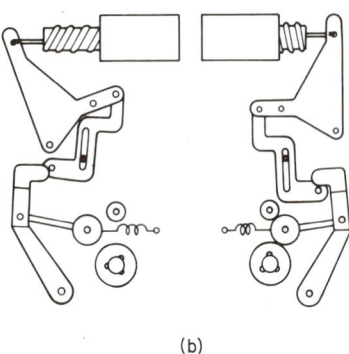

(b)

Figure 9.7. (a) Two solenoids switch in alternately to apply alternative pinch wheels and effect direction change; (b) the same mechanism releases spring-loaded idler wheel to drive appropriate take-up capstan

The capacitor is part of a circuit known as a *bistable*. This is a transistor circuit that operates like a two-way switch; it remains in one state until it is triggered, whereupon it changes to the opposite state until it is triggered again, whereupon it reverts to the original state, and so on. This bistable controls two power transistors, one in series with each solenoid; each time it is triggered by the capacitor discharging, it switches off one transistor and its solenoid and switches on the other. Thus the solenoids are alternately switched each time the tape stops. This affords a safety factor too, because if the tape should start to tangle, the circuit operates to switch off the drive.

Add-on units

As well as complete cassette players and combined radio-players, there are a variety of units available for use in conjunction with existing equipment. Blaupunkt and Philips make models that are designed to be played back through a car radio. They consist of the mechanical equipment, switching and preamp, but minus a power amplifier. A connection must be brought out from the car-radio audio circuits, usually the top end of the volume control, to the player switching. Inserting a cassette operates the switch to switch out the

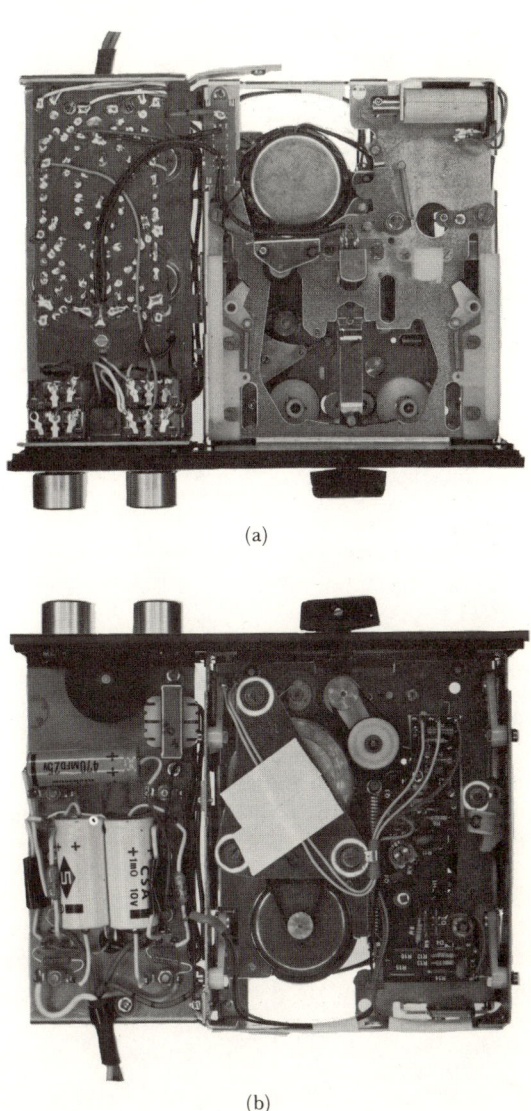

(a)

(b)

Figure 9.8. Radiomobile 302 CS cassette player, (a) top and (b) bottom views. In top view tape hubs, playback head, pinchroller and solenoid can be seen. Bottom view shows motor, drive-belt, flywheel and take-up drive pulleys

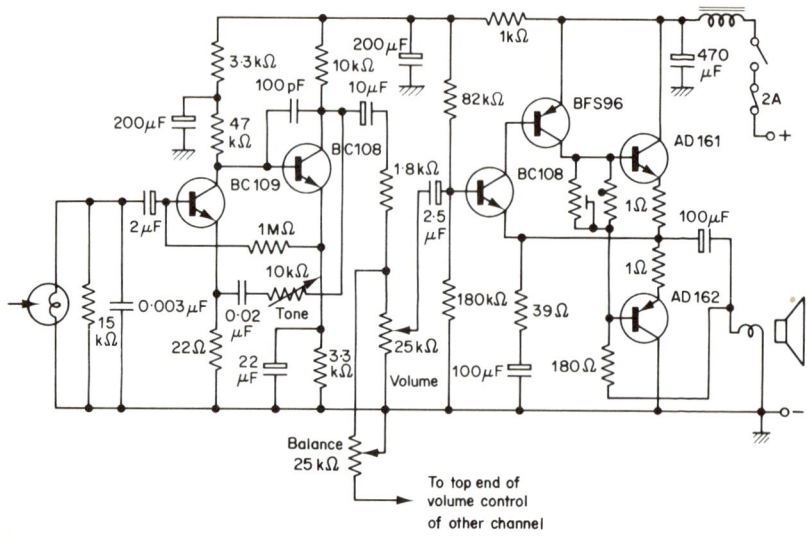

Figure 9.9. Typical circuit of playback amplifier for one stereo channel; the other channel is identical

radio and switch on the player circuits. Because the dashboard aperture will already be occupied by the radio, these units are made to be mounted under the dash. A typical circuit is shown in Figure 9.9.

Another unit consists of a mounting bracket to take an existing portable cassette recorder. This is plugged into the unit and obtains its power supply from the car battery. Playback is via a car radio as with the previous unit, but in addition recordings can be made from the radio direct if required, or from a microphone. The recorder can be quickly disconnected when desired and used as before as a portable on its internal batteries. A few car cassette players include a facility for recording from a microphone, or from radio if a combination unit. This could be useful for recording memos, dictation etc., while on a long journey.

Chapter 10

Cartridge Players

The cartridge format has hitherto proved to be the most popular form of tape system for mobile use, even though as mentioned in Chapter 9 the cassette is rapidly catching up. There are a number of quite fundamental differences between the two systems; it is not just a matter of a different size and shape of tape magazine.

Instead of having two spools or hubs with tape being transferred from one to the other and then back again, the tape is stored on a single hub that has a tape-supporting cheek on one side but is open on the other (Figure 10.1). The ends of the tape are joined together by a short section of metallised foil-tape to form an endless loop. Tape is pulled out from the centre of the spool by the action of the tape-drive spindle and pinch-wheel. It is then fed back on to the outside layer, and is taken up. The spool is not driven in any way by the player as is the take-up hub in a cassette recorder; it turns only by reason of the tape being pulled from it, in the same manner as the feed hub of a cassette.

At first glance this would appear to be an impossible arrangement. The circumference of the spooled tape is greater at its outer layer than

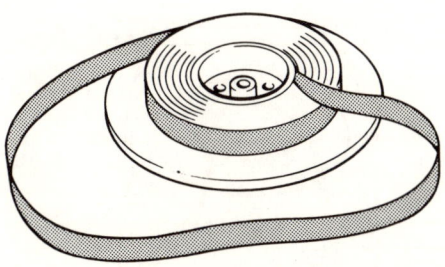

Figure 10.1.   Endless tape on cartridge spool which has only one cheek; tape is pulled from the centre and taken up on the outside

its inner one, hence at one revolution more tape should be taken up on the outside then can be pulled from the inside. So, before the first revolution could be completed it would seem that the tape would tighten and the spool jam to a halt. This in fact would happen were it not for the special tape that is used, containing lubricants. The result is that adjacent layers of tape slip over each other and enable more tape to be pulled from the centre than would be given up by a single revolution of the spool.

The tape is continually kept taut by this means and so is less likely to tangle than in the cassette. Another factor is that the amount of tape on the spool is always the same, hence the load on the mechanical transport system is constant. This is in contrast with the cassette or open-reel arrangement where the load varies as one spool fills and the other empties, which can result in long term speed variation. The system does however impose greater wear on the tape than do others, and this is much accelerated when the lubricant wears off as it does in time. Dirt is the enemy of all sound recording systems, but cartridges are especially prone to it because dirt on the tape reduces the effectiveness of the lubricant.

As with the cassette, the tape passes along an exposed side of the cartridge casing, but it is driven differently. Instead of the drive spindle being inserted into the casing behind the tape and pressure being applied from the front by the player's pinch-wheel, the drive spindle is applied to the front of the tape and the pinch-wheel is mounted behind it. Each cartridge thus has its own pinch-wheel internally mounted.

The tape passes from the spool centre, around a pulley wheel and along the head-aperture behind which is mounted the pressure pad. From there it passes over the pinch-wheel and back to the outside of the tape-spool. See Figure 10.2.

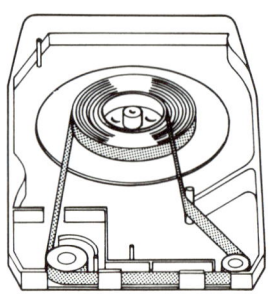

Figure 10.2. Inside view of cartridge

Tracks and dimensions

Standard 0.246-inch (6.25 mm) tape is used, as for open-reel machines. The tape-speed is $3\frac{3}{4}$ in/s (9.53 cm/s), which is the same as that of single-speed open-reel recorders, and twice that of cassette players. There are eight tracks recorded across the width of the tape, these being used to give four stereo channels. As the tape is less than twice the width of cassette-tape, and there are more margins between the tracks, the width of each track is less than in the cassette. The tracks are numbered from top to bottom, with the stereo pairs not adjacent, as in the cassette, but interleaved in the following manner (Figure 10.3): channel 1, tracks 1+5; channel 2, tracks 2+6; channel 3, tracks 3+7; channel 4, tracks 4+8. The head gaps are therefore widely separated to read these tracks, compared to the close spacing in a cassette head. (Because all cartridge systems are stereo there is no necessity for compatibility with mono players, which is the reason for the adjacent stereo pairs in cassette systems.)

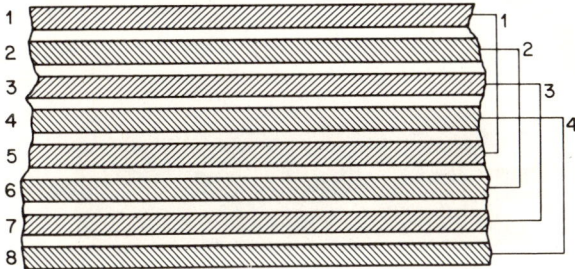

Figure 10.3. Track disposition showing stereo pairs

The drive-system

As there is no drive to the spool from the player, the drive-system is greatly simplified. The complicated wheel trains and clutch arrangements of the cassette player are eliminated. There is no rewind because the tape eventually returns to the starting point again when it has been played through. A few players incorporate a fast-forward facility. This cannot be done by direct drive of the spool, as in cassette and open-reel machines, because there is no way of driving it other than via the tape. Fast-forwarding can only be carried out by running the flywheel and drive spindle at a higher speed, and the easiest way of doing this is by switching out the motor governor.

It follows that the only drive required is that of the tape-drive

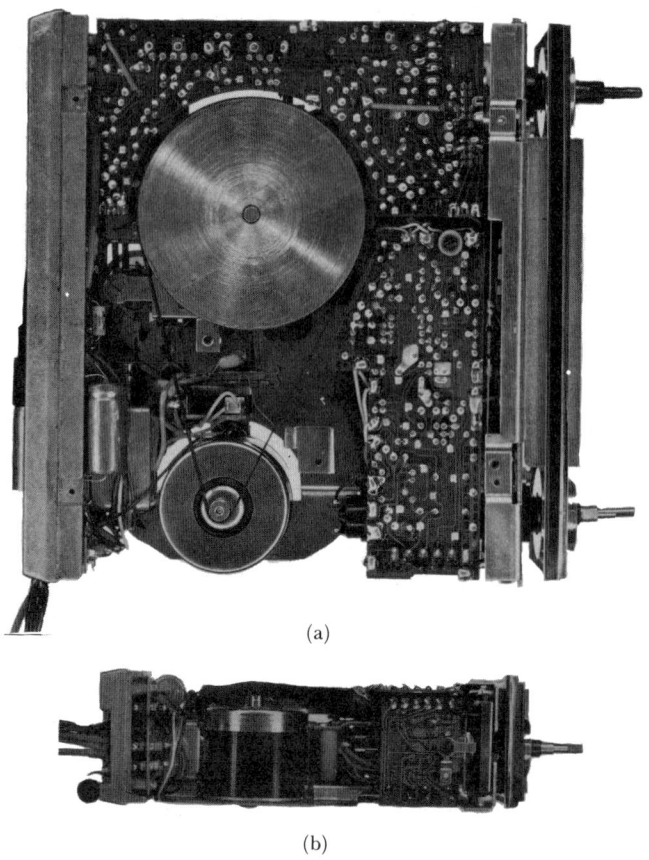

(a)

(b)

Figure 10.4. Radiomobile 108 SR cartridge player (a) bottom and (b) side views. Motor, drive belt and flywheel can be seen

spindle, so all that is needed is a flywheel and spindle belt-driven from the motor. Even the arm which, in the cassette machine, carries the pinch-wheel and playback-head to apply them to the tape is not necessary, as engagement of the drive-spindle against the tape and its internal pinch-wheel is achieved by just pressing the cartridge into place. The cartridge position is maintained by means of a roller mounted on a sprung arm which engages with a notch in the cartridge side. Some models use another long roller, also spring loaded, to bear against the top or bottom of the cartridge case and thus prevent vertical movement while in the playing slot.

Unlike the cassette, which was intended originally for portable and home players using top-loading, the cartridge was designed specifically for slot-loading in car equipment. Because there are no tape capstans to insert into the housing, and the drive spindle is pressed against the leading edge instead of being introduced into the case, the pivoted sub-chassis needed in the cassette player is not required. This results in further simplification.

Track-changing

When the tape has come to its end, it will carry straight on and start again, and go on indefinitely until it is stopped. However, it is necessary to change to the next channel, and this is accomplished automatically. Between the start and finish of the tape is spliced a short length of metallised-foil tape which shorts out a pair of contacts as it passes over them. This passes an energising current through a solenoid causing retraction of a spring-loaded plunger.

As shown in Figure 10.5, the plunger is coupled at its free end to an escapement mechanism consisting of a pawl and toothed ratchet wheel, and when it retracts it causes the pawl to move the ratchet wheel through a quarter of a turn. The bottom of the wheel is formed into a cam with four steps; underneath this is the head bracket, which is spring-loaded from the chassis. Each quarter-turn of the wheel depresses the bracket further, and the head is lowered to read the next pair of tracks. After the final and lowest position, the bracket springs back to the top position to restart the cycle. This is the basic arrangement; various makes have slightly different mechanical features, but the principle is the same in all cases.

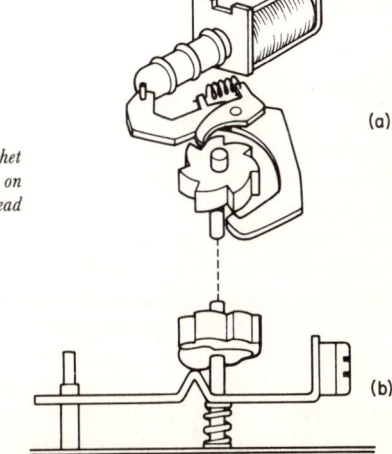

(a)

(b)

Figure 10.5. (a) Solenoid operated ratchet mechanism for track changing; (b) cam on underside of ratchet wheel controls position of head bracket

Associated with the toothed cam-wheel is an insulated disc carrying an electrical contact. This shorts across each of four pairs of wiping contacts in turn, which are wired to four panel lamps. One of these lights up for each channel, thus indicating which channel is being played at any time. If desired, the track can be changed by means of a button on the control panel. This shorts out the tape contacts and so energises the changing mechanism. To select any particular channel it is necessary to go through the sequence until the desired one comes up.

Since the playback head is not a fixture as it is with cassette and open-reel recorders, but moves vertically, the reset accuracy may deteriorate with wear, strain and other factors. Adjustment is therefore provided to position the head exactly relative to the tape tracks. If not so positioned, the head gap loses part of the track and overlaps the adjacent margin producing a loss of volume and increase in background noise. If badly out of alignment, it may even encroach on the neighbouring track so that it is heard as well as the desired one. With most players the adjustment is an internal one and consists of a set-screw which alters the position of the head-bracket relative to the cams, or the head relative to the bracket. (In the latter case the screw must not be mistaken for the azimuth adjustment screw, which is present on all recorders to tilt the head until the gap is perfectly vertical. Adjustment of this is described in Chapter 17.) In some models the adjustment is brought out to the control panel in the form of a 'fine tuning' control. If fitted this must be adjusted for maximum volume and clarity.

Another control sometimes found is a 'repeat' button. When this is selected, the tape contacts are open-circuited so that the metal end-foil does not initiate a track change. The track just played will be repeated until the control is released.

Quad and the cartridge

The eight tracks of the cartridge afford an ideal format for discrete quadrasonics, where four separate channels are required. Several quad models have been produced and a number of quad cartridges are available that give two programmes of full quadrasonic reproduction. At the time of writing the repertoire is rather limited, but new ones are being added and in time there will no doubt be a wider choice extending beyond the pop range that now seems to predominate.

The quad players contain four separate amplifiers and of course four speakers, two of which must be mounted in front and two at the rear. Just as the volume and tone controls for stereo two-channel players are ganged so that a single control operates the potentiometers in both amplifiers simultaneously, so the controlling elements in all four amplifiers are operated from single controls in quad players. There is usually an extra balance control; this is in addition to the left/right balance of the ordinary stereo player, and is a front/back control. Thus overall balance can be achieved to give the most satisfactory result.

The playback head has four independent magnetic circuits and gaps instead of two; these first read tracks 1, 3, 5, and 7. For the second programme, the head moves down to read tracks 2, 4, 6, and 8 (Figure 10.6; compare Figure 10.3). Track changing from the first to the second programme is straightforward because the head must only drop one track, as for an ordinary stereo tape. In going from the second back to the first, the head must jump three positions, i.e. the top gap must jump from 2 to 3 to 4 to 1. A special circuit including another solenoid is used to effect this change by producing three pulses to actuate the main changeover solenoid three times. It does this only on alternate switchings, so that the head moves only one position when going from programme 1 to 2, but three positions when going from 2 to 1. This circuit is controlled also by the manual track change switch so that the correct head position can be achieved either automatically or manually.

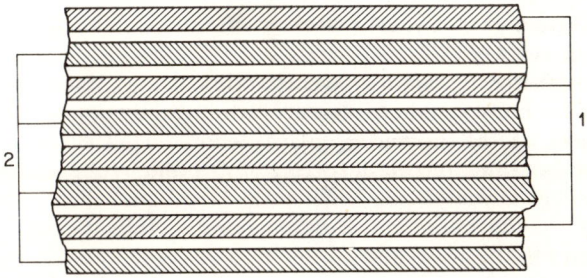

Figure 10.6. Quad tracking showing arrangement of the two four-channel programmes

Quad players can also play back ordinary stereo cartridges. To play these the special track-change circuit must be switched out so that the head advances one position at a time. The extra head sections must be switched out too, otherwise we would have another pair of tracks playing through the rear speakers at the same time. These rear channels can be paralleled with the front ones, or connected out of phase (see Chapter 8) to give a simulated quadrasonic effect, or just switched off; it depends on the make of the equipment.

The necessary switching is done automatically by the cartridge casing itself. At the top left-hand side of a quad cartridge there is a channel, an inch wide by about a quarter of an inch deep. A feeler, coupled to the switching in the player, senses this channel or the lack of it when the cartridge is inserted.

Comparison of cartridge and cassette systems

A number of different cassette and cartridge systems have appeared over the years. There have been the RCA, R3M, Philips and DC international types of cassette; and the Fidelipac, Conlay, Lear-Jet, and MGM types of endless-loop cartridge. Of these, the Philips cassette and the Lear Jet cartridge have finally emerged as the standard types. Another cartridge, the Japanese Hipac, was introduced quite recently, this having an endless loop of 0.15-inch (3.81-mm) tape, the same size as cassette tape, running at 1 7/8 in/s (4.76 cm/s). By using just the single tape spool, this cartridge is less wide than a cassette, though it is slightly longer. In view of the fact that the Philips cassette and Lear Jet cartridge are now so well established it seems unlikely that the Hipac or any other format could become a serious contender.

The technical differences between the cassette and cartridge systems have been well covered in this and the preceding chapter, so we will here make a few general observations as to the main features and advantages of each.

At first glance the cartridge seems a crude system, but it works, and works well. The constant mechanical loading, higher tape speed and larger flywheel of the cartridge player should all contribute to a superior short and long term speed stability and frequency response. In practice, however, the differences are slight when comparing specifications between the two systems in models by the same maker. For example the wow and flutter quoted for a cassette player is commonly 0.35%, while that for a cartridge player is 0.3%. In most cases a frequency response of up to 10 kHz is claimed for both systems.

The reason for such small differences in performance, in spite of the potential superiority of the cartridge, is probably that the cassette system has been the subject of much research and development to bring it up to hi-fi standards. Indeed the best home hi-fi cassette units give results comparable to the high-class open-reel tape machines of a few years ago. While the more modest car cassette player cannot boast this level of performance, some of the benefits of these developments have been applied to bring the standard up.

The cartridge on the other hand, was designed and intended for car entertainment, with simplicity and convenience as the prime objectives. It has not been developed for high-quality applications. Recently, home cartridge players have appeared, some with improved specifications, but they still appear to be aimed at medium-quality audio systems rather than the expensive hi-fi installation.

So, like the internal-combustion engine, the cassette with all its inherent technical drawbacks has been developed to give a performance at least as good as its rivals. It must be remembered that the tape-width, although less than the cartridge, accommodates fewer tracks with less margin wastage; the track width is actually greater, giving less background noise and drop-out susceptibility.

Another feature that must be considered when comparing systems is the fact that cassettes can be recorded by the user either in the car or at home, to be played back at home or in the car later. Many homes have a portable cassette recorder, and there is the growing popularity of the radio recorder whereby recordings of radio programmes can be made directly without external wires or connections. Thus a traveller can record music, plays, talks of his choice at home, to play back while he is driving, or he can dictate notes and memos while driving if his car system is equipped to record. While there are some cartridge systems that will record, these are very rare, and the format does not lend itself very well to recording.

The cartridge has a marginal advantage in convenience in that, once it is in, it will continue to play without further attention, repeating itself indefinitely. The cassette must be turned over to play the other side unless the player has an auto-reverse facility, in which case it too will go on playing until stopped. Playing times are 80 minutes maximum for a cartridge (all tracks) and 60 minutes per side for a cassette. These are maximum times, and most pre-recorded tapes are much less than this. An average length is about half the above figures. Most tape recordings are available in both forms, but the cartridge is slightly dearer. When buying the original equipment, though, it will be found that the cassette player is more expensive than a comparable cartridge unit, because of its greater mechanical complexity.

Perhaps the most important point of comparison for car use is that of size. Modern cars seem to have limited storage space, and what there is is usually taken up with maps, guides, dusters and other necessary items. Cartridges are bulky when compared to cassettes so there is little likelihood of being able to accommodate a collection of any size. Quite a large number of cassettes, however, could be stored without taking up too much space.

So far the cartridge doesn't come out of the comparison too well. However when considering quadrasonics it is the only practical choice. Quad cassettes are being developed, but the discrete ones are running at present into problems owing to the difficulty of putting eight very narrow tracks on 0.15-inch tape with ultra narrow margins. Special circuits are needed to overcome the noise and cross-talk between channels. Other quad cassettes are available using the SQ matrix system (as used for SQ discs) and with the normal four tracks. The four channels are encoded into two tracks, but the channel separation is poor without very complicated circuitry to enhance it. So it's back to the cartridge. Before investing in quad equipment, though, it should be noted that quad cartridges are rather expensive at present and run for only half the time of their stereo counterparts because they use four instead of two tracks at a time.

Cassette/cartridge converters

For those who want the best of both worlds one or two makers have produced an ingenious device that enables cassettes to be played on cartridge machines. An example of this is the Belair SCP 580 Stereo Cassette/Cartridge Converter, which is distributed by the Oscar Radio Co. See Figure 10.7.

Figure 10.7. Belair SCP 580, enables cassettes to be played in any cartridge player

The unit is the same width as a cartridge, but longer, and the front end is the same shape. It is pushed into the cartridge slot in the player just like an ordinary cartridge. This leaves a section protruding into which the cassette is dropped, and on which is the single control button for starting and stopping the unit.

The mechanical drive system is similar to that of an ordinary cassette player, with a flywheel/drive spindle and a clutch for the take-up capstan, all inside the unit. There is no internal motor because drive is obtained from the cartridge-player drive spindle. A rubber pressure-roller similar to the pinch-wheel in an ordinary cartridge presses against it, and is coupled to the cassette drive spindle with a gearing ratio to provide the correct cassette tape-speed. There is no rewind, but a fast-forward facility is obtained by releasing the 'play' control while the cartridge unit is still running. Rewind can of course be achieved by turning over the cassette and then fast-forwarding.

Also included in the unit is a pre-amp that amplifies the output of the cassette playback head. This signal is then fed to a transfer head, located at the leading edge of the unit to face opposite the playback head in the cartridge player. There is thus an inductive coupling between them and the signal is fed into the cartridge player's amplifying circuits. The system is two-channel so that stereo reproduction is obtained. Five transistors and a zener diode are used in the electronic circuitry.

Power for supplying the pre-amp is picked up from the cartridge player. It will be remembered that there are two contacts in every player, situated so that the tape passes over them, that operate the track-change solenoid when the metal foil appears at the end of the cartridge tape. A pair of matching contacts in the converter unit connects with these to provide the supply. It is true that the contacts in the cartridge player are in series with the solenoid, which therefore passes current when the pre-amp circuits are connected across them. However, the current drawn by the pre-amp is very small, just a few milliamps, and is insufficient to cause the solenoid to operate. A voltage stabilising circuit is included in the unit to compensate for differing voltages from 9 to 24 V. Thus the unit can be used in any cartridge player without modification.

The frequency response is rather less than would be obtained from a good cassette player, 40–7000 Hz being specified, with wow and flutter a little more at 0.5%. However the audible effects of these differences are slight, and a small price to pay for the versatility conferred.

Chapter 11

Motor Control Circuits

Whatever the type of player, whether cassette, cartridge or disc, it is essential that the recorded material be driven at the correct constant speed if the reproduced music is to be at the proper speed and pitch. Minor speed variations may not in themselves be noticeable, but the accompanying pitch variations are, even slight ones being objectionable to a musical ear.

A flywheel is commonly used to smooth out small speed changes, but this of course must be driven at the correct speed to start with, hence the need to control the motor.

Electro-mechanical governors

The most common type of control is contained within the motor itself, and consists of a mechanical governor controlling a pair of contacts mounted on the rotor (Figure 11.1). A short sprung arm has a small weight, and also one of the contacts, fixed to its free end. The other contact is mounted on another arm sprung against the first one. Normally the contacts are closed and, as they are in series with the armature, permit current to flow and the motor to run.

When reaching a certain speed, the weight, attracted outward by centrifugal force, overcomes the tension of the arm causing it to move away from its mate and separating the contacts. The rotor immediately slows, whereupon the weight falls back, the contacts re-make and the speed increases. This happens many times a second, and the motor speed is kept at a constant average level, although the instantaneous speed is continually oscillating above and below it. The mass of the flywheel is too great to respond to these rapid changes and so it effectively smooths them out to the average speed. If the flywheel should be undersized, as it sometimes is in portable cassette machines, it may be partially affected by the fluctuations and pass on a speed-change ripple, just as a low-value smoothing capacitor in a

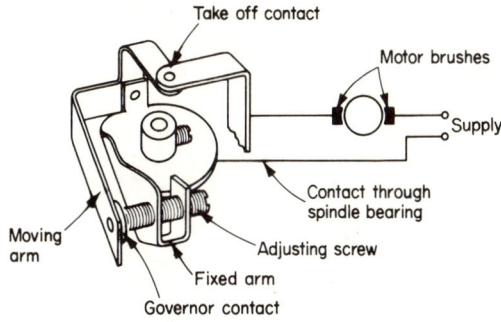

Figure 11.1. Electro-mechanical governor for mounting on motor rotor shaft. The contact on the moving arm serves as a weight and the end of the adjusting screw as the other contact. Separate weights and mating contacts are often used

power supply circuit will permit a hum ripple to appear on the supply line. Thus the wow and flutter figure will be greater than with a better machine having a larger flywheel.

Some means of adjusting the governor is necessary so that the correct speed can be set. This is provided by a grub-screw threaded into the stationary arm. The tension between the two arms, and thereby the mechanical resistance acting against the weight, can be varied by means of this screw. If the tension is lessened the weight moves earlier and the speed is reduced. The screw is accessible through a hole in the motor casing, and should be adjusted with the aid of a timed length of tape or a stroboscope.

The operation of the governor entails the continual making and breaking of the contacts. This, along with the commutator, produces interference in the form of a background 'hash' that can get into the amplifying circuits. In fact it can be quite troublesome, needing capacitive and inductive filters in the supply leads and careful routing and screening of leads to minimise it.

Electronic control circuit

Of recent years electronic transistor control has found more favour and has been increasingly used. Dirt and oxidation of the contacts as well as displacement of the arm can all lead to erratic running with the electro-mechanical governor, such problems being eliminated with the purely electronic control. Furthermore one source of interference is abolished, although that produced by the commutator of the motor remains.

The simple basic motor control circuit is almost identical in different models and makes, only component values varying. The circuit is shown in Figure 11.2. It can be seen that the motor is connected in series with transistor TR2 and resistor R5, and so the current through the motor is controlled by TR2. Forward bias for TR2 is supplied by TR1, which is connected to its base from the supply line. Bias for TR1 is obtained through the network R1, R2, and R3 connected from the supply to the collector of TR2.

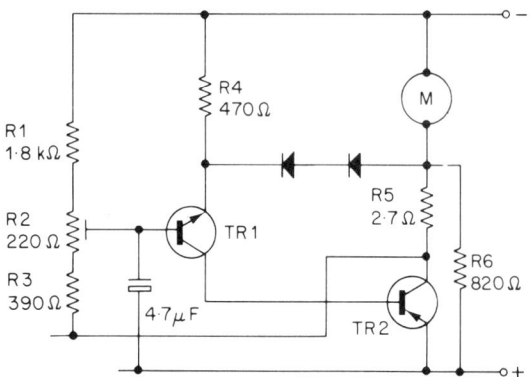

Figure 11.2. Simple electronic motor control circuit. It uses voltage variation across the motor or R5 caused by supply fluctuation or speed variation to bias TR1 and control current through TR2

If now there is a drop in the supply voltage, there is a fall in the voltage across the motor, and this is communicated in full to the emitter of TR1 via the diodes. It is also applied to the base through R3 and R2, but to a lesser extent because of the potential dividing action of R1-3. Thus there is a net *increase* in voltage applied to the base/emitter circuit of TR1 because the difference between the base voltage and emitter voltage is greater. This rise in forward bias increases the conduction of TR1, which therefore increases the forward bias applied to TR2 so that it passes more current to the motor. Hence the original supply voltage drop is compensated for. Should the battery voltage rise, the reverse process will operate and the current will be reduced.

There is no theoretical difference between a motor and a generator; a motor can be used to generate and vice versa. It follows that when a motor is running it is also generating and the polarity of the generated current will, according to Lenz's Law, oppose that of the applied current. There is then some cancellation, and if there were no friction or other losses the resulting total current in the motor would be zero. This of course is impossible in practice, and a forward current flows to supply the energy needed to overcome friction and the applied load.

If now the load (either applied or that resulting through losses) increases, the motor slows and the opposing generated current (termed back e.m.f.) is reduced, so the total current in the circuit rises. Returning to the control circuit, any increase in current due to slowing of the motor produces an increased voltage drop over R5. As the resistor is effectively connected between the emitter and base circuits of TR1, the drop results in the base becoming more positive. Its conduction is thereby increased and with it that of TR2, so as before the current through the motor is raised to compensate.

The circuit will therefore apply more power to the motor if the supply voltage either falls or slows through an increased mechanical load. It will be noticed that R2 is a variable resistor, and by this means the motor speed can be adjusted. The diodes are temperature-conscious and so compensate for any temperature variations that would affect the operation of the transistors. R6 is provided to give an initial starting bias. (When switching on, both transistors are cut off, having no forward bias, hence without R6 the motor would not run.) Once the circuit is operating R6 has a negligible effect.

Motor servo-control

The simple circuit previously considered operates by sensing a d.c. voltage change across the motor and using it to control the series transistor. A more accurate form of control uses an alternating voltage generated by the motor as the feedback signal. There are various methods of applying this principle; one of them, as used in the TEAC AC-9 cassette-player, is shown in Figure 11.3. The generator consists of a toroidal washer with 30 segments, thus providing 30 poles, mounted on the motor spindle adjacent to a coaxial magnet and generator coil. The motor runs at 1010 r.p.m., which means that the generator frequency is 505 Hz ($1010 \times 30 \div 60$). The magnetic field of the generator is at 90° to that of the motor so there is no mutual interference.

This signal is applied to the input of the control unit, which takes the form of an integrating circuit. The load across the generator consists of C1, R1 and R2. At 505 Hz, the reactance of C1 (0.1 µF) is 3150Ω and the resistance of the two resistors is 940 Ω. The voltage applied to the following diode will therefore be proportional to the ratio between these values.

If the motor speed alters so also will the frequency of the generator, and the reactance of C1, which is dependent on frequency, will

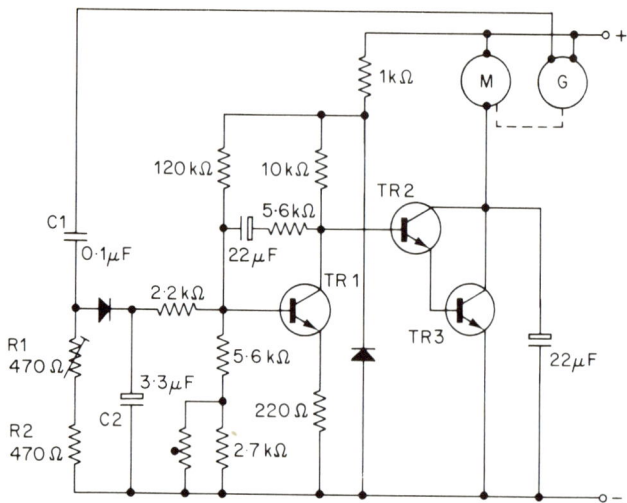

Figure 11.3. Servo circuit used in TEAC AC-9. A frequency is produced by a generator incorporated with the motor proportional to the motor speed. A control voltage is derived from this by the integrating circuit in the input

likewise change. Thus the ratio is altered and the resultant voltage changes too. This is rectified by the diode and smoothed by C2 to provide a control voltage for the following amplifier. The voltage can change from about 3 V at 600 Hz to 2 V at 450 Hz. An increase of frequency gives a higher positive voltage to forward-bias TR1, which because there is a phase reversal over this stage reduces the bias of the output stage and cuts the motor power. The circuit does not operate on voltage differences to produce an 'error signal' when the speed strays, as does the previous one, but the control voltage derived from the generator frequency is always present. It is thus free from the 'hunting' effects of the former.

A degree of voltage stabilising is given by the 1-kΩ resistor and diode across the supply from which the collector voltage for TR1 is taken. Thermal stability is afforded by the thermistor connected across the lower base-bias resistor of TR1.

Brushless motors

All d.c. motors need a commutator and brushes to convey the energising current to the rotor. Wear takes place here, and also interference is generated that can be picked up by the amplifying circuits. Speed stability even with governor circuits is not as good as in brushless types because of the uneven drag of the brushes on the commutator.

The alternative is to use a rotating magnetic field, produced by the stator, which is followed by the rotor or which induces a current in the rotor windings. This principle requires alternating current, and synchronous induction or hysteresis motors, which are of this type, are found in mains-operated playing equipment.

A modified version can be run from a d.c. source if an oscillator and transistor switching circuits are employed. An example is the Radiomobile Model 106 to 108 range of cartridge players. As shown in Figure 11.4, the stator comprises three motor coils set at an angle of 120° to each other, and three secondary coils also at 120° to each other, but displaced 60° from the motor coils. There is also a single primary coil. The rotor is simply a permanent magnet, but at one end there is an aluminium disc across the diameter of which is fixed a high-permeability ferrite rod.

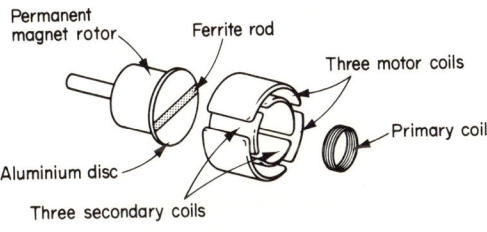

Figure 11.4. Diagram of brushless motor used in Radiomobile cartridge players

The supply circuit (Figure 11.5) consists of an oscillator TR1, with a control transistor TR2. There are three switching circuits using a total of six transistors, the output of each going to one of the motor coils. The three secondary coils are each connected through a diode to the input of one of the switching circuits, and the primary coil is fed from the output of the oscillator.

The operation is as follows. Oscillations from TR1 are fed to the primary coil, and a magnetic flux is conveyed through the ferrite rod to whichever of the three secondary coils happens to be within range. The voltage thereby induced is applied to the diode in the input of one of the switching circuits. These are normally cut off, and the rectified voltage provides forward bias to switch the circuit on.

The associated motor coil is thus energised and, owing to its advanced position, the produced field interacts with that of the rotor to pull it around part of a turn. The ferrite rod is now moved into the range of the next secondary, which is activated, switching on the

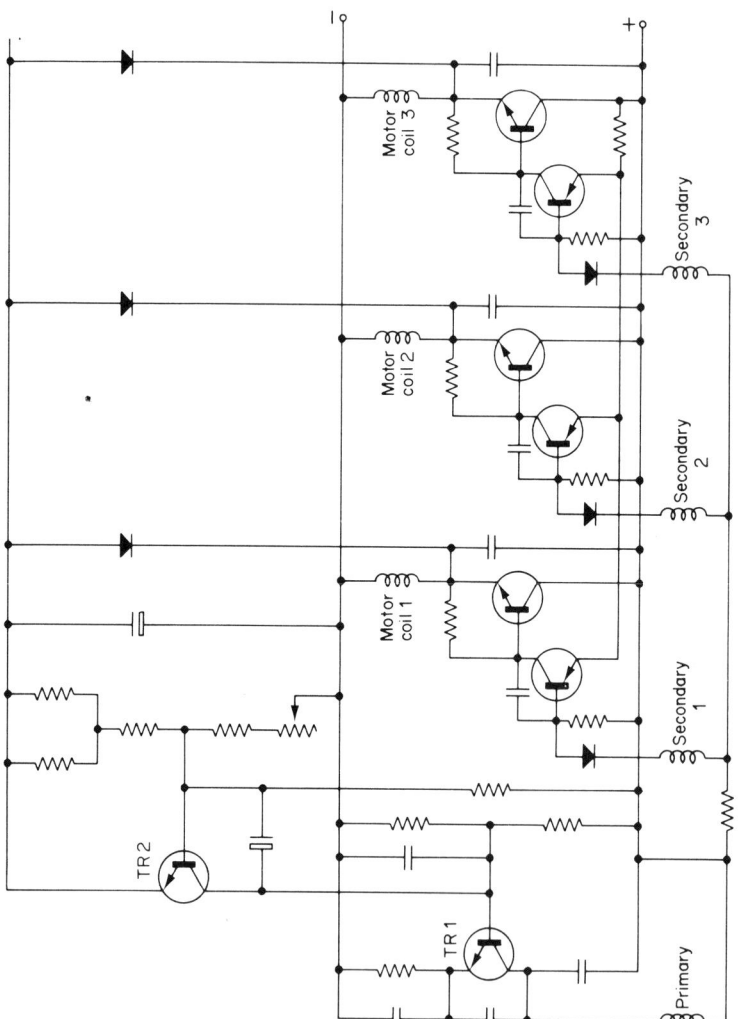

Figure 11.5. Control and supply circuit for Radiomobile motor. Primary is coupled to each secondary in turn by the ferrite rod, thus energising each motor coil in sequence and producing a rotating field. Back e.m.f. from the coils forward-biases TR2 which controls level of oscillation of TR1, thus regulating transistor current through motor coils

associated circuit and energising in turn the next motor coil, which thereby produces a further part-revolution. Hence each motor coil is energised in sequence, setting up a rotating field for the rotor to lock on to.

Speed control is achieved by sampling voltage pulses from the motor coils, applying them to an electrolytic capacitor via isolating diodes to prevent pulses from one coil reaching the others and upsetting the operation of the motor. These pulses (generated in the coils by dynamo action) are proportional in voltage to the speed of the motor, hence the voltage across the capacitor likewise depends on motor speed. This voltage is applied across a resistor network which supplies base-bias for the control transistor TR2 which in turn biases the oscillator. The transistors are connected so that the forward bias on the oscillator is reduced when the control voltage is increased.

When this happens, the signal generated by the oscillator is reduced, and with it the voltage applied as forward bias to the switching circuits. Current through these is therefore less, and so too the power through the motor coils. The frequency of the oscillator is not important to the operation of the motor or the speed-control circuit.

There are other types of servo system where a synchronous motor is run from a precisely controlled frequency derived from an oscillator. An a.c. signal is generated from the motor, and the frequency of this is compared with that of the oscillator in a discriminator circuit. Any difference is used as an error signal to correct the oscillator frequency. These are very accurate, but also complicated and used only in the better hi-fi tape systems.

Chapter 12

Disc Systems

Recordings on magnetic tape are by far the most convenient means of reproducing music in the car, having the advantages of compactness and long playing time. A 10 or 12-inch disc would need a player at least that size, which would be almost impossible to accommodate, while 7-inch discs give only 10 minutes or so per side. Additionally disc players are far more susceptible to vibration and shock, being purely mechanical in nature, than tape systems.

However, before the present tape systems were developed, car disc players were produced, and some may well be still in use. One of these was the Philips Auto-Mignon, which we'shall take a brief look at.

The unit consisted of a turntable and pickup unit minus amplifier. It was designed to be connected to a car radio so that the pickup output was fed through the receiver's audio stages. Power was taken from the radio's on/off switch. There were two push-operated controls, the right-hand one being the radio/gram changeover switch; as well as being connected to the radio's audio stages, the output from the radio's detector was taken to it so that it could switch to the pickup or back to the radio. A multi-cored screened lead terminating in a plug and socket carried the various connections between the unit and the radio, and this had to be soldered into the radio at various specified points in its circuit. Subsequently the units could be parted by just unplugging the lead. The circuit is shown in Figure 12.1.

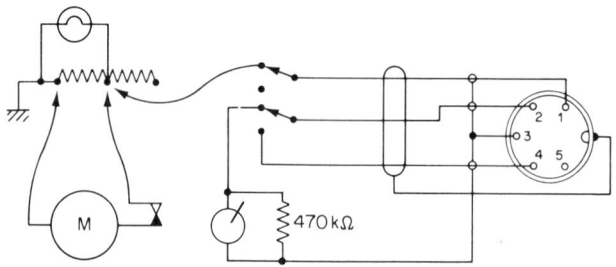

Figure 12.1. Circuit of Auto Mignon

The instrument was designed to work from 6 V, but an internal resistor allowed 12-V operation, either negative or positive earth. Only 7-inch 45 r.p.m. records could be played, and these needed to have the centre break-away portion removed to give a 38 mm hole.

The operation of the unit is as follows. A record is introduced through a slot in the front of the instrument level with the turntable surface (Figure 12.2). The centre boss lies below the level of the turntable and so does not interfere with the sideways loading of the record. When located on the turntable, the leading edge of the record engages against a striking pin on the main actuating lever. This is roughly Y shaped and is pivoted at its centre; it is sprung so that the slight record pressure causes it to jump back by a toggle action (Figure 12.3).

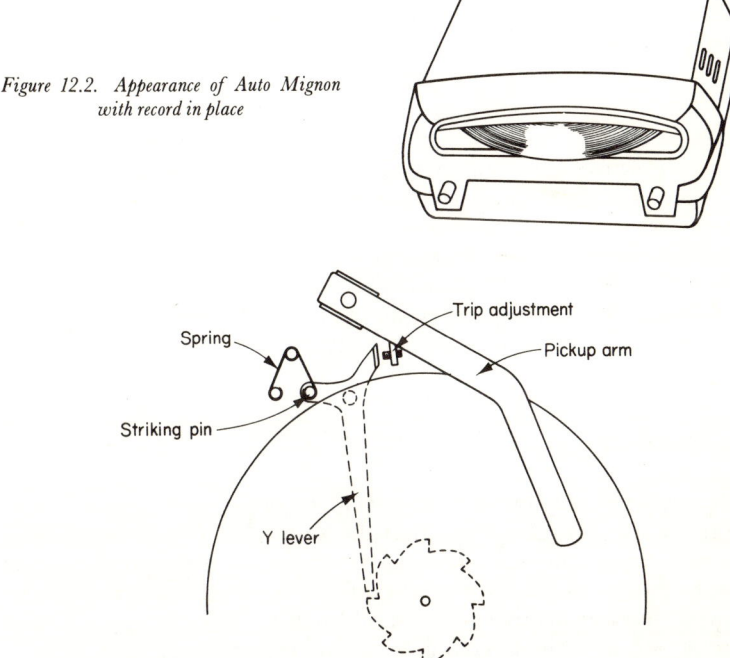

Figure 12.2. Appearance of Auto Mignon with record in place

Figure 12.3. Y actuating lever with striking pin and trip mechanism

The lever movement produces several independent actions. The pickup stylus rests in the bristles of a small nylon brush mounted at the end of a lever. This swings clear, cleaning the stylus as it goes, and the motor switch is operated. The turntable centre-boss is held down against the tension of a concentric spiral spring by a catch-lever engaging with circlips and washers on the boss spindle, so the catch-lever is released allowing the boss to rise and engage with the record hole.

No inward movement of the pickup arm is necessary because it rests with the stylus precisely over the record run-in groove. The head is pivoted so that it moves vertically at the end of the arm, hence the next action is to release the head by means of a long thin lever running inside the pickup so that it is pulled downward by a small spiral spring between the head and arm (Figure 12.4). The stylus makes contact with the groove and the record is played through to its end.

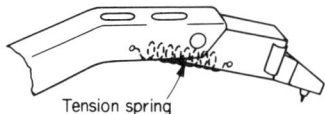

Tension spring

Figure 12.4. Pickup arm showing swivel head

Now comes the switching off cycle. A tab near the pickup pivot engages against one arm of the Y actuating lever when the pickup travels inward on the run-out groove. This pushes the long arm of the Y lever into the toothed wheel at the centre of the turntable which then jerks it back to its rest position. The centre boss is pulled down, the pickup head is lifted clear of the record and the arm swung back to the start position, and the brush returns to protect the stylus. Finally the striking pin on the lever pushes the record off the turntable to be partially ejected and the motor is switched off.

Special features

The trip lever in an ordinary auto-changer or player is in two sections that are friction coupled so that the knock-off tab is pushed away when it approaches the striker on the turntable as the pickup moves across the record, and prevents premature tripping before the run-out groove. Such an arrangement is easily upset by movement or tilting of the player, so a single-section lever (actually the long arm of the Y lever) is here used. To ensure that it trips at the right time, the tripping position can be set by adjusting a screw on the pickup tab that engages with one of the short Y arms.

The problem of speed variations as the car takes bends, mentioned in Chapter 9, has been considered here. What happens is that on left-hand bends the deck 'catches up' with the turntable, thus reducing the relative turntable speed, while on left-hand bends the opposite takes place and the relative speed increases. With the tape deck we described, two contra-rotating flywheels compensate for each other. This is not possible with a gram unit because the turntable is, in effect, the flywheel. Instead two idler wheels are mounted on either side of the motor capstan, both engaging with the inside of the turntable rim as shown in Figure 12.5. If a single idler were used in position 1, a tendency for the turntable to increase in relative speed would pull the idler away against its spring and lessen its traction, thus allowing the increase to occur. A single idler in position 2 would be similarly affected by a speed decrease. By using two idlers on either side of the motor capstan, when one pulls away the other is pushed harder into contact, and so the motor is able to maintain control of the speed and keep it constant.

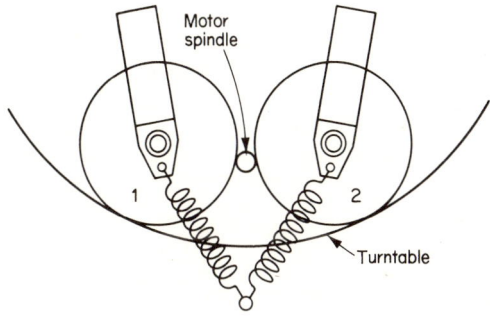

Figure 12.5. Double idler wheel arrangement

The whole unit is well sprung on three spiral springs to minimise vibration and shock. Groove jumping does not occur because the stylus pressure is not maintained by gravity, as in a normal player, but by a spring.

The Discatron

A portable disc player need not have the conventional turntable and pickup arrangement at all. One departure from the usual was the Discatron player. This was not a car player but a portable; however, the principle is of interest. The 7-inch record is posted through a slot as with the Auto-Mignon. It is supported on a tapered spindle through the centre (small) hole from one side, and three rubber-tyred wheels at three points of the rim at the other (see Figure 12.6). The record is held and played vertically, being introduced from the top of

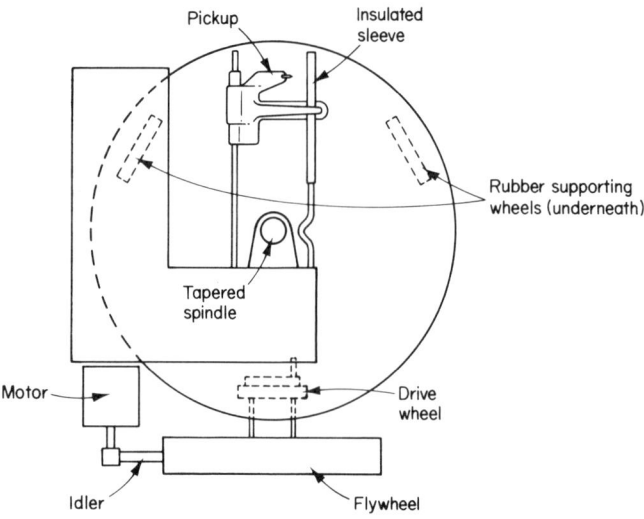

Figure 12.6. Plan view of the Discatron. Record is supported by supporting and drive wheels from beneath and tapered spindle from the top. Pickup travels on a carriage along a transverse rod

the instrument. One of the three rubber wheels drives the record, being on a spindle with a flywheel, which is driven via a conventional idler wheel from the motor.

The pickup head is mounted not on an arm but on a carriage that slides along a transverse steel rod over the record surface. A pair of leaf springs extend from the pickup carriage to contact a parallel bar running close to the rod. These have two functions, to maintain downward pressure on the record and to electrically actuate the auto-stop mechanism. The first section of the bar is covered with an insulating sleeve, so when the pickup head reaches the end of the record, the springs run off the sleeve and contact the bare bar. This completes the circuit to a solenoid, which causes a plate to move into the path of a striker pin on the flywheel. The solenoid is mounted on a lever that also forms part of the latching mechanism, so that when the striker hits the plate, the lever is jerked forward thereby releasing the latch. The 'reject' control is mechanically linked to the lever and so the same result can be obtained by depressing the 'reject' button, thus rejecting a record before it is completed.

The transverse rod and bar, with the pickup carriage and tapered centre-spindle, are carried on an assembly that is pivoted at the centre. When the start button is depressed, the assembly pivots forward into the playing position and is latched down. It is this latch that is released when either the auto-stop or the reject button is actuated. A further necessary operation which occurs when the latch is released is that a small lever moves along the main transverse rod and thereby restores the pickup carriage to the starting position ready for the next record.

Both the Auto-Mignon and the Discatron used crystal pickup heads with sapphire styli, although the Mignon was also available with ceramic head and diamond stylus.

Chapter 13

Installation

Installation of a car audio system entails the fitting of the player or radio, an aerial in the case of the latter, and from one to four loudspeakers. Then there is the wiring of the units and interference-suppression for radio reception.

Mounting the radio/player

Many of the specialist radio manufacturers supply installation kits to match their own range of equipment to a large selection of cars. It is well worth using the appropriate kit as this makes for a professional-looking job with the units appearing to be tailor-made for the car. Check, though, exactly what the kit contains beforehand; some may include items not required because they have already been supplied with the radio or player initially, such as a loudspeaker, while others may not include optional items that may be desired.

Faceplates, knobs, bezels and loudspeaker grilles can generally be changed to match the styling of the car and the other instrumentation. Some of the smaller manufacturers do not offer this service, and you have to take the equipment as it stands.

There are three principal ways to mount the radio or player, but in some cases (such as in commercial vehicles) it may prove desirable to adopt a more unorthodox fitting. The most common position is behind an aperture in the instrument panel (see Figure 13.1). Most modern cars have a dummy panel covering the radio opening which just needs to be removed in order to mount it. It is advisable to keep this panel safely in case the car is changed in the future, and it is required to remove the radio. In some cases holes may have to be drilled in the instrument panel to accommodate the control spindles, but before any drilling or cutting is attempted, *make sure there is sufficient space behind the fascia to accommodate the unit*. There will be few problems with modern radios, but the players, especially the cartridge units,

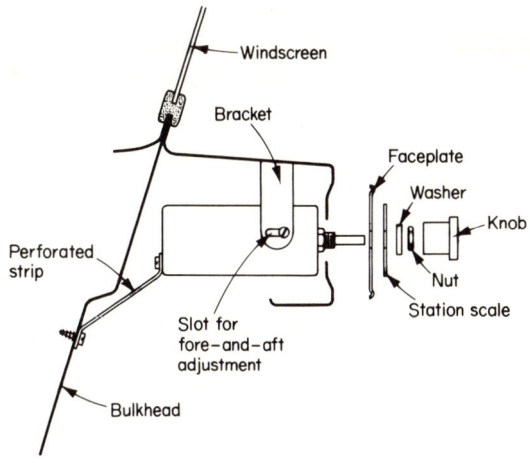

Figure 13.1. In-dash fitting using flexible internal bracket and perforated rear strip to bulkhead

are deeper and the space in some cars may be very restricted between the instrument panel and the bulkhead.

Actual fixing differs from one model to another and from one car to another. Older radios and most players need to be secured both at the front and at the rear. A common method is by means of a pair of bolts, one on each side of the unit near the front, that pass through side panels in the instrument-panel aperture. The holes for taking the bolts are slotted to facilitate fore-and-aft adjustment of the unit. In other cases brackets are fitted to the sides of the instrument and can be bolted into the car. Some cars have bendable brackets already fixed in the aperture, and these can be adjusted to match with the unit fixing-holes.

Rear fixing is by means of a bolt at the back or near the rear edge of the instrument. A length of perforated mild-steel strip is supplied, and this is bolted at one end to the unit. It is then bent back to a convenient point on the bulkhead, where a hole is drilled and the strip secured to it by a self-tapping screw. In some cars a threaded bush and a bolt will be found on the bulkhead for this purpose, thus saving the drilling and tapping. The strip will in most cases be longer than required, so the excess may be cut off before fitting permanently. Some modern radios are so small and light that the rear fitting can be dispensed with, but all players should be well-secured to prevent vibration-induced wow.

The second fixing method is to sling the unit under the dash or parcel-shelf (see Figure 13.2). It can if desired be fitted on the top of a

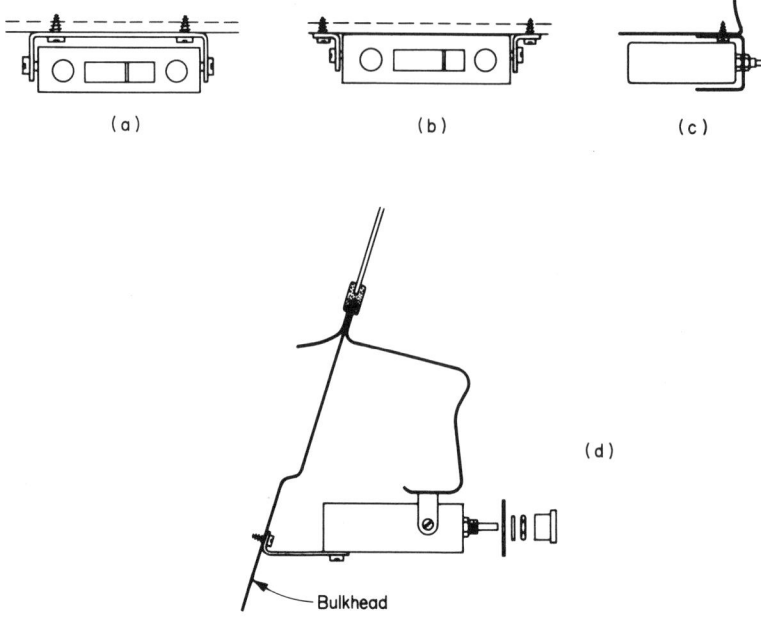

Figure 13.2. (a) Under-dash fitting using gimbal; (b) under-dash mounting with side L brackets; (c) box-type face-plate for under-dash support; (d) complete under-dash fitting

parcel shelf, but this takes up valuable room which is so scarce in many cars. Underslinging is not perhaps quite as elegant as the through-the-panel method, and means that the controls are lower. Before deciding on this position make sure that the controls can be comfortably reached whilst driving, without causing a hazard. Ensure too, in the case of tape players, that there is sufficient space in front of the unit, otherwise it may be found that the gear lever makes it impossible to insert a cartridge! Some players are too high to mount in the panel aperture, and so must be fitted elsewhere.

A gimbal bracket is often supplied for underslinging. This fits to the sides and passes over the top of the unit. The bracket is fitted first by self-tapping screws through the top to holes drilled in the underside of the dash or shelf, then the instrument is inserted into the bracket and the side bolts fitted. If fitted to a shelf, the shelf must be solid enough to support the weight—many aren't.

The gimbal bracket allows the angle of the instrument to be adjusted as required. If the dash underside is sloping, this can be compensated for, or it may be considered desirable to tilt the unit upward slightly to facilitate operation of the controls. Tape-players should not be inclined too far from the horizontal, as this can cause

speed irregularities and other mechanical malfunctions; about 20°
should be considered the maximum tilt, unless the maker states
otherwise.

Two L brackets, one on each side, can also be used to undersling a
unit, or some manufacturers supply a special faceplate made in box
construction with an open back. This is first screwed in place, then the
instrument can be introduced from the rear and secured by the
control spindle bushes and nuts. Yet another type of fixing uses a
metal tray with high sides and drilled front. This is really an extension
of the box-faceplate.

Sometimes it is convenient to mount the radio in one unit with the
loudspeaker, under the dash. Boxes are made for this purpose by some
radio manufacturers. These are underslung, the loudspeaker
aperture pointing downward to the floor, either directly or at an angle
(see Figure 13.3). If there is sufficient depth between the underside of
the dash and the transmission hump, a box can be chosen that allows
the loudspeaker to face outward. This is better acoustically, as the
high frequencies will not then be absorbed by the carpeting.
Front-facing speakers are usually elliptical in shape, to reduce the
depth required for mounting.

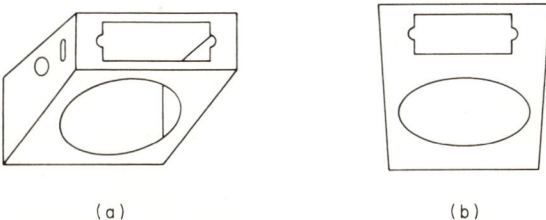

(a)   (b)

*Figure 13.3. (a) Casing for fitting radio and speaker in same unit; speaker
faces downward with slight forward angle. (b) Panel for radio and speaker
(front-facing)*

The third fixing method is by means of a centre console that fits
over the gear-box and rises to meet the bottom of the instrument panel
(Figure 13.4). Many cars have such a console built in with the heater
and other controls, and a space is provided for fitting a radio or
player. In such a case mounting is much the same as it is for in-dash
fitting. For others, consoles are specially made for a particular car and
are available from firms such as Radiomobile, who provide a range
for many popular models. Both radio and speaker can be fitted easily,
and the console is secured by a few self-tapping screws to appropriate
locations on the car bodywork. A feature of these consoles is the tray
that surrounds the gear lever, utilising otherwise wasted space to
store maps, guides, sunglasses and other small objects.

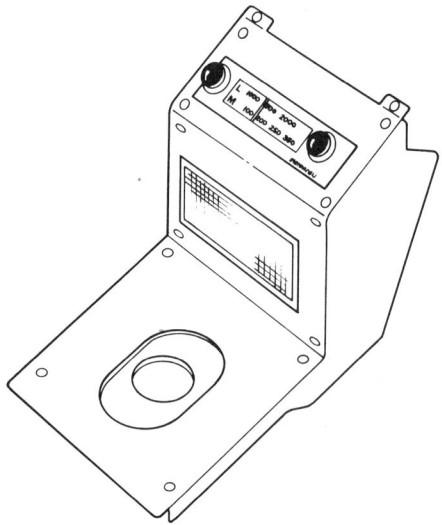

Figure 13.4. Console fitting for gearbox

Loudspeakers

Having decided on the location of the radio or player, the next consideration is the mounting of the speakers. It would be as well not to start installing the player until the speaker locations have been determined, because the situation may call for some modification of the player mounting.

For radios, only one speaker will be involved unless the radio has f.m. and a stereo multiplexer. A central position, if possible, is the most satisfactory for both driver and passenger, and this requirement is met by the combined under-dash radio/speaker mountings and gearbox consoles previously mentioned.

Other than these, an under-dash fitting using the most convenient of the various speaker housings for the car is the easiest and most satisfactory arrangement. It is preferable to have the speaker facing outward, as this gives the best frequency range in the higher registers, but if this unduly interferes with leg room or occupies too much parcel shelf space, downward facing mounting may be necessary.

As pointed out in Chapter 8, more than one speaker can be used for radio. This will not give stereo reproduction, but it can give improved results, especially if the mounting positions are not ideal. Thus a speaker can be used on each side, or one in the front and one at the back. These can be controlled if desired by switches and faders as described in Chapter 8. It may be worth giving some thought to the possibility of a radio-only installation being changed for a radio/stereo player in the future. If two speakers are installed, one on each side, they will be ready for the change to stereo later without incurring much extra work. Any centrally located speaker would be of no use and would have to be removed when such a change was made.

Pod speakers can be fitted to the upper horizontal part of the fascia, beneath the windscreen. This position, being the nearest to the listeners' head level, is probably the best for preserving the upper frequency response and therefore giving greatest clarity to the reproduction; it must be remembered that the high-frequency dispersion of normal loudspeakers is very directional. The point to watch, though, is that the driver's view of the road ahead is not unduly obscured. Hence the speakers should be as low as possible for use in this position, one of the elliptical types being most suitable. This mounting position should be avoided though in cars that have a high front fascia—or for short drivers! Another point to consider is that the wiring will be conspicuous and untidy-looking unless taken through a hole in the fascia top; this hole, together with the mounting holes, will not be easy to conceal if the speakers are later removed.

Another possibility is flush-mounted units in the kick-panel, or scuttle, one on each side of the car. Growing in popularity is the door-mounted loudspeaker. Special units are let into the door panels (see Figure 13.5), and although acoustically not ideal, as the legs of driver or passenger will obscure them and cause high-frequency absorption, they are convenient as they take up no extra room. The extreme side positioning also renders true stereo impossible, but some limited effect can be obtained.

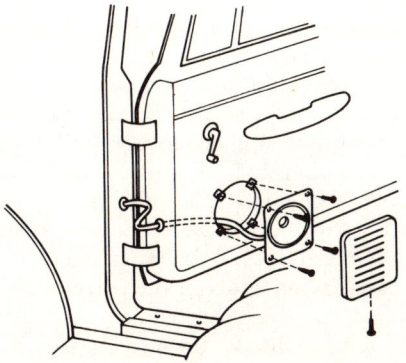

Figure 13.5. Door-mounted speaker. Fitting is by four spire clips in door panel. Cable holes in door and doorframe are staggered by 4 inches with a loop left to prevent cable fatigue

The loudspeaker units must be thin enough to be so mounted, and it must be remembered that rain water runs down the interior of the door from the windows to escape at the drain holes at the bottom. Speakers designed for this type of mounting therefore have drip shields over the upper part. Loudspeakers without this protection would soon have their cones reduced to a soggy mess after a heavy storm or a car-wash! The polyplanar speakers described in Chapter 5 are especially suitable for this type of fixing because, being made of polystyrene, they are weather-proof; they are also very thin.

When fitting speakers in doors, there are several points to watch. Make sure that the seat does not cover the speaker grilles when the door is shut. See that the window winding handle does not foul against the grille at any part of its revolution. Check that the rear part of the speaker does not interfere with the window winding mechanism, the window itself at any part of its travel, or any door catch or lock mechanism. Obviously these matters must be investigated *before* cutting and drilling the panels. In most cases the main speaker hole will be quite critical in size. If made too large, it may remove part of the material needed for the fixing screws, or may not be completely covered by the grille. So accurate cutting is essential. The screws will be secured by spring clips at the back.

When installing quad systems, the rear pair can be door mounted in the same manner as the front ones. This also is not acoustically ideal. In addition to possible masking by rear passengers, the position is just below the heads of the front occupants and so hardly to the rear at all. It has been found with quad reproduction that the most realistic effects are obtained when the rear speakers are higher than the heads of the listeners. This is probably due to the fact that in the concert hall the bulk of the reverberations come from the ceiling and the upper part of the rear walls, the lower reverberations being absorbed by the audience itself.

Even if the front speakers are door mounted, therefore, it would be better to fit the rear ones on the rear parcel shelf. These could be of the pod-type, one at each end angled inward, or they could be flush mounted. Fitting in either case is quite straightforward, the pod speakers being screwed down to the shelf with screws and spring clips underneath, and the flush units needing a cut-out hole in the same way as the door-mounted ones. Care must be taken to see that pod speakers do not cause blind-spots in the driver's vision to the rear. Being situated at the ends of the window, they could obscure a vulnerable point. There should be no problem, though, if wing mirrors are used. Flush-mounted speakers are better in this respect, and acoustically are quite satisfactory in spite of the upward facing direction, because the sound is well reflected forward by the sloping rear window.

The suggestion made in Chapter 8 for roof-mounted speakers over the head of the driver and front passenger gives the best stereo effect of all, but can pose problems when installing. Screwing to the roof is obviously out of the question as the screws would come out through the top. The only answer is to use magnetic feet on the speaker housings. As these would need to contact directly with the metal of the roof, small holes would have to be cut in the head-lining for them to penetrate. They would have to be right first time, although there would be some latitude in positioning because the speaker housing would well cover them. Subsequent removal could be an embarrassment, although the situation would be no worse than door-mounted units or other forms of panel mounting. Wiring could be taken above the head lining and down the door pillars behind the trim.

Aerials

The aerial can be mounted on either of the front wings, side pillars or back wings, or on the roof. It is more usual to fit it in the front as this involves less work in running the cable. Most aerials have sufficient cable for front mounting only, so rear fitting means changing the cable, extending the existing length by removing the plug and joining on, or fitting a ready-made extension as supplied by some makers with plug and socket. Lengthening the aerial lead will increase the capacitance and may put it outside the range of the aerial trimmer, so some series capacitance may have to be introduced as described in Chapter 6.

To minimise interference pickup, the aerial should be sited on the opposite side to the distributor. With rear-engined vehicles this gives a choice of sides when fitting the aerial at the front. Some owners prefer the appearance of a rear-mounted aerial; this is quite in order but does entail the extra work mentioned. For front-engined vehicles, rear-mounting gives less vulnerability to ignition interference, but if the engine is well suppressed there should be little problem with a front-mounted aerial on a.m. For f.m. receivers interference is a greater problem, and rear-mounting may be worth-while. There may be some advantage too, in fitting the aerial on the nearside. One of the difficulties with mobile f.m. reception is that interference is caused by other cars. Nearside mounting may give a little extra screening by the car body from vehicles passing on the other side.

Having decided where the aerial should be sited, check that there is sufficient clearance underneath, especially if the aerial is a retracting or motorised one, as these can descend a good way below the surface. Make sure too, that there is access beneath the chosen spot sufficient to enable the aerial to be introduced from the underside. Some non-retractables, roof and pillar mounted types are not fitted from the inside, but do need internal exit space for the cable to pass. Some car bodies have box sections with no access to the inside, so look out for anything like this before drilling. A bracket is provided on some retractables and motor aerials to steady the bottom end. These must be fitted to the bodywork on the inside by self-tapping screws, so a check should be made that it is possible to drill for and fit these.

Having made sure of the above matters, the hole can be drilled in the required spot. Usually this is an inch in diameter, but some are smaller; check the maker's instructions. This is usually rather an anxious moment, because a mistake or just a slip can have rather nasty results. Firstly, then, use a centre punch to put a dimple in the correct place; then drill a small pilot hole, and finally the full-sized hole.

The casing of the aerial to which the braiding of the cable is connected must be in good contact with the car bodywork electrically. To facilitate this many aerials include a serrated edged saddle or bar which bites into the underside of the metal when it is tightened up. It is best not to rely on this, especially as it is not found in all models, so clean around the underside of the hole down to bright metal before assembling the aerial. Then assemble according to the maker's instructions, and bolt up tight.

Roof and pillar aerials need only small holes for the fixing screws and a slightly larger one for the cable to pass through. In each case mark the positions carefully, and use the centre punch to dimple the surface to avoid a wandering drill.

Connecting up

The speakers can be connected first, and in the case of a radio ordinary lighting flex can be used. Wiring should be in accord with normal electrical practice; avoid anything like wire-whiskers that could short across the leads and also avoid anything that could short one of the leads to the car bodywork. One of the speaker wires will most likely be earthed inside the radio or player, so if the other were accidentally shorted to chassis it would put a short across the speaker. The probable result would be destruction of the output transistors.

Front-mounted speakers pose few problems because they are close to the radio or player and so do not require long runs of wire; a foot or so tucked out of the way behind the dash and parcel shelf is usually all that is needed.

In the case of rear speakers, the wiring must be brought up to the front to the radio or player. One method is to drill a small hole in the floor and pass it underneath the car to come up through another hole in the front. Although avoiding awkward internal runs, the external wiring is rather vulnerable to damage by stones, jacks and other hazards. It should too be supported in at least two places to avoid drooping and greater damage risk. Generally, internal wiring is the best plan. From the rear parcel shelf it can pass behind the rear seat-backs and beneath the seats themselves, which can be lifted out for the purpose. Then it can run along the floor under the carpet. If it is laid alongside the transmission hump it is unlikely to be damaged by being stepped on. It can be taped in place with insulation tape stuck across the wire at suitable intervals. As tape will not stick on dirt or grease, both of which are likely to be present on the metal floor, wipe around the area with a rag dipped in methylated spirit before applying the tape. The wire can then be brought up behind the carpet on the bulkhead, and from there behind the dash to the radio. If taped or otherwise secured, it will not be disturbed and misplaced when the carpets are removed for cleaning. Alternatively it can be run along the floor adjoining the side or scuttle, and up behind the front kick panel. Do not run it in such a manner that it could get tangled in the pedals.

When wiring door-mounted speakers special care must be taken to see that the wire, which must bridge the hinge and therefore be flexed each time the door is opened, is not strained, damaged, or affected by fatigue after a number of door closings. Figure 13.5 indicates how the wiring should be carried out. Holes should be drilled in the door frame and the door edge, not opposite each other, but displaced about 4 inches apart vertically. They should be grommetted and the cable passed through, formed into a part-loop and fed into the other grommet. The looped portion ensures that the twisting action of the door opening is distributed along the length of the loop, hence does not produce fatigue at one point.

An important matter in the wiring of more than one loudspeaker, whether stereo or mono, is phasing. All the cones must move in the same direction at the same time. With mono, when all the speakers used are of the same type, this means that the same terminal on each speaker must be connected to the same terminal of the amplifier or radio. This is unaffected by faders or other devices that are merely inserted into the appropriate parts of the circuit; phasing must still be observed. Hence the wiring must be coded by being of two different colours in order to ensure the correct connections.

With stereo the same thing applies, although the speakers do not go to the same amplifier terminal because of the two separate channels. The amplifier output socket will be coded in some way to show phasing, so terminals of the same phase must be connected to the same speaker terminals as before. Many of the complete systems include colour-coded wiring and instructions as to the correct connections, and these should be carefully observed. The same thing applies for quad; all speakers must be connected in phase to the appropriate amplifier terminals.

Few problems arise where speakers are all of the same make or are clearly marked as to phase. However, if different types are used for front and back, or if any are unmarked, the phasing must be determined. This can be done simply with the aid of a small dry battery such as the 4.5-V flat torch type. Observe the centre of the speaker cone either from the front or back, then momentarily touch the battery across the speaker terminals. The cone will jump either forwards or backwards according to the polarity of the battery. Mark with a positive sign the speaker terminal that produces forward motion of the cone (towards the grille) when the battery positive is connected to it. Do not use a car battery cell for this purpose because the current flow will be too great and would damage the speaker. Thus marked, the speakers can then be connected all in phase. It doesn't really matter which way they are connected provided they are all the same, so that the cones move in unison.

The aerial wiring is straightforward enough because the cable is already connected to the aerial and a plug is fitted to the end by the makers. The exception is the long run to a rear-mounted aerial. In such a case a complete extension lead is the quickest answer, but the plug and socket may produce a lump under the carpet, and may get parted or even damaged by being trodden on. If an extension is used, try to arrange for the coupling to lie somewhere where it will be undisturbed such as in the well under the back seat.

If a joint is made, first make sure that the extra cable is of the special low-capacitance car-aerial type. The inner conductors should be soldered together and taped over, then the outer braidings pulled down to cover the joint, enmeshed with each other and soldered in a few places. To facilitate this, do not strip the braiding back when exposing the inner conductor, rather push it back so that it can be returned to its original position. If a joint is not covered with braiding, even though there may be a continuous connection from one braid to the other, it will be unscreened and may pick up interference. When soldering, keep the cable straight otherwise the inner conductor or braiding may penetrate the insulation when it is softened by heat. Also, apply the iron only for a few seconds sufficient to make a good joint. Joints made in this way are perfectly satisfactory, but if there is any doubt as to one's ability to carry them out, it is best to use an extension lead.

As to running the cable, avoid if possible the engine compartment, because ignition interference is strongest here. Another thing to avoid is running the aerial cable in the same harness or adjacent to other wiring for any length, especially ignition wiring. Of course it is not always possible to avoid other wiring completely, but the greater the separation the better for interference reduction. These points may have but little effect when receiving strong local stations where the signal-to-noise ratio is high, but they could have a much more marked effect when receiving weak and distant transmissions.

The wiring of both loudspeakers and aerial will be done at the same time as the speakers and the aerial themselves are installed; it has been described separately only for the sake of clarity.

After the interference suppression components have been fitted, as described shortly, the final job is to connect the power supply. Remember that the earthing is including in the power circuit as well as the aerial input circuit, so this must be of very low resistance. Any resistance here will be common to both power circuit and aerial circuit and could result in noise voltages being developed over it and applied to the input. Where the unit is screwed directly to the car bulkhead via the rear staying bracket a good earth will be made, but make sure that the bolts and screws at both ends of the bracket are tight. If mounted on a parcel-shelf or on a wooden dashboard panel, it may be necessary to run an earth wire to the nearest available part of the bodywork and connect it by means of a self-tapping screw. In such a case, the wire should consist of a length of copper braid such as supplied for the purpose by some car-radio accessory manufacturers. Braiding stripped from heavy screened cables would also be suitable.

Before connecting the power lead, check that the polarity setting of the equipment is correct for the car; it is very common for the wrong polarity to be fitted, and checked only after the unit has been switched on and the smoke cleared away!

The power lead is in two sections linked by a bayonet-type plug and holder, which also serves as a fuse-carrier. No contact can be made without a suitable cartridge fuse, so make sure a fuse is in place and that it is of the rating recommended by the manufacturer. The supply end of the cable should then be pushed through one of the grommetted holes in the bulkhead and connected into the car junction box usually situated just inside the engine compartment. Two auxiliary outlet points are usually available here, one switched by the ignition key and the other unswitched. It is the latter that should be used, as otherwise the radio will not be usable when the engine is switched off.

Some authorities recommend disconnecting the battery before doing any installation or wiring work on the car. This may perhaps be advisable when working on a strange car, because one doesn't know exactly what may be encountered in the way of frayed and bared power supply leads that may short if disturbed. Normally disconnection should not be necessary, but there is some truth in the saying that it is better to be safe than sorry!

Interference suppression

No suppression is required for tape players, but all radio installations require it. A number of routine measures should be carried out, and in most cases will eliminate interference on the a.m. stations. There are three main suppression points, one of which will probably be suppressed already. The main source of interference is the distributor, and this is the first point to be dealt with. A resistive suppressor of about 10 kΩ in value should be fitted in series with the lead between the coil and the distributor centre h.t. connection. Modern cars already have distributor-suppression incorporated by law, so this measure will only be needed on the older models.

The next point to be suppressed is the ignition coil. A 2 μF capacitor should be connected between the chassis and the terminal that carries the lead to the ignition switch. This component should be metal-cased, the case being firmly clamped to the bodywork. In the case of transistor ignition, no suppressor should be fitted to the coil. Next, a 0.5 μF capacitor suppressor of similar construction to the last one should be connected from the D terminal of the dynamo to chassis. No connection should be made to the F terminal. The leads between the capacitors and the terminals should always be kept as short as possible.

This completes the routine suppression measures; now a test can be made of the complete installation. The vehicle should be tested away from buildings from which electrical interference might be picked up. First, before completing the mounting of the radio, the aerial trimmer should be adjusted. To do this, a weak station should be tuned in at the high frequency end of the medium waveband (somewhere near 200 m or 1500 kHz on the dial). Now adjust the trimmer for maximum volume, with the aerial fully extended.

The radio can then be finally mounted in place. Switch on the engine and rev it, with the radio off-tuned so that it is not receiving a transmission, and the volume up full. Do this with the receiver switched in turn to medium and long waves. There should be no interference. Next, operate the wipers, heater, and direction indicators in turn to see if they generate any interference. If all is quiet the suppression measures are adequate and the installation is complete.

Some interference may be noticed from either engine or ancillary equipment, so it must then be decided whether the level is acceptable. When a radio is off tune it is working at maximum sensitivity and will amplify noises that would be swamped by even a weak radio signal. This can be noted in the case of the background noise generated by the radio itself, which can be very prominent under no-signal conditions but which disappears when a station is tuned in. So tune in a weak station and note whether the interference is now still audible and at what level. If it is sufficient to be obtrusive further suppression measures must be taken; these are described in Chapter 14, together with those needed for f.m. suppression.

Chapter 14

Interference Suppression

Whenever an electrical circuit is switched on or off, the equilibrium of that circuit is disturbed. Usually a spark is generated at the switch contacts and energy is thereby released, causing motion of the electrons in the associated circuit. The effect is similar to dropping a stone in a small pond; waves travel outward to the edge, are reflected back to the middle and outward again through several cycles before the energy is dissipated. So too, electrical energy flows backwards and forwards in what is termed an oscillation in the circuit until it is expended.

As with the waves in the pond, the frequency is of a random nature, but because the start is sudden the transient waveforms are steep; steep waves mean high frequencies, so they range well up into the radio band. Thus radio frequencies are generated that will be accepted by the tuned circuits in the radio receiver and so cause interference.

The spark itself radiates interference as it is the prime generator of it, but much more is radiated by the associated leads through which the oscillations are flowing (Figure 14.1). They serve, then, as aerials to transmit the waves generated by the spark, and this must be taken into account when devising suppression measures. This radiation can be picked up by nearby metallic objects such as bowden cables, pipes and body panels, then re-radiated. This secondary radiation, as it is called, can then find its way into the radio circuits due to proximity of the re-radiating body.

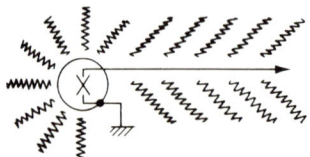

Figure 14.1. Sources of interference radiation. The spark source itself radiates, but the connecting lead acts as a transmitting aerial, radiating more than the actual source

Large masses of metal, such as body panels and the road wheels, can build up electrostatic charges during periods of dry weather. Periodically these charges discharge to adjacent metalwork, producing oscillation in the same manner as the spark discharge. Here then is another source of interference.

It can be seen that there are numerous potential interference sources in a car. As interference is produced by anything involving switching and sparking, the ignition system (both primary and secondary circuits), the generator commutator, voltage regulator (or in the case of an alternator, the control regulator), wiper and heater motors, petrol pump, clock, instrument stabilising unit, direction indicators and any other similar device can give trouble. The starter motor can give heavy interference because of the large currents flowing, but this is only momentary and so can be ignored.

Suppression methods

Resistance suppressors (Figure 14.2a) are wired between the generator of the interference and the radiating cables. The resistance reduces the amplitude of the oscillations but does not completely eliminate them. Any wire between the suppressor and the generator will still act as a radiating aerial, so the suppressor must be connected as close to the spark source as possible. This is why resistance is built into plug caps and distributor rotor connections. If there is any appreciable d.c. current flowing in the circuit, the resistance will produce a voltage drop and so a power loss. The resistance value, then, must be chosen to give a compromise between impeding the interference currents and offering minimum impedance to the wanted d.c. currents.

Chokes or *inductances* (Figure 14.2b) work in a similar manner to the resistance suppressor; they are wired in series with the source and its cables, as close to the source as possible. However, the impedance of an inductance is zero at d.c. and rises to a very high value at radio

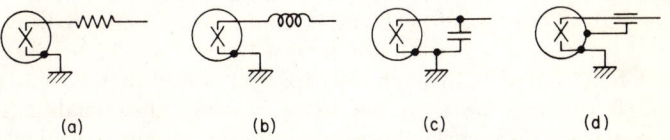

(a) (b) (c) (d)

Figure 14.2. (a) Resistor suppressor minimises flow of interference energy to connecting lead. (b) Inductive suppressor offers a high impedance to high-frequency oscillations but a minimum to d.c. currents; especially useful for v.h.f. interference suppression. (c) Capacitive shunt serves as a 'short-circuit' to high-frequency currents. (d) Co-axial capacitor wired close to the terminal eliminates radiation by the connecting lead of ordinary capacitor; useful for v.h.f. suppression

frequencies. Thus it offers effective suppression to radio interference, yet causes no losses to d.c. currents. If used in a.c. circuits it impedes the wanted current as well as the interference; however, as the impedance rises proportionately to frequency, low inductance values offer little opposition to the low-frequency wanted current, but a much higher impedance to the high-frequency interference. They can still be used in a.c. circuits, then, provided the inductance is kept low.

A factor that limits the efficiency of choke suppressors is their self-capacity. Any coil or winding possesses capacitance between adjacent turns and layers. Capacitance has the opposite effect of inductance (its impedance drops as the applied frequency rises), so being effectively in parallel with the choke it allows the high frequencies to pass. The self-capacitance is not great, though, and a well-designed inductor is a very effective suppressor if used properly.

Capacitive suppressors (Figure 14.2c) are wired not in series but in parallel with the interfering source. A capacitor does not pass d.c. but its impedance to a.c. currents falls as the frequency rises. Thus, for radio frequency interference, the capacitor is a virtual short-circuit. As it in no way impedes the passage of d.c. currents in the circuits across which it is connected, it is a convenient and often-used means of suppression. Because the lead from the source to the capacitor is carrying interference currents, it can act as a radiator, hence it must be kept as short as possible. The inch or two normally needed to connect a capacitor will have no great effect on medium and long-wave reception, but for short-wave, and especially v.h.f. in the f.m. band, it can be serious.

To overcome this problem, special *co-axial* or *lead-through* capacitors are used (Figure 14.2d). These are connected in series with the lead-out wire from the source, right close to the source terminal. The capacitor is not actually in series with the lead-out wire as this would obviously block the d.c., but the capacitor surrounds the lead, which passes through the middle of it and is connected internally to one of the capacitor plates. If this device is connected right up to the terminal of the interference source, the lead will be effectively suppressed and only the source and the terminal can radiate. The outer plate of the capacitor should be connected directly to the casing of the interference source, not to nearby bodywork, because the interference currents through the capacitor would then have to pass through the bodywork to the source casing, thus enabling this return-path to radiate. To short-circuit the interference effectively the capacitor must connect directly across the source, i.e. from its terminal to its case, and take in no external path.

Many capacitors, being wound from rolls of metal foil, possess inductance. This is in series with the capacitance, and because it offers impedance to high frequencies means that the capacitor is not a complete short-circuit to them; hence its effectiveness as a suppressor is limited by its self-inductance. The amount is not great, but can be sufficient at v.h.f. to cause trouble. Non-inductive capacitors can be made by doubling back the foil on itself so that the inductance of one part is cancelled by that of the other. This is the type that should be used for interference suppression, especially at v.h.f., ordinary capacitors having only limited effectiveness.

Earthing straps made of thick copper braid are used to interconnect panels or metal components to the bodywork. These are effective in dealing with secondary radiation from parts such as the bonnet cover that may not be in good electrical contact to chassis. Static between panels can be prevented by fitting earthing straps between them, and sometimes it may be necessary between the differential housing and the bodywork. It is assumed that the engine block is in first-rate contact with the bodywork, because the block is source-earth in the case of ignition interference, and all affected metal parts must have a very low resistance path back to it. If there is any doubt on the matter, a heavy braid should be connected between the block and the nearest main metal member, usually the bulkhead.

All braids should be tinned with solder at their point of contact with the metalwork. If this is not done electrolytic action may take place between the dissimilar metals copper and steel in the presence of acid deposits, and cause corrosion. Even if only mild, the contact resistance would be appreciably increased thereby nullifying the effect of the strap.

Screening of interference sources, radiating cables, or radio circuits by earthed metalwork effectively blocks coupling by electromagnetic radiation. Hence the receiver aerial cable, the most vulnerable component, is screened with metal braiding; the radio too is encased in metal. Sparking plugs are buried in the engine block and so are well screened, but their leads are not and neither is the distributor. Siting the aerial on the opposite side of the car puts the block between it and the plug leads and distributor, and so affords a measure of screening. The car body also screens the aerial from the ignition interference source.

A particular problem arises in the case of glass-fibre bodies. The only answer is to line the engine compartment with metal foil. This should be done to all accessible places including the bonnet, and all sections should be linked with braiding. A strap should also be taken from the block to the nearest foil.

Preliminary measures

All a.m. radio installations need suppression at three points as a matter of routine (Figure 14.3). The first is the h.t. lead from the coil

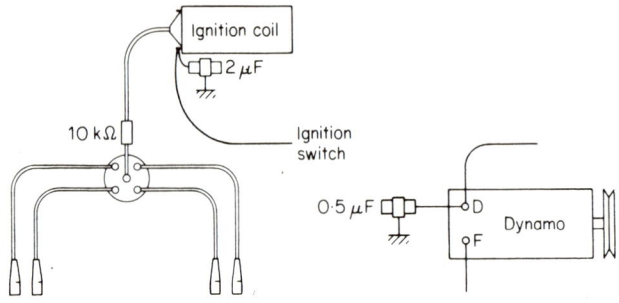

Figure 14.3. Routine suppression points for a.m. reception

to the distributor; if a resistive brush to the rotor arm is fitted, no further attention is necessary, if not, a 10-kΩ series suppressor should be fitted as close to the distributor as possible. In some cars the lead is composed of carbon granules and therefore constitutes a series suppressor. The coil is the next point, needing a 2 μF capacitor connected from the l.t. lead from the ignition switch across to the bodywork as close as possible to the coil, preferably on the same bracket. This must *not* be fitted to transistor or capacitive-discharge systems. Finally, the dynamo requires a 0.5 μF capacitor taken from the D terminal, which is the output lead, to the frame. No capacitor should be connected to the F field terminal; if in doubt, the D terminal has the thicker wire connected to it because this carries the whole output current, whereas the F terminal wire carries only the field energising current. All capacitor wires must be kept as short as possible.

If interference is still present, the first thing is to make sure that the car ignition system is in good condition, especially the rotor arm, distributor points and spark plugs. If these are worn or maladjusted, excessive interference may be generated. Likewise loose connections anywhere in the electrical system will give trouble, but these should give some indication of their presence by erratic operation of the circuit concerned.

Next, check that the aerial is in order, especially if it is not a new one but was already installed. The individual sections of the telescopic mast may be oxidised and so not make good contact with each other, thus restricting the effective length of the aerial to the bottom one or two sections. A common fault is leakage between the aerial and the earthing. This can be measured by an ohmmeter and it should read infinity; leakages are usually due to dampness in the insulator and are worse in wet weather. A short between aerial and the bodywork may be caused by a wire-whisker from the braid shorting in the connection to the aerial or in the plug. Check cable continuity by measuring from the aerial to the tip of the aerial plug, and also check the screening by metering the resistance between the plug body and an earthing point. In each case the resistance should be a fraction of an ohm. Most car radio troubles are eventually traced to the aerial, so it is wise to eliminate it early in the proceedings.

Identifying the source

Tracking down the source of the interference is not difficult as the symptoms can readily be identified. Ignition interference produces a sharp rapid ticking noise that varies with engine speed. If the engine is revved then switched off, the noise stops immediately.

The dynamo causes a whining noise that increases as the engine is revved. The sound is quite different from ignition, and it can be confirmed by the fact that it dies down when the engine is switched off unlike the abrupt cessation of ignition noise. An alternator makes a very similar noise to a dynamo.

Next comes the voltage regulator. This causes quite a distinctive sound that can best be described as a chattering effect. It is heard only when the engine revs are high, and it does not cut out when the engine is switched off, only when the revs fall below a certain level.

Another source is the instrument voltage stabiliser. This device, which is not to be found on all cars, gives more accurate instrument readings by stabilising the supply voltage from the battery so that they are not subject to the fluctuations of voltage resulting from various states of battery charge. The stabiliser consists of a bi-metallic strip with a small heating element that continually opens and closes a pair of contacts. This happens so rapidly that the damped gauges behave as if a lower but constant voltage were being applied to them. The unit is usually mounted at the back of the instrument panel just where it will generate most interference for the radio. The noise is a continuous sizzle which appears with the ignition turned on but the engine not running. It is often worsened by vibration, as can be found if the instrument panel is struck with the flat of the hand. It is possible to determine whether a stabiliser is fitted by observing the petrol gauge when the ignition is turned on. If it registers immediately, there is no stabiliser, but if it takes a few seconds, one is present.

Interference from other ancillary equipment can readily be identified by switching the particular items on and off. The heater motor, wipers, and direction indicators are the main culprits. An electric clock will give a ticking noise over the radio just like the sound of a clockwork one, and of course it is on all the time when everything else is switched off.

Static due to charges in the body panels is only present when the car is in motion and will be heard when the engine and all other electrical equipment is switched off. It can be identified by coasting down an incline with the engine off. Another similar effect, though, can be caused by a poor electrical connection or a bad earthing contact in one of the circuits. This may only appear when the car is in motion but will disappear when the particular circuit is switched off. There may also be some other symptom such as erratic or below-standard operation of the circuit concerned. An example is that of a dim lamp, which is most likely due to a poor earthing contact—this could also generate interference.

Further suppression measures

Having carried out the routine suppression, and then identified the source of any remaining interference, further suppression must be applied. There may of course be more than one source, so each one will have to be dealt with in turn. (See Figure 14.4.)

In the case of ignition interference, further h.t. lead suppression should be tried. A set of 5-kΩ resistive suppressors should be wired, one in each plug lead close to the distributor, or (if available) the type that plugs into the outlet spouts of the distributor. If not already

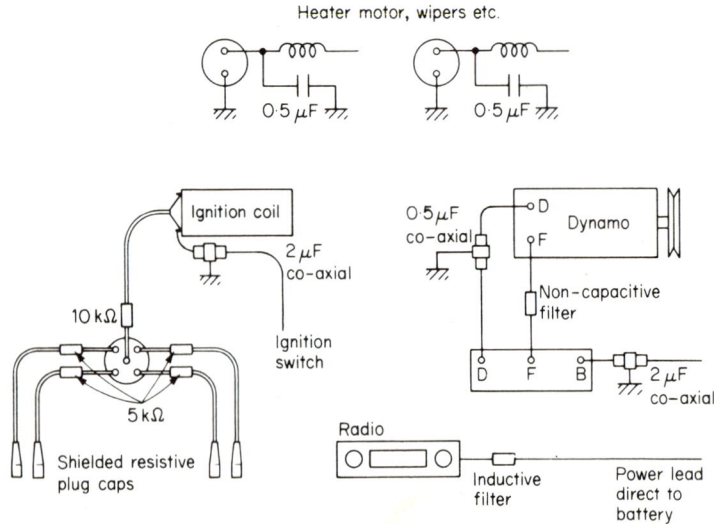

Figure 14.4. All possible suppression measures. Rarely necessary except for f.m. (v.h.f.) reception

fitted, shielded plug connectors that include resistance should be used. Carbon leads should be replaced in stubborn cases with wire ones and the extra suppressors fitted. However, the total resistance of the h.t. circuit (including the 10-kΩ coil/distributor suppressor, 5-kΩ plug lead and resistive plug cap) should not exceed 20 kΩ otherwise the engine performance might be affected. Special h.f. inductive filters were at one time made for inclusion in plug leads. They suppressed interference without introducing too much resistance. However it seems that they are now no longer available from any of the usual sources.

Next, a 0.5 μF capacitor suppressor can be tried from the ignition switch to chassis, which will bypass any interference being picked up by the lead from the switch to the coil (but not with transistor systems). This lead is already bypassed at the coil end by the 2 μF coil suppressor. If interference persists, and the coil is mounted on the bodywork, take an earth strap directly from the coil bracket to the engine block. Improvement may be made by substituting the ordinary 2 μF coil suppressor with a lead-through type. Sometimes the power supply lead can pick up interference, although the supply should be well filtered inside the radio. Taking the power lead direct to the battery instead of through the junction box has been known to improve matters in difficult cases, but supply lead filters are also available, and can be tried.

Loudspeaker leads can also pick up noise and feed it into the set. This is rare, but if all else fails try re-routing the leads or rewiring with screened leads. The screen should then be connected to chassis, but use twin screened lead so that the screen will not have to be used as one of the loudspeaker wires. Do not overlook the possibility of secondary radiation by the bonnet; an earth strap from it to the bulkhead—or better still two, one each side—should eliminate this possibility.

If the trouble is dynamo interference, fit a 0.5 μF suppressor to the D terminal of the voltage regulator. The lead from this terminal goes to the dynamo and is bypassed at the dynamo end by the 0.5 μF suppressor already fitted. The value of this could be increased to 1.0 μF and a lead-through type substituted. In stubborn cases an inductive filter could be tried in series with the F terminal lead, but no capacitive suppressor should be used on either dynamo or voltage-regulator F terminals.

Voltage-regulator interference can usually be checked by wiring a 2 μF suppressor from the B terminal to chassis.

Coming now to the instrument voltage stabiliser, a 0.5 μF suppressor can be tried wired from the terminal that feeds the instruments to chassis. This is not always successful, so a choke connected in series may be required as well. Should this prove especially troublesome, the stabiliser can be dispensed with and a transistorised one used instead. These are available commercially, but one can easily be constructed with very little trouble. Figure 14.5 shows a circuit using a single transistor, a zener diode and two resistors. It will generate no interference, and is likely to operate even more accurately than the bi-metallic strip; it may be found that the instruments take a few seconds longer to reach their proper readings on first switching on. No special layout is required and construction can take any convenient form. A heat-sink should be provided, though, to conduct heat away from the transistor.

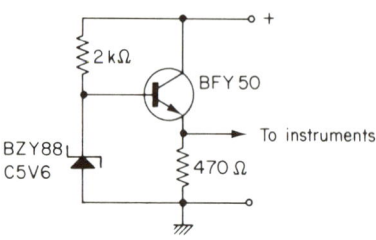

*Figure 14.5. Circuit for transistorised instrument
voltage stabiliser*

Most ancillary interference can be dealt with by wiring a 0.5 μF suppressor from the offending item terminal to chassis. If this does not do the trick, an inductive suppressor connected in series in addition to the capacitor should. Suppressors are available from Bosch that combine an inductor and a capacitor in a compact form; these are particularly useful for suppressing small motors and other noise sources.

This brings us to the final source, that of static. Determining the precise source can only be done by a process of trial and error. Try bonding the wings, the bonnet and, if the aerial is at the rear, the boot lid. The exhaust system and also the steering column are other possibilities. Tyre static is another source. Friction can build up a charge between ground and the car bodywork that leaks only when it has reached quite high potentials. This can not only cause radio interference but also result in an electric shock when someone dismounts.

The dangling chain once popular as a prevention for travel sickness can serve to discharge static to ground, but its effect is rather uncertain. The most effective cure is to provide a conductive path from the tyre tread to the car body. Painting the inside wall of the tyre with a lead paint or rubber conductive paint should do the trick. It is not necessary to paint the whole wall, several wide strips will do.

It may be that the wheels themselves are not in good contact with the body due to the wheel bearings. Packing them with graphite grease should make them conductive. Alternatively special springs made for the purpose can be fitted inside the hub caps. These form a bridge between the hub-cap and the axle.

In the case of the rear wheels it could be found that the back axle is not in electrical contact with the body, and if this is so it will be necessary to fit a copper braid strap from the axle to the body. The top bolts of the differential housing should prove a convenient anchoring point. Static appears mostly in long dry spells, when any dampness that may have provided a leakage path has dried out. This is probably one reason why static interference is not much of a problem in the UK!

F.M. suppression

The suppression methods described for stubborn cases of interference on a.m. radio should be regarded as routine treatment in an f.m. installation. All capacitive suppressors should be of the lead-through type. Suppression measures can be summarised as follows. A 10 kΩ suppressor in h.t. lead to distributor. 5 kΩ suppressors in all plug leads, and suppressed shielded plug connectors. A 2 µF lead-through suppressor on the ignition coil l.t. lead terminal (except with transistor systems), and an earth strap from the coil mounting to the engine block. A 0.5 µF lead-through suppressor from the dynamo D terminal and the same on the regulator D terminal. A 2 µF lead-through from the B terminal of the regulator, and a non-capacitive filter in series with the F terminal lead. Combined inductive/capacitive suppressors on clock, wipers, heater and other motors including the instrument stabiliser, or a transistor unit in place of the latter.

Chapter 15

Mobile Public Address

As its name implies a public address system is a means whereby the natural voice of the speaker is amplified to reach a larger audience than would be possible without it. Two common uses for a mobile system are: commentaries given by the driver or courier to motor-coach passengers, and the sound-car by which announcements are broadcast to the public at large.

We will consider each of these applications separately, but they have certain factors in common. The basic equipment required is a microphone, an amplifier with a high output, at least 20 W rating, and one or more loudspeakers of suitable type and ratings. Microphones are made in various types. Crystal microphones are the cheapest, have a high output and work into a high impedance. They are fragile, however, being vulnerable to damage by vibration, shock and dampness. They also have a resonant peak in the treble part of their response curve that can make some voices sound harsh and unpleasant, sibilants being particularly affected. Moving-coil microphones can be obtained in any impedance to suit the amplifier, and are robust. They are dearer than the crystals, and are available over a wide price range. They also have a resonant peak, though usually less pronounced than that of the crystals; with the better ones, the peak is well damped.

Other microphones used for high-quality indoor installations are the ribbon and capacitor types, but the one best suited for mobile p.a. is the moving-coil.

Acoustic feedback

This is a feature of all situations where there is a microphone working in the same volume of air as a loudspeaker that it is feeding. It is initiated by sounds from the loudspeaker that are picked up by the microphone, amplified and fed to the loudspeaker, which reproduces them at higher volume, to be picked up again by the microphone and so on. In just a second or so, the sound builds up into a loud whistle or howl, the frequency of which depends on the dominant resonant frequency of the system; and the volume, on the maximum power rating of the amplifier.

Feedback can be a major problem in indoor installations where the speakers are operating at high volume levels, but it is less so in the mobile uses we have mentioned. It can occur in a coach, but is less likely with a sound car where the microphone is inside the car and the loudspeaker outside.

Good p.a. practice consists of mounting the loudspeakers so that the sound from them does not easily reach the microphone: they should be either angled away from it or well separated from it. Operating a microphone near a loudspeaker is inviting trouble. Microphones with a peaky response will feedback sooner than those with a level response.

If you turn the volume up on any system, a point will be reached where feedback will occur, so matters should be arranged so that the normal operating volume is well below the feedback level. If operated only just below, a ringing sound accompanies each spoken word and intelligibility is greatly reduced. Intelligibility is the main object of any p.a. installation, mobile or otherwise, so it is better to use rather less volume and maintain clarity than to have it loud and yet not understandable. Another mistake often made by operators is to speak too close to the microphone. This causes distortion that reduces intelligibility. About six inches distance is the minimum for this class of work.

Coach installations

Commentary facilities are usually an extra for a music system supplied by either a radio or a tape-player. Such combined units need two controls, one for the music and the other for the microphone. One can then be faded out in favour of the other. A microphone has a very low output and needs an amplifying stage of its own in addition to the normal audio amplifier stages in the radio or player-unit. The signals from the microphone are amplified by this stage before they are applied to the volume control. Thus when the control is turned down the noise generated by the stage is also decreased, so maintaining the same signal/noise ratio. If this were not done the microphone signals would be swamped by amplifier noise at the lower volume levels.

The impedance of the microphone must match that of the input stage. Most transistor amplifiers will accept between 600Ω and 50 kΩ input, unless specifically designed for other values. High-impedance crystal microphones are not suitable for transistor stages, nor are low-impedance moving-coil types of 30–50 Ω.

The loudspeaker is often mounted at the front of the coach near the roof and facing down the coach to the rear. This will give the best overall coverage if only one speaker is to be used. It may be rather prone to feedback if the microphone is near. Audibility towards the rear of the coach is poor, and if more volume is used to reach the back (assuming this can be done without feedback), it may be too loud for those in front.

The best way of sound distribution in a coach, although it is an expensive one, is to mount individual speakers in the luggage rack over each seat. These can be flush-mounted, with the rear protected from the luggage by a box. A switch can be incorporated so that each passenger (or pair of passengers) can switch off if desired. This is much appreciated by those who prefer to travel in peace and quiet.

A compromise arrangement is to mount speakers at intervals down the coach on the ceiling or rack as before. These can be fed at a lower volume than the single one at the front and so will be less obtrusive to those who do not wish to hear.

When connecting a number of loudspeakers, the impedance must be carefully watched. Paralleling reduces the impedance to a half in the case of two, a third in the case of three and so on. Transistor output stages do not like speaker circuits with a lower impedance than that specified, which incidentally is the reason why all speaker wiring must be run in a manner to avoid all possibility of short-circuits across the feeders. Obviously a large number of speakers cannot be connected in parallel as the impedance would drop to a small fraction of what it should be.

If on the other hand they are connected in series, the impedance is now the total of all of them which will be too high. Although not likely

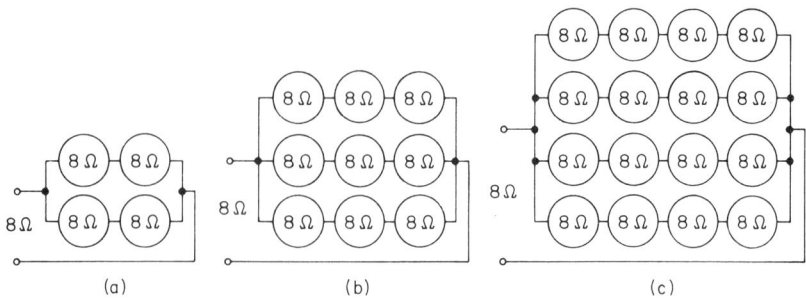

Figure 15.1. The impedance of a loudspeaker circuit can be matched to the amplifier by series-parallel connection of loudspeakers of the same impedance; this can be done with (a) 4, (b) 9, or (c) 16 speakers

to damage the output stage, the power available in the circuit will be only a fraction of the rated output, and must be shared by all the speakers.

The difficulty can be overcome by a series-parallel connection (Figure 15.1). If four speakers are connected thus, the impedance is the same as for a single speaker. The same is true of combinations of nine, sixteen and twenty-five. There must be the same number of groups in series as there are speakers in each group. It follows that switching a speaker off is in effect removing it from the circuit and will upset the power distribution to the others. If it so happened all the speakers in one group were switched off the whole circuit would be open and none of the others could operate at all.

To prevent this a dummy load must be wired in conjunction with a two-way switch so that switching the speaker off also connects the load in its place (Figure 15.2). The load is made up of a 5-W wire-wound resistor of approximately equal resistance to the speaker impedance. Value is not critical to within an ohm or two but if not exact should be slightly higher. Thus for an 8-Ω speaker a 10-Ω resistor would be suitable.

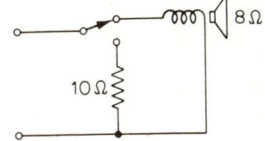

Figure 15.2. Where switches are provided for each speaker, a two-way switch must be used that connects a dummy load equal to or a little higher than the speaker impedance

Sound-cars

The other mobile sound application is the sound-car for making public announcements. A straight amplifier is required here, with no radio or tape facilities. Higher powers (at least 20 W) are required for this purpose, as the sound is intended to carry for some distance. All mobile p.a. amplifiers for sound-car use are transistorised so that they can deliver high powers with minimum drain from the car battery. Valve amplifiers were very restricted in this regard. The current drain when sound is not actually being reproduced is quite small and the amplifier can be left switched on between announcements. Many units designed for this purpose, though, include a switch on the microphone that switches the amplifier on and off. This enables the driver of the car to use the unit with the minimum of distraction.

The main difference from other mobile sound systems is in the loudspeaker. Usually a single unit is used, but sometimes two may be mounted to cover different directions. It must be efficient (that is, have a high conversion factor of electrical signal into sound), it must be weatherproof, and it must be capable of handling the high powers applied to it from the amplifier.

This rules out ordinary cone loudspeakers, which are not weatherproof or, except for the larger hi-fi models, rated for high powers. Those that are need a large baffle which would be impracticable for mounting to a car exterior. Efficiency is also not a strong point, in fact the mechanical force applied to move a mass of air with an initial area equal to that of the cone is rather like using a sledgehammer to crack a walnut or driving a car downhill at full throttle in bottom gear! While cone loudspeakers have other advantages their efficiency is less than 5%, which means you have to put at least 10 W of electrical energy in to get 0.5 W of sound energy out.

A much more efficient unit is the horn loudspeaker (Figure 15.3). This has a small moving-coil driver linked to a diaphragm fitted at the narrow end of a horn that widens out in an exponential manner. The horn effectively couples the small area of the diaphragm to the large area of air at the open flare. It thus serves the same function as the gear train in a gear-box, and efficiencies of 50% or more can be obtained. The horn length is such as to prevent rain reaching the driving unit unless it is tilted upward, and so is reasonably weatherproof.

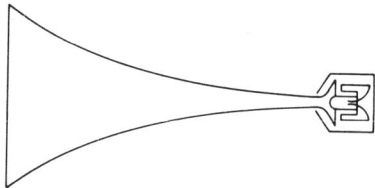

Figure 15.3. A horn speaker: the diaphragm of the moving-coil unit drives the column of air in the horn and affords an efficient coupling with the outside air mass

A large horn can be somewhat unwieldy, even though it can be mounted without too much trouble across the roof of a car. The present practice is to use re-entrant horns, that is horns folded up to form a more manageable unit (Figure 15.4). These can be roof-mounted or fitted to the bumper.

The main disadvantage of a horn speaker is that the bass response

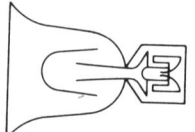

Figure 15.4. A re-entrant horn reduces the horn to more manageable proportions, and is also more weatherproof

is governed by the length of horn and area of the flare; the larger these are, the better the response. To keep the size within practical limits means a severely restricted response. That is why the reproduction sounds harsh and rather like a telephone. As high quality is not of prime importance for this application, the restriction is acceptable in view of the other advantages.

Chapter 16

Setting up a Workshop

With the present extent of public interest in mobile audio systems, there is a need for specialist service depots to install and repair this type of equipment. Such a depot may be associated with an existing radio and television business, or with a garage, or it may be independent. It may serve the public direct, or it may take on work for the motor trade or radio dealers.

One matter will have to be decided right at the start, and that is whether to undertake installation or confine work to equipment repair. This will be largely determined by the facilities available. A covered area off the road big enough to accommodate at least a couple of cars will be required. If installation and in-situ testing can be carried out it will add to the profitability of the business and enable a complete service to be offered and advertised. On the other hand if there are no facilities for it, or it is decided to not to do actual work on the car for other reasons, it should not prove a major obstacle to the success of the enterprise because the majority of mobile audio systems are owner-installed and can just as easily be removed by the owner when service is needed.

The size of the workshop and its facilities is another thing that needs advance consideration. A large room solely devoted to mobile audio may be required if a large work turnover is planned and the business is to specialise in it. If it is to be an extra service in an existing service depot, however, it may just take the form of a special bench fitted up for the purpose. In the latter case the organisation and paperwork will be integrated into the normal workshop routine.

Test equipment

The first item of equipment required is some form of power supply. For the sake of convenience this could take the form of a stabilised 12-V mains unit, with a current rating of about 3 A. Stabilising is not absolutely essential, because the voltage applied to the units in the car varies over quite a wide range and minor voltage deviations will be of little consequence. However, it must be remembered that the current taken by different items that may be used with it can vary extensively. A car/portable radio make take just a hundred milliamps or so, whereas a quad tape player with four amplifiers and a motor may take several amps when being tested at high volume. A mains unit with poor voltage regulation may give a dangerously high voltage at the lower load currents.

Car audio and radio units have no smoothing circuits of their own to remove mains hum, so a good degree of smoothing is necessary in a mains unit. A small amount of residual hum will of course be acceptable, as the unit is to be used only for testing and not for customer demonstration, but too much may upset certain audio measurements and adjustments.

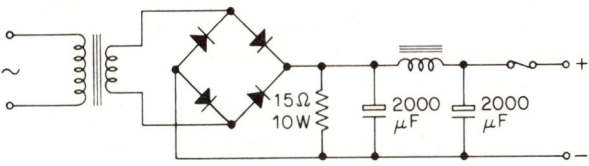

Figure 16.1. Circuit of power unit to supply d.c. bench test voltage

A mains unit can quite easily be made up if a suitable transformer is available; see Figure 16.1. A bridge circuit of four rectifiers can be used, and it is preferable to use an inductor rather than a resistor for smoothing. The use of a resistor would mean poor voltage regulation, which is one of the things to be avoided as we have seen. An inductor will provide rejection of hum frequencies without introducing too much series resistance. Finding a suitable component may not be too easy unless it is obtained specially for the purpose. One could try using a heater winding on an old mains transformer that had an open-circuit primary or h.t. winding. High-value reservoir and smoothing capacitors are needed, and the reservoir must have a ripple current rating equal to the maximum d.c. current to be supplied by the unit, a point sometimes overlooked when making up mains power units. A degree of stabilisation can be simply obtained by connecting a resistor across the d.c. output, which will bleed about an amp. This will tie the output voltage down when operating with a low-current load. The bleed current will have to be taken into account and added to the maximum output current required when choosing the transformer and rectifiers. Should the ratings of these be rather tight, the bleed resistor can be switched out of circuit when a high-current load is being supplied, and switched in for low-current ones. Suitable values are 15Ω at 10 W power rating.

A much simpler solution to the power supply problem is to use a car battery and an ordinary charger. The charger can be permanently connected to the battery and a pair of leads brought up to a bench socket to supply the equipment being tested. The charger can be switched on at night or, if a trickle charger, can be left on while the battery is being used. Hum will be smoothed out to a great extent by the battery itself, which will also keep the voltage down. Care must be taken to ensure that acid splashes and residues that appear around the battery fillers do not get in contact with clothing, so it is usual to locate the battery under the bench at a remote corner. Don't forget, though, to occasionally top it up and clean off the terminals. A further advantage of using batteries is that work can continue during power cuts.

An aerial will be required for each bench. While in theory this need only be a short length of wire similar in length to a car aerial, it is best to fit a proper car aerial at some convenient point. This then duplicates the conditions of the car installation including the input capacitance of the aerial cable.

There can be problems if the building is steel-framed or in a poor reception area. Mounting the aerial near a window may help if it does not entail lengthening the lead more than a few feet. Another problem can be posed by electrical interference. Some fluorescent lights can be very troublesome in this respect, and it may mean trying different lamps or even complete fittings, or using only incandescent lamps for the workshop lighting. Interference will be worse where the signal strength is low. Some experiment may be needed to find an aerial position that gives reasonable signal pickup and minimum interference; don't be afraid to try some unconventional ones; in one case the best position proved to be horizontal, a few inches from the floor.

There is one consolation though if the signal is weak: if a radio is made to work reasonably well under these conditions it should be perfectly satisfactory in the customer's car.

Another requirement for each bench will be a pair of loudspeakers. As a general rule equipment brought in for repair comes in minus the speakers, and it is but rarely that speakers give trouble, unless damaged. The bench speakers should be of 8-Ω impedance and thus be suitable for all classes of instrument; 4-Ω units may be satisfactory for most players, but could be rather low for the odd one or two. As noted before, it is better to have too high an impedance than too low with transistor output stages. The speakers can be conveniently mounted on the bench and leads fitted ready for connection to the equipment under test.

There will of course be the usual workshop tools and fittings, bench lamps, soldering irons (including a 12-V model if work on cars is to be undertaken, so that it can be run from the car battery). Also needed will be a vice, an electric drill, and a good collection of hand-tools, pliers, cutters, screwdrivers and so on. A grindstone is also useful for tool-grinding and other purposes, but this may be included with the drill.

The proper operation of any tape mechanism depends on the pressures and tensions of various mechanical components. Spring-loaded levers such as the carriage carrying the heads in a cassette player, pinch-roller mounting, and many others must all engage with the specified tensions. Tension adjustment can be made by bending the associated spring or moving its anchorage point. If too great, the tension can cause excessive wear, sluggish operation due to friction, and in some cases jamming of the mechanism. Insufficient tension on the other hand can cause slipping and lack of traction.

To adjust the tension correctly, a pressure gauge is required. This is a cylindrical tool with an internal precision-made spring and calibrated scale rather like a spring balance. A sliding probe is made to bear against the point where tension is to be measured, and the pressure is then read off the scale. With some gauges the probe appears at both ends of the instrument to enable both 'push' and 'pull' tension to be measured.

Gauges are usually supplied in sets of two or three, each one covering a limited range of pressures, so that the complete range normally encountered on tape machines can be measured between them. It is surprising the number of professional workshops that do not carry a set of gauges, yet they are inexpensive and take the guesswork out of all spring tensioning. They are to be strongly recommended.

Also necessary are test tapes, both cassette and cartridge. Elaborate checks on frequency-response, noise and other specifications are usually confined to the servicing of hi-fi equipment and so are not necessary here. All that is required is music in stereo, and also a tape for adjusting the head azimuth. The latter can be made by recording a fixed tone from an audio generator at about 6 kHz on a recorder that is known to have correct head alignment. A tone at a lower frequency, say 2 kHz, can be also recorded to check wow and flutter, but more of these tests in Chapter 17.

Test instruments

In addition to the bench equipment so far described several items of test instrumentation will be required. The first and most important is a reliable multi-range meter. This should be capable of measuring volts, resistance and also current. A.C. ranges are included in most meters but are not so important for this class of work, except perhaps a low-voltage a.c. range for indicating output during alignment of radio stages or tape-heads. A limitation with many meters is that the current ranges do not go very high. When working on 12-V equipment it is often necessary to make current checks, and these could run into several amps. It is essential then to choose a meter that has a high d.c. current range, 10 A being a useful one. Do not count on using, for separate current readings, an ordinary ammeter as used in battery chargers or in cars, since these have a poor degree of accuracy. Other than a good current range, the requirements for this type of work are not very exacting and a number of medium-priced meters being offered would be quite suitable (see Figures 16.2 and 16.3). A factor desirable for any workshop testmeter, whatever the purpose, is robustness. Such an instrument gets a lot of hard use and many knocks in the course of its life, so reliability and ruggedness is

*Figure 16.2. Avo Model 8 multi-range meter has a current range of
10 A, necessary for car audio servicing*

Figure 16.3. Eagle EP50LN multi-range meter has a 12 A current range

important. Many of the cheaper meters that may have an adequate range-specification, and may be quite suitable for occasional amateur use, just would not stand up to daily life in the workshop.

The alignment of radio circuits, as well as fault-finding, calls for the use of an r.f. signal generator. Here again the requirements are not too stringent. An a.m. generator that covers the i.f. frequencies and long and medium wavebands will serve the majority of alignments. For f.m., a separate f.m. generator is desirable, but as pointed out in earlier chapters the proportion of f.m. receivers is small, and of these the number needing complete alignments will be a minute fraction. Hence an f.m. generator may be justified for a large depot handling a considerable amount of work, but hardly worth-while for a small one. If one is obtained, choose a model that has stereo signal facilities, because the main interest in f.m. car radio is to receive stereo broadcasts. F.M. alignment can be undertaken with an a.m. generator provided the ranges extend up into the v.h.f. band (up to 100 MHz).

An audio generator can be very useful and should form a part of every car audio workshop's equipment. Frequency accuracy is not essential, neither is a low harmonic-distortion content. Square-waves, which are essential for hi-fi audio testing, are not needed with this class of equipment. So quite a modest generator should fill the bill. An accurately calibrated output attenuator is desirable, because then a signal of known voltage level can be fed into the circuits to check on sensitivity specifications.

A most useful item of workshop equipment is a circuit tracer. This consists of a sensitive amplifier and loudspeaker with a demodulator that can be switched in or out of circuit. The tracer probe can be used in all parts of an audio amplifier right back to the tape heads, and in most parts of a radio circuit, and will pick up any signals that are present there. Thus stages causing loss of signal, noise or distortion can be identified by probing the stages before and after, in a matter of minutes. This instrument can be quite inexpensive and is a 'must' for every test-bench.

A similar device is the circuit injector, which comprises a random untuned square-wave oscillator. It is usually housed compactly in its own probe and so makes a convenient 'pocket' instrument. Not only can injection be made into all audio stages, thus indicating any that are inoperational, but also, because the harmonics of the square wave extend up into the radio frequencies, it can be used in the pre-detector circuits of radio receivers. It is a crude yet effective device that can aid in quickly locating defective stages.

Other items of equipment may prove useful and can be obtained if desired, but those mentioned are the most important and should be regarded as essential.

Spares and manuals

The stock of spares will include a range of preferred resistor values. These are: 1.0; 1.2; 1.5; 1.8; 2.2; 2.7; 3.3; 3.9; 4.7; 5.6; 6.8; and 8.2 Ω and their decades. There are 6 decades of these 12 values, which gives 72 values from 1 Ω up to 8.2 MΩ. The apparently odd values are chosen because they progress in 20% increments and so percentage-wise are equally spaced. There are intermediate values at 10% intervals but these are less often encountered. Resistors can be obtained in all power ratings from $\frac{1}{8}$ W to 10 W, but those of $\frac{1}{2}$-W value will be most useful: they are small enough to replace $\frac{1}{8}$-W and $\frac{1}{4}$-W sizes in most items of car equipment, but with sufficient power dissipation for the majority of circuit applications. Some 1-W and 5-W values should be stocked in the lower values under 500 Ω.

Capacitors are diverse in type and values and there is no need for a workshop specialising in car audio and radio to stock every available one. For a start, voltage ratings need be no higher than 25 V. Preferred values are the same as for resistors, but there are also 'round-figure' ones. Exact values are not so critical and it is usually sufficient to stock alternate values in the preferred range. Basic units are: microfarads (μF; 10^{-6} farad), nanofarads (nF; 10^{-9} farad) and picofarads (pF; 10^{-12} farad). Picofarad values are not much used for transistor radio and audio units, the usual range being from 10 nF to 500 µF; the values from 1 µF to 500 µF are electrolytics.

A range of transistors needs to be stocked. This can be a problem as many foreign types are not available or even listed in the UK. The most popular ones in use at any given time can be best discovered by looking through current service manuals. There is not a big choice of output transistors fortunately; in current models, the AD 161 and AD 162 complementary pair are very popular, but for earlier stages the range of types is much greater.

Apart from resistors, capacitors and transistors, spares will be for specific makes and models and not usually interchangeable with other models just as with car spares. The most usual replacement parts are: drive belts and idler wheels, motors, pinch-wheels and playback heads. Experience will have to be relied on to determine those spares in greatest demand in any given area. If installation is to be undertaken, fascia panels and knobs for various popular models together with aerials, extension cables, suppression components and general fixing hardware will be required.

Service information including circuit diagrams is essential for rapid fault diagnosis and repair. Service manuals may be obtained from the manufacturers or importers by writing on a business letterhead, explaining the specialist service you are offering and requesting copies of all manuals available. Some are free while others make a charge for them. A number of makers are very reluctant to part with service information and many supply only to dealers stocking their products. This is a very short-sighted policy, but it exists. There are a number of firms who deal in service manuals; their adverts can often be found in magazines such as *Practical Wireless*. These may be able to fill in on the models not otherwise obtainable. Build up as comprehensive a library of manuals as possible as soon as possible. Unnecessary delays in repairs will result by waiting until a particular model comes in for attention before acquiring the service information.

Chapter 17

Repairs and Maintenance

It will be appreciated that the repair and servicing of radio and tape playing equipment is a task requiring knowledge, skill and experience, and is not therefore something that can be adequately learned from a book leave alone a single chapter. We can, though, deal with some of the straightforward symptoms, faults and tests in a complete installation and outline some of the principles and practices involved in bench repair work. Before undertaking the repair of anything other than simple installation faults, readers should have a basic knowledge of theory as covered in the first three chapters. Test equipment as described in the last chapter is desirable, but especially a reasonably accurate multi-range meter.

Radio installations

If a radio has just been installed in a new vehicle by its owner and it doesn't work, the chances are that the polarity is wrong. So frequently a radio is changed from one car to another without checking the polarity, and the result is a blown fuse and possibly burnt output-transistor emitter-resistors. Transistors can also be damaged, but usually the fuse protects them. After polarity conversion, check the quiescent current (under no-signal conditions with the volume turned right down) against the maker's figure and adjust if required by means of the internal preset. If polarity is uncertain, find the large-value supply-line electrolytics and check with an ohmmeter which pole gives a zero reading to the casing.

A common fault is the aerial. If stations are weak and there is a high background hiss, the trouble is most likely the aerial or its cable. Check continuity from the aerial rod to the tip of the aerial plug with an ohmmeter; it should read a fraction of an ohm. Check also for leakages from the case of the plug to the tip. This should read infinity, but may read a few thousand ohms or less. Often the cause of the leakage is damp dirt in the terminal block at the base of the aerial, especially in wing-mounted aerials. Strip, clean and seal the block to prevent further entry of damp.

Another check is to measure the resistance between the bottom and top rod of the aerial. Oxidation often causes poor surface contact between succeeding rods and in many cases the bottom one is virtually on its own. Clean and smear with light grease. For interference problems consult Chapter 14, but in cases where interference has suddenly appeared check the earthing of the aerial cable braiding by taking an ohmmeter reading from the plug casing to an earth point. It should be a small fraction of an ohm; if not, check the contact between the earthing saddle under the aerial mounting assembly and the metalwork of the car.

Complete silence from a radio, without any hiss or noise, could be either power supply failure or the speaker circuit. Most radios have an illuminated dial or other lamp indication, so this gives an immediate check on the power. If power is present and the lamp lit, switch off and disconnect the loudspeaker leads from the radio. Connect an ohmmeter across them, switched to the lowest ohms range. A reading of a few ohms should be observed, and there should be a crackle in the loudspeaker as the meter is connected. No reading means either open-circuit leads or speaker, while a reading of around an ohm and no crackle indicates a short circuit. Sometimes a short circuit may not completely cut the sound but give distortion and very low volume. If an ohmmeter is not to hand, a crackle can be produced by connecting a dry battery momentarily across the speaker leads; a 4.5-V flat torch battery is quite suitable and convenient, but do not use the car supply.

If aerial, supply and speaker are in order, the trouble must be in the radio itself, and it must be removed for bench testing.

Tape-system installations

The presence of power to a tape installation can be seen, in the case of a cartridge player, by the track indicator that lights up to show which track is being played. Not all cassette players have illuminated power indication, but the presence of power can be quickly discovered by operating the rewind control as a slight noise nearly always accompanies this operation.

As the majority of tape players are stereo, there are two speaker circuits and one can serve as a check on the other. If there is sound in one channel and not in the other, the leads can be changed over to see if the sound changes channels. If it does, the speakers are eliminated and the fault must be in the amplifier. When both speakers are dead, a player fault is indicated as it is very unlikely that both would develop a defect at the same time. In many cases, though, the leads are soldered into a single plug and it is not convenient to make the change; in such cases the circuit should be tested with a meter or battery.

Loose connections are an ever-present possibility with mobile equipment. The effect will depend on what part of the circuit is affected. Those in the power supply (including connection to the junction box), the contact of the fuse in its holder, and also the earthing of the unit to the car frame (easy to overlook this one), will produce crackling and speed variation. Where a tape player is fed into the audio stages of a car radio, any loose joints in the interconnecting lead will produce crackling, momentary loss of sound and, if the screen of the lead is affected, possibly ignition interference.

Poor connections in the speaker circuit rarely produce crackling, but there will be momentary breaks in sound in the affected channel. Trouble of this nature within the player generally gives rise to crackling or tearing noises, which can often be brought on by tapping the casing of the unit.

Radio fault diagnosis

From car installation we turn to workshop repair. Whatever the fault, the only sure way of diagnosing it (and diagnosis is the main part of the work, repair is usually straightforward), is by a systematic process of elimination. True, one can sometimes arrive at the trouble by an inspired guess, but more often guessing and random tests get you nowhere and waste valuable time. If as a result of experience you have found that a certain symptom in a particular model is due to a fault in a particular component, a 'stock fault' as it is known in the trade, then by all means go straight for that part the next time without spending time on preliminary tests. Such action is based not on guesswork but knowledge and experience.

The radio receiver can be considered in two sections, the r.f. circuits before the detector, and the a.f. circuits. Readers are referred back to Chapters 1 and 2 if they are not familiar with these. To start with, then, we must determine in which of these two sections the fault lies. Let us assume we have no sound at all. An audio signal injected into the volume control from an audio generator or signal injector will produce a loud healthy note from the loudspeaker if the a.f. circuits are in order. If it does not, we must isolate the defective a.f. stage either by using the injector to feed in a signal to successive stages, or by taking voltage measurements on the collector, base and emitter connections to each transistor. These can be compared with the figures given in the maker's manual; if one is not available, a rough

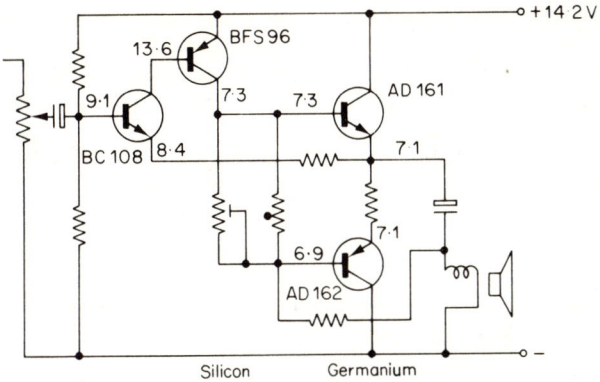

Figure 17.1. Voltages on transistor electrodes in typical car audio circuit; note the different base/emitter voltages for silicon as compared with germanium transistors

guide is that the collector should be about half the battery voltage, the emitter around 1 V, and the base 0.2 V higher than the emitter for germanium transistors and 0.6 V higher for silicon types; see Figure 17.1. The common meter lead should be clipped to supply +ve for PNP transistors and −ve for NPN. Precise voltages vary and are not too critical, but these base/emitter differences are important and indicate a fault if absent or incorrect. There may be a fault in the bias network or a short-circuit base-emitter junction in the transistor. A high emitter voltage with low collector potential indicates a leak in the transistor or too high a base bias possibly because of an open circuit in the bottom leg of the base potential divider. If the emitter and collector voltage are about the same, the transistor is most likely short-circuited. Examples of fault conditions are given in Figure 17.2.

Abnormal voltages exist in directly coupled stages where collectors are taken directly to following base circuits, the collector voltage being much lower than usual. Where two or more stages are d.c. coupled, a fault almost anywhere can affect the voltages on all the transistors and we cannot localise the particular stage where the defect may lie. Fortunately there are not so many other components in such circuits, so testing each one in turn is not too long a job. With a.c. coupled circuits voltage measurement should in most cases quickly identify the faulty stage, whereupon components can then be tested to reveal the culprit.

When measuring resistors or checking capacitors for leaks in circuit, remember that most likely there will be a parallel path in the circuit that will reduce the reading and so may mislead (Figure 17.3). Often the transistor will provide such a path giving a lower reading

190

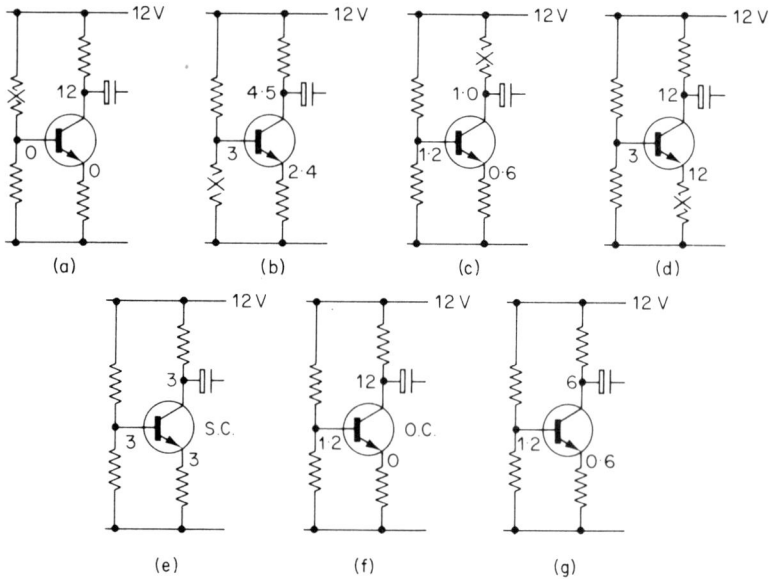

Figure 17.2. Effect on circuit voltages of various fault conditions (voltages shown are approximate, actual values will depend on component values): (a) o.c. top bias resistor; (b) o.c. bottom bias resistor; (c) o.c. collector load; (d) o.c. emitter resistor; (e) s.c. transistor; (f) o.c. transistor; (g) normal readings

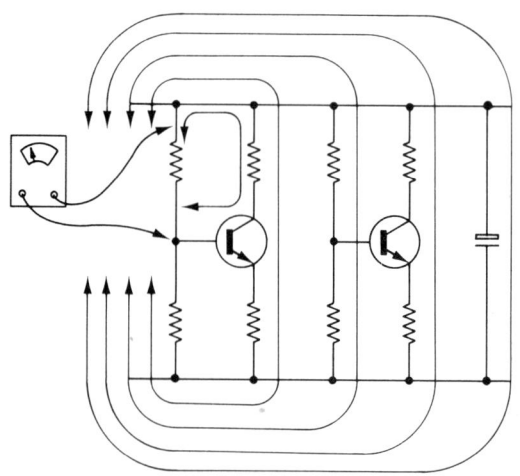

Figure 17.3. Numerous parallel paths exist across most resistors in a transistor circuit, thereby making resistance readings misleading; one end must be disconnected for accurate measurement

with the meter connected one way than when connected the other way. The supply line can also give a low-resistance path by reason of the transistors connected across it and also the leakage of electrolytic capacitors and base-bias networks. The only way to get an accurate reading is to disconnect one end of the component.

The potential across a complementary-pair output stage (see Chapter 1) is half the supply voltage because the transistors are in series with respect to the supply. Base/emitter potentials are the same as for ordinary transistors. Most cases of distortion originate with the output stage; a fault in a transistor or associated component may cause unbalance between the two halves of the stage, and this may be reflected in unequal voltages. Incorrect current is a frequent source of trouble, so this should be checked with all suspect output stages. Biasing, including faults in directly coupled driver stages, could be the cause, or one or both of the transistors could be to blame.

Working back from the detector, if the a.f. circuits are found to be in order we come to the i.f. circuits and the oscillator. Voltage checks can be made as before; also the signal injector is very useful as it generates both r.f. and a.f. signals. An r.f. signal generator can be used, but it must be tuned to the i.f. frequency of 470 kHz for a.m. circuits. When using this method, signals are fed into base and collector of successive stages to discover the point where they disappear. As we work back to the aerial the sound should get louder as each stage adds its gain.

An alternative method is to use the signal tracer. This picks off the signals if they are present, so we start from the frequency changer and work forward to the detector. The sound gets louder once more because we are adding more stages the farther on we go. It may be noticed that signals injected into or picked off the base of a transistor are less than on the preceding collector although we would expect them to be the same. This is because the impedance of a base circuit is lower, and therefore the signal voltage is less. A common cause of trouble in i.f. and mixer circuits is the transistors themselves. Unless there is a leakage a replacement can be connected temporarily across the old one by touch-soldering its three wires on to the print. The fourth wire if present is a screen and can be ignored for testing. If the old transistor is leaky it must be disconnected before a replacement can be tried.

Circuit alignment

The i.f. tuned circuits may be out of line, in which case a realignment will be required. A 470 kHz signal modulated with an a.f. tone from a signal generator is fed into the base circuit of the mixer transistor. The receiver volume control must be turned up full and the output of the generator kept low. A low-reading a.c. voltmeter should be connected across the loudspeaker, then each i.f. coil in turn should be tuned by its iron-dust core, starting from the detector. Tuning is for maximum reading on the output meter; when all the cores have been tuned, the procedure should be repeated.

Remove the generator and meter connections and tune over the dial to check that the local stations come in at the right places. If not, correction at the high-frequency (low wavelength) end can be made by the oscillator trimmer capacitor, while adjustment at the low-frequency end is by the oscillator coil core. These adjustments affect each other and so may have to be repeated. Some receivers have separate oscillator adjustments for medium and long wavebands while others do not, so there must be a compromise between the two in alignment and calibration of the scale. Finally the pre-mixer r.f. circuits are aligned. A weak broadcast signal should be tuned in and the r.f. circuit appropriate to the band should be adjusted for maximum volume.

These paragraphs give just the basic alignment routine; there may be variations between models and if a maker's manual with alignment instructions is to hand this should be followed. F.M. alignment should not be attempted without the maker's instructions and suitable equipment.

Tape-player fault diagnosis

The amplifier stages of a tape player are very similar to the a.f. circuits of a radio, so the same test procedures will apply. As there are two identical amplifiers in the same stereo unit, we can use the good one (usually there will be a fault only on one) to check voltages and compare with the defective one. This can be extremely useful if there is no maker's service manual available. Resistance readings can in many cases be taken without disconnecting the component, because the parallel paths will obviously be the same for both amplifiers and resistance measurements can simply be compared with those of the good amplifier. Remember to connect the meter leads the same way round in both cases otherwise different results may be obtained due to the transistors in circuit.

We must mention now one of the most common faults of all with tape equipment, which should therefore be checked before anything else if the appropriate symptoms are encountered; that is, dirty heads. Oxide from the tape is deposited on the surface of the head, and this builds up into a hard encrustation which holds the tape away from the head surface and bridges the magnetic gap. The result is a considerable drop of signal level which is worse at the higher frequencies, thus giving a weak muffled effect. The remedy is to clean the head with methylated spirit on a piece of soft material. Special tools are made for the purpose, but one can easily be made up by gluing a small square of felt on the end of an ice-lolly stick. The head is rarely externally accessible with car tape-players and the cover will have to be removed to reach it.

Head-cleaning should be part of a regular maintenance routine. When it has been neglected and a heavy deposit has built up, cleaning in the manner described is the only solution. There are special head-cleaning cassettes and cartridges, however, that will keep the head clean if run through on the machine regularly, say once every half a dozen tape playings.

Head positioning is also important. The magnetic gap must always be perpendicular to the line of tape travel. The magnetic pattern on the tape consists of a series of vertical stripes made by the original vertical recording-head gap (see Chapter 3). If the playback head gap is not also vertical it will to a certain extent bridge adjacent stripes diagonally and thereby increase the effective width of the gap. The result is loss of high frequencies. Adjustment of the azimuth, as it is known, is made by rocking the head to one side or the other. With cassette recorders this is done by means of set screws in the flange at the base of the head. There may be two screws, one each side of the head, that have to be turned in opposite directions (Figure 17.4), or one screw adjustable with the other fixed and spring loaded against the flange.

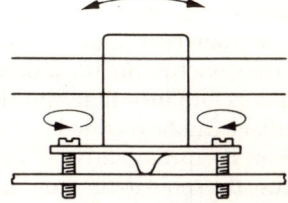

Figure 17.4. Principle of azimuth adjustment; mechanical details vary, especially in cartridge players

Adjustment can be made with an ordinary music cassette, if one has a keen ear, by setting the screws to give maximum treble response. It is best, though, to make a special tape for the purpose. Simply record a section of a cassette with a 6 kHz note from the audio generator on a recorder that is known to be correctly aligned. This can be followed with a section at 8 kHz. The azimuth is adjusted for maximum output at 6 kHz using either the ear or an output meter across the speaker terminals. A fine adjustment can then be made using the 8 kHz note.

It is not often that this adjustment is needed with a cassette machine unless there has been physical strain or misuse. Sometimes though, as the head surface wears, the gap is distorted in shape, and the treble may be improved by a slight alteration of the azimuth setting. Complete head replacement eventually is required where wear is visible and the treble response poor even after cleaning and adjustment. Sometimes wear takes the form of cavities around the gap. These can collect oxide dust from the tape and so need cleaning far more frequently than normal.

With cartridge players, the head is moved physically at each track change, and therefore the chance of the azimuth getting out of correct alignment is more likely. Some machines have the head azimuth adjustment brought out to the control panel so that the user can himself adjust for maximum treble. Otherwise, the setting should be checked and corrected if necessary each time a cartridge player is brought into the workshop for repair.

Vertical position of the head is also important. If the head of a cartridge player is not in vertical alignment the gaps will overlap the edges of the tracks and there will be a reduction in volume and an increase in noise. If it is even further out, the gaps will encounter the adjacent tracks and there will be a second programme heard in the background; this is called *cross-tracking*. Many cartridge players have a control usually labelled 'fine tuning' that adjusts the vertical position of the head; this should be set for maximum volume. It is unlikely that vertical displacement of a cassette head would occur unless by physical damage.

A not uncommon fault with cassettes is tape tangling and spillage. How to deal with this is described in Chapter 9, but prevention is better than cure, and the risk is greatly reduced if the tape is kept taut in the cassette; any slack should be taken up by turning one of the tape hubs before insertion into the player. In the case of a cartridge any spillage can be rectified by pulling more out, strange though that may seem. If tape is gently pulled out from the centre of the spool this will cause the spool to turn and take up more than was pulled out, because the take-up is on to the outer edge. This process can be continued until all the slack is taken up.

Mechanical faults

A large number of mechanical troubles are due to stretched or greasy drive belts, and hardened or perished idler-wheel rubbers. It is always wise to check the condition of these components in any case where there is slow or erratic running. Any sign of oily deposits on any friction drive surface should be removed with methylated spirit. The motor or its governor circuit can also be responsible for these symptoms, motors with mechanical governors being especially prone to trouble after a long period of use. Before getting too involved in the player itself though, try one or two other cassettes or cartridges first, because any stiffness or fouling of the tape hub or spool could give the same trouble.

Regular speed variations are described as 'wow' and are usually due to some rotating component. It may be eccentric, have a stiff bearing or be fouling something and thus cause a varying load during rotation. To locate the trouble, watch the mechanism in action and try to match the speed of the wow with the rotation of one of the parts; the one that matches is the source. A closer examination will then reveal the cause.

Wow can also be caused by oxide deposits on the drive capstan or pinch roller. These must be cleaned by hand because there is no friction, hence cleaning action, between them and a cleaning tape, which will only clean the head and tape guides. Deposits on the guides can cause the tape to stick and drag. This may produce slowing, or in some cases an audible squeak. Another effect is for the tape to proceed in a succession of jerks as it is alternately held and released. This happens very rapidly and causes a form of distortion known as flutter. Felt pads that press the tape against the head-face are especially likely to cause this, if they get matted and hard. Note that with cassettes each one has its own internal pressure pad while the pinch roller is part of the player, while in the case of the cartridge the roller is internal.

The take-up spool in a cassette player can sometimes give trouble. If the torque is too great the take-up spool tries to pull tape past the capstan faster than the capstan speed will allow and the result can be slowing or stalling. If the drive is too weak the spool may stop under load causing tape spillage. The felt clutch washer is often the culprit having become hard or matted with oxide dust. Cleaning and fluffing up the surface with a file or other abrasive tool will usually effect a cure.

Oil is the worst enemy of any tape machine; it can perish rubber idlers and pinch rollers, it can get on the friction drive surfaces and cause loss of traction, and it can form a film on the playback head and affect the frequency response. Actually very little oil or other lubricant is necessary. Motor bearings are of the oil-sealed type and so usually are the flywheel top bearings. Other spindles and pivots run in nylon, which needs no oil. An occasional spot may be required on a pivot or linkage that shows need of it, but it should be kept to the minimum.

As cartridge players are simpler than the cassette machines, there are fewer repair problems and mechanical defects are usually self-evident. Makers' service manuals usually give information on the mechanical assembly, exploded diagrams, spring tensions and various adjustments, as well as the circuit diagram and other electrical data. So the advice given in the last chapter is repeated: build up a library of as many manuals as you can if you intend to offer a public service for the maintenance and repair of mobile audio equipment, since it will save much time and effort.

With all repairs, though, always remember that the golden rule is to follow a systematic procedure of elimination in tracking down the fault. If as sometimes happens it proves stubborn, re-check your tests or devise others to establish more positively the stage or section where the trouble must lie. A common experience is to be misled by jumping to conclusions and taking things for granted. Short-cuts may sometimes be permissible, but, when faced with the difficult fault, prove every step in the diagnosis. Finally you will be rewarded by the isolation of the offending part, and then be able to make an effective and positive repair.

Index